KYRGYZSTAN
Reflections of a Winter's Journey

This edition 2018

Acknowledgments

I owe this book and all my travels to the many people who have helped me along the way. The kindness and generosity of people, often most pronounced in those who have least, never fails to humble me. I extend particular gratitude to those whose stories fill the following pages. I also thank my parents for tolerating my nomadism and their assistance with this literary venture. I thank Dr Tracy Rihll whose words long ago encouraged me to pursue writing. Thank you to Stuart Fraser and Janyl Madikova for taking the time to read parts of the manuscript and their valuable suggestions on how to improve it. I am also very grateful to Alex and Paul Boxall for their assistance in matters technical. Lastly, I would like to thank all those whose writings and scholarship I have drawn upon, and that have made my experience and understanding of the world fuller, and hopefully, this book more interesting.

Leon Whiteley was born in 1982. He studied Ancient History and Egyptology at the University of Wales, Swansea, and Anthropology at the University of Oxford. In 2008/9 he cycled 25,000kms through twenty-one countries from South Korea to Germany. After writing this book he spent the next five years living in China.

"Is there anybody there?" said the Traveller,
Knocking on the moonlit door;
And his horse in the silence champed the grass
Of the forest's ferny floor.

Walter de la Mare.

Preface

<u>Locating Asia's Lost Heart</u>

Kyrgyzstan is 'The land of the Kyrgyz', people with a nomadic pastoralist past. Through the centuries they've drifted south from Siberia and now reside in the nation of their name. Kyrgyzstan lies at the very heart of Asia, nearly in the centre of Eurasia's great expanse. Having existed as an independent state for a mere two decades, Kyrgyzstan can only be understood as part of the regional context to which she belongs. Most narrowly, she is one of the five post-Soviet Central Asian states or 'Stans.' However, Kyrgyzstan is also part of a cultural continuum that extends deep into modern China, includes Mongolia, and also the wider Turkic-speaking world. In both historic and prehistoric times what is now Kyrgyzstan was part of a nomadic cultural complex that dominated the breadth of Eurasia from the Korean Peninsula in the East to the Hungarian plain - and often beyond - in the West.

That world has long been in retreat, and always it remained obscure to those on the periphery. The periphery being the encircling settled civilizations of China, Persia, and Asia's largest peninsular - Europe. The latter, along with its island offspring in the Americas and Australasia, has long considered itself the centre of the civilised world, but this has far from always been the case.

Beyond the borders of settled men, Central Asia remained in the shadows, made opaque by distance and disinterest. Since records began it was recounted as the land of an ominous other, mysterious and threatening. Nearly 2500 years ago, the 'father of history', a Greek called Herodotus described 'a region of which no one can give accurate account'. He wrote of bald-headed men who subsisted only on cherries; mountains 'inhabited by a goat footed race'; and the 'one-eyed'[1] Arimaspian people. Looking in from the other side, and rather more intimately positioned, was a Chinese princess forced to marry a nomad king. She lamented 'Being in a far corner of the earth… a tent is my house, of felt are my walls; raw flesh my food. With mare's milk my drink. Always thinking of my own country, my heart sad within. I wish I were a yellow stalk and could fly to my old home.'[2]

Seven hundred years after Herodotus, the Roman historian Marcellinius described those from the Asian interior as 'having no fixed abode, no home or law or settled manner of life, but [they] wander like refugees in the wagons in which they live. In these their wives weave their filthy clothing, mate with their husbands, give birth to their children and rear them to the age of puberty. No one if asked can tell where he comes from, having been conceived in one place, born somewhere else, and reared even further off.'[3]

He was writing about the Huns. Their eruption into the West, and that of the Mongols nearly a thousand years later, cemented Central Asia's status as synonymous with a dark and brooding barbarism; the people who lived there were objects of fear and revulsion; they 'who make deep gashes in their children's cheeks, so that when in due course their hair appears its growth is checked by the wrinkled scars.'[4]

Unfortunately, stereotypes of Inner Asians as the barbaric 'other' are not limited to the ancient past. In the Seventeenth Century settled Europeans believed that 'Tartar babies were born with their eyes closed like dogs, and did not open them until several days after birth'.[5] Today, 'Russian mothers still use the threat "the Tartars are coming" to frighten little children into bed or into doing their homework.'[6] Even the modern Western 'comedy' *Borat*, with its mockery of Kazakhstan, expresses a contempt for Central Asia that in our politically correct age would have brought public outrage had it been directed at any other region on Earth.

However, such notions of backwardness or inferiority are misplaced. Historically, we know that 'nomads were in general much better fed and led much easier, longer lives'[7] than their agricultural neighbours. Indeed, many Greeks and Romans even sought to improve their lives by joining the Huns and other Central Asian peoples. Similarly, citizens of China frequently melted into the Eastern Steppe for the same reason. Moreover, the nomadic peoples who drifted or fought their way into the territory of sedentary states invariably settled, and, in fact, some of the greatest powers of settled civilisation were born of vigorous nomadic interlopers.

The violent, swarming advances of Eurasian nomads - like the Huns, Mongols, or Tartars – which periodically bludgeoned against the borders of settled civilization, might be seen as anomalies when compared to the encroachments of settled peoples going the other way. From this perspective we can view the 'civilised' sedentary peoples as the aggressors, who, in pursuit of agricultural land constantly expanded into the realm of the nomads. It was a process that only came to an end at the beginning of the Twentieth Century when the remaining nomadic Kazakh, Kyrgyz and Turkmen were forcibly settled.

It also cannot be ignored that the highpoints of Greek, Indic and Chinese classical civilisation all reached their peak at very much the same time. Whilst conceivable that this occurred independently and in total intellectual isolation from each other, it seems far more likely that a degree of 'cross-fertilization' was facilitated by the common border they shared with Middle Asia, which must to all intents and purposes be considered a 'fourth civilisation' whose contribution to the other three has long been overlooked. The famous Greek, Demosthenes, was himself half Scythian; the first Central Asian people to appear in Western records. Zoroaster, the founder of Zoroastrianism, once the dominant religion of the Persian world, is also believed to have hailed from somewhere in Central Asia. New evidence is even beginning to hint that written Chinese, long thought to be utterly indigenous in origin, may have found its innovation from the same source that brought bronze working and chariot technology to the Yellow River Valley; Steppe people entering China from the northwest in the Second Millennium B.C.[8]

Why then, is this 'fourth civilisation' so neglected in the historical record, reduced largely to a succession of violent incursions? There are a number of reasons for this. Firstly, we get our history from what has been written down, and it was the sedentary peoples on the periphery of Central Asia who were doing most of the writing. Thus the perspective gained from historical documents, whether European, Indian, Chinese, or Persian, has been unanimously one-sided. It was these centres of civilisation that Western imperialism first made accessible to Western scholarly intrigue. So perhaps it is unsurprising that their history has prevailed over that of the Asian interior. Any desire to uncover the history of Central Asia was inhibited not only by a paucity of texts, but by geopolitics, and raw, inhospitable terrain.

Indeed, geography plays a huge part in understanding Central Asia. To a great extent it is the formidable natural barriers which encompass Central Asia that have defined it. Mountains, deserts, and endless steppe served to partially seal the region off from surrounding civilisations. Of course, this does not mean it was impassable. Central Asia's most memorable moniker 'The Silk Road', testifies to the fact it was regularly traversed. However, it was hard going, as illustrated by this early Chinese account: 'Our envoys clasp the emblems of the mighty Han and starve to death in the hills and valleys. They may beg but there is nothing for them to get, and after ten or twenty days man and beast lie abandoned in the wastes never to return.'[9] When Marco Polo made his way across the region over a thousand years later the journey was equally testing and fraught with risk.

Right into modern times nature proved a serious obstruction to reaching the region. The expansion of the Russian Empire from the west, and the British Empire's forays from the south, were literally advances into uncharted territory.

Today, very close to Urumqi, the capital of modern China's Xinjiang province (Historically and culturally part of Central Asia), lies the Eurasian 'Pole of Inaccessibility'. This is a geographical construct, the claim of which is all in the name: Urumqi is further from the nearest coastline than any other city on Earth.[*]

For the author at least, this geographic fact seems synonymous with notions of total and utter isolation. Perhaps this assumption is a product of growing up on an island and belonging to a people once famed for their maritime exploits. A similar perspective was probably held by those who first coined the term. However, a branch of the Silk Road had passed that way for thousands of years; something attested by the Buddhist frescoes in nearby caves and the ruins of many ancient cities. Likewise, the old Mongolian word from which the modern name 'Urumqi' derives means 'beautiful pastures', showing the area has long been both accessible and desirable to pastoralist people. Inaccessibility from the ocean did not deprive the region of either people or civilisation. However, with the advent of

---

[*] Approximately 1600 miles.

the 'Age of Discovery' it did protect Central Asia from the predations of Western colonial interests, which were largely facilitated via naval power.

This explains to some degree why Central Asia has seemed so obscure to the Western observer. It was never accessible to the West in the way much of the rest of the world has been. However, Central Asia was still colonised, and it still played a significant part in British imperial history.

At the same time as 'Britannia ruled the waves', Russia was rolling inexorably south across the steppe into Central Asia. Such a trajectory seemed to be setting course for the Sub-continent, and this caused considerable alarm for imperial officials in British India. The stage was set for the geopolitical tussle that has gone down in Western history as 'The Great Game.' To the Russians it was 'The Tournament of Shadows.' The 2000 miles which divided the British and Russian Empires at the start of the 19th Century had, by its end, been reduced in some places to a matter of metres.

The borders pegged out by Russian Cossacks soon solidified under the Soviets into an Asian Iron Curtain. The territory of Soviet Central Asia was delineated. Afghanistan, although in part culturally contiguous with its northern neighbours, remained as a buffer state between the British and Russian Empires.

The Great Game of the 19th Century merged into the Cold War of the Twentieth, and the dynamic regional geopolitics of the Twenty First has even invited the term 'The New Great Game.' That history repeats itself can be read in the failed foreign interventions in Afghanistan, as successive great powers (Britain – USSR – The 'West') try to impose conformity upon the last untamed corner of Middle Asia.

However, despite being the pivot on which so much has swung, swathes of Central Asia - and I refer to 'The land of the Kyrgyz' - remained relatively unknown to the West. From the British perspective 'The Great Game' largely revolved around Afghanistan and the small city-states in what is now modern Uzbekistan. This was the world of settled people. It was this Central Asia, the one evoked by Elroy Flecker's much quoted 'Golden Journey to Samarkand' that filled the imaginations of the 19th Century British public. It was southern Central Asia's searing deserts, criss-crossed by camel trains, and dotted with shimmering Silk Road caravansaries.

By contrast, the Turko-Mongol nomads, the Kyrgyz and the Kazakhs, did not muster nearly as much attention. Already firmly within the Russian sphere of influence they invited no comparable intrigues of British imperial espionage. Thus they are largely absent from the romantic yarns spun in that Silk Road struggle. Presiding over no towns and displaying no ostensible trappings of state power they were geopolitically inconsequential. Heirs to the formidable steppe empires which had at various times overcome all of the surrounding civilisations, the nomads were now considered little more than primitive tribes of shepherds living in felt tents; their home the wasteland between world powers. Once sealed into the amorphous Russian construct of Turkestan[10] whatever peripheral place they held in the West's collective consciousness was where they remained, and slowly faded from.

Today, Oxford University has separate libraries for Japanese Studies, Slavonic Studies, Latin American Studies, Chinese Studies, and many other regions, but just a sprinkling of texts related to Central Asia, and most of those deal only with Afghanistan or Mongolia.[*] This is not a bias peculiar to Oxford; rather it is a reflection of the limited number of books on the region that are in existence. This under-representation becomes all the more striking when one considers that Central Asia constitutes approximately one-seventh of Earth's landmass.

With the collapse of the Soviet Union some seventy years after its institution, a part of the world appeared that had all but been forgotten. 'Turkestan' re-emerged as five independent nation-states; Kazakhstan, Kyrgyzstan, Uzbekistan, Turkmenistan, and Tajikistan. This is the tale of a trip through one: 'The Land of the Kyrgyz.'

---

[*] Rather than any specific school or library on the region, there is only TOSCCA, The Oxford Society for the Caspian and Central Asia, which holds infrequent seminars. That its sponsors are BG group ('a world leader in natural gas') and the Foreign Office gives an indication of the nature of the interest.

Introduction

'The Past is a Foreign Country'

With considerably less success or prestige than paper, gunpowder, or the Mongol hordes, I took my first trip on The Silk Road in summer 2007. It was an attempt to get back to Britain overland from India. I knew nothing about Central Asia other than that I would have to pass through it to reach Europe. There were other ways of course. I could have gone to the north via Russia or through Pakistan to the south. However, I was curious to see something of these countries whose names conjured up no concrete images in my mind. When the idea formed I had not yet visited either Russia or Pakistan, but their mere names were loaded with assumptions, expectations, and nearly a quarter of a century's accumulated stereotypes and media images. These five 'new' countries though, were an empty canvas, and for me that made them an incredibly attractive proposition. I was looking for an adventure and that made Central Asia's obscurity irresistible. Only the suffix 'stan' gave me anything to go on; and which to this Western boy had connotations of the wild and potentially dangerous that only made them more alluring.

Nearly a year of backpacking had already left me feeling the world was a little more familiar than I wanted it to be. Bangladesh and Pakistan had certainly seemed like back-alleys on the tourist trail, but Kyrgyzstan was the first place I felt I had truly left it.

It was exciting to be in a place virtually no one I knew had even heard of. I saw no tourists or youth hostels, no safe retreat where you could be with 'your own kind' and view the 'strange' land through a filter of familiarity. I had become disappointed that travel was not as difficult as I had hoped it would be. The paths all seemed well-trodden and comfort too easy to acquire.

Kyrgyzstan on the other hand felt fresh. I had not known what to expect so everything was new. I had left China through a desolate

Martian landscape, so rugged and unforgiving it was no wonder the Chinese regarded it as the world's end. I was crammed onto a bus divided into three rows of bunks, two tiers high, and all too small to reasonably accommodate a human being. Upon crossing the border, the road became a rutted washboard. The sun set in a blood red haze over brooding unfinished peaks and a vista that seemed to have escaped from prehistory.

And who were these people on the bus I wondered? They broke bits from circular-shaped bread as broad as dinner plates, sharing it round. Smiles revealed gold capped teeth in every combination; in ones and twos, or until whole mouths shone like a jeweller's shop window. I was unable to put them under any pre-existing category in my mind. Their faces were neither stereotypically Asian nor European. They displayed every variation; plump and thin, eyes slanted and round, skin dark to light, yet some common theme seemed to unite them all. Patterned headscarves and loose, brightly coloured traditional dresses sat side by side with jeans, leather jackets and mobile phones.

Morning broke over a beautiful, empty land. Rolling green plateau washed into waves of hills that lapped softly beneath sharp, ice white peaks. It seemed like a land unmanaged by man, as crisp and clean as the day after its geological formation. Above was the vast blue bowl of the heavens, so unfathomably deep and extensive it was no wonder the nomads had worshipped it as *Tengri* the 'Sky father.'

On that first visit, away from the ravages of Russian 'development', I found the nature seemingly untouched. With just an old Soviet army map and a bus ride to the trail head, I was transported to another time; trekking through alpine meadows that seemed unblemished even by animal tracks; to come across a vast turquoise lake, set in an epic basin of weather-sculpted rock, yet without the slightest hint of another human being for miles around. When I did encounter people in those hills, they were hardy mountain men riding horses against faultless backdrops, their sheep speckled on otherwise empty hills.

There was no need to frame a photo as every view was faultless. The English word 'landscape' was originally a technical term used by artists to describe an idealised vista, one worthy of painting. This idealisation of landscape began at a time when Europe was rapidly industrialising. Thus, nature was looked upon with increasing nostalgia. In Kyrgyzstan I found that this nostalgia could be fully indulged. 'Landscape' was everywhere, not just at selected spots already trampled as the masses sought to find scenic solitude together.

I had traced a raging river in search of a bridge. Instead I was found by a Kyrgyz lad on his horse. Without a word of shared language, saddle or stirrups, he carried me and my weighty rucksack across the torrent. On the opposing bank he rode to a break in the black velvet forest that flooded down from the surrounding hills. Where the trees stopped a carpet of green began. The grass looked as manicured as a golf course yet was as wild as could be; trimmed by grazing animals rather than by machine. Coloured flowers sat amongst it like scattered jewels. With the appearance of a large white mushroom sprouted a traditional Kyrgyz felt tent of the type commonly referred to as a *yurt*.

A pair of grinning children scampered outside playing with a dog, whilst wood smoke wafted lazily from the yurt-top into *Tengri's* azure infinity. It was as idyllic a scene as one might imagine; the wholesomeness of *Little House on the Prairie* transferred to a nomadic abode in the valleys of Kirgizia. I dismounted awkwardly as the boy leapt down nimbly beckoning me into the yurt. The children looked on at the curious stranger to arrive in their midst. Inside, I was greeted by a rotund Kyrgyz woman in colourful dress and headscarf, and her wiry husband with his thick moustache and strong Mongolian features.

It had seemed a little early for lunch but I was enjoined to eat. Broth was poured from a bubbling fire-blackened pot into bowls for everyone. The whole family crowded in, crouched on the floor rugs under a halo of light that streamed through the yurt's smoke-hole or *tunduk*. The soup was steaming hot. Bubbles of oil and specks of red spice submerged potato, pasta-like pieces, and chunks of tender meat still on the bone. It was delicious, and accompanied by tea served in cups without handles, as is common throughout Asia.

I had only a few words of Russian with which to converse, but my notebook and pen allowed for an entertaining form of cross-cultural *Pictionary* by which to communicate. The camera too, a humble point-and-shoot, was also a source of genuine fascination and pleasure. It seemed hard to believe that I was in the former USSR, the very ideology of which had been progress through technology and science. Indeed, the Soviet Union had moved from peasant to space-age society in mere decades. Yet there I was, in the former superpower's backyard feeling like I had made first contact between two disparate worlds, centuries apart. The family stood for photos with military formality, staring sternly into the lens but then never failing to be amused at the image which appeared on the screen. I felt I had slipped into history, and history more than anywhere, was a place I had always wanted to see.

When I had been fed to bursting I doubted I would have the energy to continue the climb, but knew I had to try before night fell. Unsure what was expected, I took out some money to pay for the meal, but it was vehemently refused. Instead I indicated that I would send the photos and offered the last of the chocolate I was carrying. The matriarch set it down ceremoniously on the low table and cut it exactingly into five equal pieces, one for each member of her family.

The youngest son then led me from that enchanted setting and through the picturesque landscape; into the dark forest and across flowered glades, over streams bridged by rock and logs, round boulder-strewn meadows, and up and down the great green folds of land until he found the path by which I could pursue my trek alone.

Kyrgyzstan was still nature's land, yet its human presence was striking and mixed. Felt tents from the distant east, of Mongolian and Siberian heritage; gingerbread cottages of the Slavic colonists, no less quaint or idyllic with their white-washed walls, wonky roofs and gently chugging chimneys. Kyrgyz horsemen with dark weathered features wore elf-like tri-corn hats of white felt, adorned with swirling black patterns. Stocky blond-haired men, tanned, with lined faces, of Slavic or Germanic stock tended horses harnessed to archaic looking carts. I was close to the middle of Middle Asia, yet more often felt I was traipsing round Tolkien's 'Middle Earth.'

It was the grandeur of the landscape and a medieval heritage that seemed so close at hand; where men still hunted with eagles, and a culture where horsemanship was still of paramount regard. Western style clothing may well have been common, but so were the *Al'kalpak* hats, headscarves and the womenfolk's traditional flowing gowns.

On postcards and such like, images abounded of a not too distant past; a warrior race of mounted nomads who lived in tune with the land; their women dressed like princesses, with tall conical hats and often depicted playing an elegant stringed instrument, the *kobiz,* from which our modern violin probably derives. These were portrayals of an idealised Kyrgyz 'golden age'; a source of identity for a recently independent people, and a selling point to visitors from lands where such simplicity was so remote as to make for appealing fantasy. It was all reminiscent of the European Middle Ages (at least as Hollywood had rendered them), but in Kyrgyzstan so many tangible elements of that world seemed to remain.

I am painting an idealised picture because that is how I perceived it. Of course, Middle Earth had Mordor, and Middle Asia has its monstrous concrete monoliths of communist construction. However, in most of the country urbanisation is sparse. In the south, the city of Osh stands at the Western end of the Fergana Valley. There the settled world of ancient Sogdia, rich in Persian influence, meets with the nomadic culture of the Kyrgyz, and mingles amongst modern infrastructure brought by the Slavic Russians. Cyrillic script sits above Silk Road *Chaikhanas* - tea houses - where the old white beards chatter; muezzins moan from the domed mosque whilst *magazines* stock bargain-price vodka. Muslim, Christian, Kyrgyz, Uzbek, Slav, Tartar, Turk, and many more; the city seemed a melting pot where multiple traditions mixed, and still resisted absorption by a homogenous modernity.

So in this land where men still live on meat and mare's milk, the products of their herds, I found an alien world, eclectic, and yet inviting. I was quick to romanticise the simplicity of life in those hills, and the call of the wild in a countryside as yet untrammelled by the opaque pay-offs of 'progress.' At the same time I marvelled at the cultural collage that had been created; *orient extremis;* the seduction of the Silk Road slumbering in the wreckage of Slavic communism. I knew nothing of these juxtaposed worlds and was fascinated by their living legacy. Nomadism and Soviet totalitarianism, both are forces that have transformed the world, and both are compelling subjects – whole ideologies, ways of life, empires won and lost are encompassed between them. The latter is officially dead and the former is slowly dying, but in Kyrgyzstan I could still see their shadows. I had stumbled into a cross-roads of cultures and civilisations hitherto obscure to me. Set in its dramatic alpine sanctuary, I found Kyrgyzstan a repository of fascinating culture and living history – If Tibet is 'the roof of the world' then Kyrgyzstan is surely Eurasia's secret garden.

After that trip I did not return to Kyrgyzstan for another two years. The realities of life and earning a living got in the way. However, Central Asia, and particularly Kyrgyzstan, was never far from my mind. I tried to indulge my new interest through books but found surprisingly little to read on the subject. To all beyond its bounds, Middle Asia was simply the middle of nowhere. When I told people about going there they regarded me as if I had gone to the moon, just without any of the associated glamour or purpose. So I stopped telling people, relishing to have found a place not yet degraded with discovery by the tourist hordes.

In 2009 I came to Kyrgyzstan again. I had been working in South Korea as an English teacher. I had liked teaching and I had loved Korea. However, there was an ease and comfort about life there that had disappointed me. The mysterious orient had turned out to be more developed, shiny and new, than Western Europe. I hungered for a more demanding environment; I wanted to be alone in far off lands, immersed in alien cultures, emancipated from the soul destroying ideal of a 'happiness' achieved through feckless consumerism. I wanted a physical challenge and a lifestyle that transcended the empty 'having a good time' mantra of my generation which I found so singularly unrewarding. Thus, I decided I would cycle back to Europe. Not for the destination, but for the journey. I was determined to taste a life of adventure, and to make good on my previous attempt to traverse vast tracts of Eurasia by the most challenging method I could conceive. To imbue travel with a sense of what travel once was - a test - not a climate-controlled bubble of in-flight movies and vacuum-packed meals; where people are transported tens of thousands of miles across continents yet their greatest deprivation is economy rather than business class.

It was a long ride. However, it is its own tale and must be told in its own time. Suffice to say, seven and a half months after leaving Korea, having ambled through the Philippines, Borneo, Peninsular South East Asia, 6000kms through China alone, and Kazakhstan, I finally reached Kyrgyzstan once more. I had been cycling with a Frenchman I had met at the Kazakh border. We cycled across the endless Kazakh Steppe to a horizon that never came any closer. It was a place apparently of no people, yet where once the armies of great tribal confederations had mustered in clusters of tents that formed felt cities; filled with banners, bows, humanity and horses. Looking out at the perpetual flat of the land, it seemed the perfect place for power to have galloped across the prairie on the back of a pony, aided by the pull of a bow. Aside from a sliver of road the land was unchanged from how it had been then. *Tengri* the 'sky father' and *Eje* the 'Earth Mother.' It was simple. The people of these lands had viewed themselves as part of nature and had considered pastoral nomadism as man's natural state of being; a harmonious relationship in which any unnecessary disturbance of nature was avoided. For them, to needlessly scuff the ground or move stones around aimlessly was to defile nature. Even burying things had to be attended by special rituals. Like the nomads we tried to leave no trace of where we had been. And like the nomads, the centre of our world was established anew each time we made a halt; a world consisting of two tents, two bikes, and a stove on which to prepare our food.

With the exception of Almaty's modern metropolis the Kazakhstan we saw was a quiet, empty land. We headed to Kyrgyzstan's remote north eastern border, a region not serviced by public transport and with no sizable settlements. Our approach was one through perfect pasture, the green-blue binary of sky and earth only broken by yellow flowers and the rare shimmering of a silver-domed mosque. It was just us and the Kazakh's herds of herbivores – reduced to distant swarms of ants against the grandeur of the landscape.

The Kazakh-Kyrgyz border consisted of a couple of shipping containers next to the gravel track. The unpaved road through the Karkara Valley is not only the backdoor to a modern state, but a time-worn trail through one of the few traversable breaks in the almost impenetrable rocky barrier of the Tian Shan. Its desolate tranquillity belies an ancient trade route, the passage of countless passing armies, and path to so many migrating peoples of which the Kyrgyz were but one. We found ourselves in a more compact country. The seamless steppe and dry flat pasturage that had rolled by with such dreamy continuity in Kazakhstan suddenly crumpled. The land folded up on itself; features formed of forest, grass and rock fought up and down the contours, whilst a broad white river weaved them all together. Even after the light and space of the Kazakh Steppe, the burning expanse of Xinjiang's Tarim Basin, the gruelling mountains of

Western China, and the cloying humidity of Oceania's jungle archipelagos, Kyrgyzstan retained its magic.

We came across a grizzled horseman; a Kyrgyz cowboy, or *chabana*. In his fur lined jacket and hat he seemed oblivious to the summer sun, as if like his well insulated herd it was a hide he could not remove. At a meander in the river, amid nature's idyllic panorama, there was the incongruous scene of a local man washing his cream-coloured *Lada* whilst animals grazed the grass on which it sat. It was the perfect snapshot of where two worlds met; the *Lada,* that metal workhorse of mechanised Russia, contrasted with the Kyrgyz herds and horses, ubiquitous with a power of far older heritage.

Later we passed a whole family on the move. A dishevelled blue truck with an open wooden trailer pulled a larger box-like blue wagon. If motor vehicles had existed in medieval times then this is what they would have looked like. The truck chugged laboriously, omitting hisses and smoke like some archaic steam-powered curiosity, barely keeping pace with the herd of plodding cows that represented the family's wealth. Flanking the cows were two *chabana* outriders and a pair of wolfish black dogs. The wooden trailer carried firewood and miscellaneous sacks, upon which sat two women. White headscarves signalled their married status, red-blue cheeks showed the rigours of high altitude living, and striped sleeves testified to the global success of Adidas. At the back rolled the box-like wagon. Like a rusty train carriage, but with only three windows and a steel pipe chimney, it was apparently the family abode; somewhere between the ancient wheeled wagons of the Steppe and a modern motor home. This convoy was the picture of pastoralists on the move. It was painted in muted black, browns, and creams on a canvas of cattle hide, horse hair and untreated timber. Even the metal of the truck and roof of the wagon had returned to the colour of mud through prolonged exposure. The only artificial hue was the blue paint on as yet un-rusted metal, and even that was the colour of *Tengri.*

With only a handful of Kazakh money until we found a town with an ATM, we lived off stale bread from our panniers for two days. We passed through shambolic villages of Slavic cottages, where there was little in the way of food to buy even if we had had the cash. We encountered great curiosity and friendliness from local people.

Always greeting us with smiles, 'Salams', and the same stock of questions; 'where are you from?', 'where do you go?', 'what is your religion?', and 'where are your wives and children?' These were questions that had been asked along this route since antiquity and where once the answers would have been 'Dawan', 'Chang'an', 'Marakanda', or 'Karakorum'. Those places remained but the names and powers associated with them had since changed many times.

If the Kyrgyz we met found the notion of trans-continental bicycle travel odd, then an absence of professed faith was thoroughly perplexing, and for us not to be married by our mid-twenties was apparently almost beyond comprehension. We were interacting with a world where faith and family are the only lens though which existence is viewed. To be seemingly without either struck them as both alien and utterly undesirable.

We cycled around the great thermal lake of Issyk Kul where we camped on deserted, warm sandy beaches with only still blue waters and the ethereal peaks of the Ala-Too for company. We rode to Song Kul also, its thawing surface splintered like a cracked mirror in a frame of snow-topped hills. Yurts dotted the shore like separate citadels in an isolated mountain kingdom. We cycled out of the mountains and into the flat, leafy green of the Chuy valley. It was like another country in a land consisting of a patchwork of ecosystems where the only constant is a mountain view. Arriving in Bishkek any notions of Kyrgyzstan as the forgotten east had to be quickly reassessed. Unlike my last visit, there were now hostels and a host of other travellers on the trail. I had not seen such a concentration of cyclists since Laos; half a dozen like Remi and I; long distant cyclists looking for a life less ordinary on the open road.

In Bishkek I also saw a darker side to Kyrgyzstan. The Russian legacy of hard liquor combined with economic hardship had taken a visible toll. Drunkenness in the backstreets was unfortunately all too common. I also met Nazda, a Kyrgyz girl of my age, and was invited to my first *Tuy,* a traditional Kyrgyz celebration, which will be described in chapter three. Leaving Bishkek, Remi and I plied the spectacular road south. We lived in the saddle, climbing and camping until our paths parted just as they had come together; at a fork in the road. Remi pushed onto Tajikistan and the mighty Pamir Highway, whilst I cycled into Uzbekistan, in an attempt to cross the Kizilkum desert at the height of summer when the temperature reached 50 degrees. I would then re-enter the remote western steppe of Kazakhstan where there were no proper roads, scattered uranium dumps, and only two places I could expect to find either people or water within hundreds of kilometres. Then, if I made it to the port of Aktau, everything rested on passage across the Caspian Sea to Azerbaijan on a rumoured freight ferry; about which no certain information was available accept that one left every two weeks, allegedly. But that is another story.

I arrived home in the UK towards the end of 2009, and by the end of 2010 I had saved enough money to facilitate another journey. It was the middle of winter and far from the ideal time to be visiting anywhere in the greater Central Asian region. Unlike my other journeys this was not to be part of some pan-Eurasian odyssey. Instead, I was going with the specific intention of writing a book. I had neither the time nor inclination to wait until spring, plus the promise of 'extreme' conditions had its own appeal. I almost felt I *should* be travelling in winter. Summer always seemed like a holiday. Winter would offer another perspective, perhaps one somehow more 'real'. Kyrgyzstan's natural beauty would be largely under snow, as would many sites of historic interest. However, whilst I had spent 2010 in the UK, Kyrgyzstan had undergone a violent revolution centred on the capital Bishkek, and later, suffered serious inter-ethnic conflict in the southern city of Osh. During my journey by bicycle I had made local friends in both cities. We had stayed in touch by email. Thus, during these troubles I was given insight into the personal face of events on the ground that went well beyond the scant reporting in the Western media. This alone, to say nothing of their life experiences in general, was to glimpse a different world. It was what I wanted to write about.

'With no significant political forces opposing the conversion of our world into a universal marketplace, the conflict of our time is the struggle to retain one's humanity in an increasingly artificial world.'

John B. Morgan

1

<u>Go East</u>

*The old world is dying away and the new
World struggles to come forth:
Now is the time of monsters.*

Gramsci.

This trip was unusual in that it started with a flight. Well, two flights to be exact. The first was from London to Istanbul. En-route the cabin TV displayed our progress with a little plane icon stuttering south west over the screen-sized Europe. The pixel plane seemed lethargic, and its movement, even over some minutes, was tedious. However, I was translating those minutes into days, thinking back to when I had made this same journey in reverse by bicycle. Then Istanbul to Berlin had meant a month of unrelenting effort in the cold and rain, as I cycled into European winter at the end of a 25,000km pan-Asian bike ride.

Such exertion was now made a mockery of as I glided effortlessly back to Istanbul in three comfortable hours. When breaks in the cloud allowed, it was possible to see Europe sweep past below. Mostly it appeared as a patchwork of muted browns, the tapestry of a landscape heavily engineered for agriculture. An observation which seemed contrary to the image of great cities and cosmopolitan life that Europe evokes. Instead, the cities were revealed as ruptures of grey which splintered in web-like patterns of urban development. I traced the threads of tarmac connecting them, and wondered could it be the same road I'd ridden fourteen months previously.

Of Istanbul I saw the airport. More than a decade before Istanbul had been my first taste of the 'Orient.' The furthest I had travelled east. It did not disappoint. I had revelled in the apparent exotica and cultural difference at this nexus of East and West. The epic and alien architecture of the Blue Mosque and Aya Sophia told of a fascinating past, but one that still stood solidly in the present. The bustle of the bazaar, the whirls of fruit-flavoured smoke from bubbling *hookahs*, and the timely wail of the call to prayer, revealed a new and intoxicating world to me. Standing on the deck of a boat as it lulled its way up the Bosporus, I took my first tantalising glimpse of Asia, and marvelled at what exciting and adventurous possibilities might be found there.

However, I've never recovered that initial enthusiasm for Istanbul. Each time I return my eyes have been opened a little wider from other travels, and I find a city increasingly sanitised and marketed for mass tourism. The mystique and taste of the exotic it once held for me has gone.

Whether the city had really changed so much, or just me, was never going to be assessed from the inside of Istanbul airport. For the airport was typically mute and 'international' in its character, cut from the same cloth as any large airport in the West or wider 'developed' world - both inappropriate definitions that Turkey seems to straddle with some ambiguity. However, it seemed to illustrate perfectly the sameness manifested by globalisation; a phenomenon which can be disturbing to the discerning 'intrepid' traveller.

The capacious white interior basked in anodyne light. It was sterile in that way shared by both the scientific laboratory and the modern shopping mall. Electronic goods and luxury fashion labels filled the façade. The ubiquitous show car was enthroned on its dais; its adoring worshippers huddled round in veneration. Here was presented the things we all, as global citizens, apparently want and should be striving for. Amidst its corporate uniformity, Istanbul, Turkey was invisible, subordinate to the logos of high-tech brands of the Far East. If there was continuity with Turkey in this temple to materialism, it was in the transit of people, ideas and stuff between continents at this watershed of cultures.

However, on the shuttle bus from the plane, the glamorous veneer of the terminal had already been proven as superficial as it appeared. Bleary eyed I had squeezed with considerable effort into the already overflowing vehicle. Some people made half-hearted efforts to accommodate those still shipwrecked on the tarmac as they tried to clamber aboard. Most just looked away. Squashed but secure I was sure I must be the last. Yet glancing back it was clear there was still half a plane load to come. A middle-aged British woman – most of the passengers were Turkish – examined the cattle truck she was expected to join with the loud rebuke that "They must be fucking joking!" The gestures of the ground crew hustling people through the jammed doors assured her they were not. She muscled on tenaciously, shouting how "Anyone with any fucking intelligence would move down to the middle of the bus to make room for the others!" There was some lacklustre shuffling and a few of the Turks shook their heads, presumably in dismay at this outburst, but gaining access to the bus remained a battle. The woman pulled her young daughter through the scrum and softly instructed her "its okay darling. It's just like India again! Hold on tightly to the rail and to mummy's hand."

Despite the dazzling showcase of uniform modernity that waited for us in the terminal, those not native to the land were already acknowledging that things were a little different here. Difference, despite its occasional discomfort is surely the essence of travelling.

Unfortunately, Istanbul was no longer different enough. Just as a drinker's tolerance of alcohol obliges him to consume ever greater quantities, travellers must constantly increase their intake of 'difference' if the habit is to remain rewarding. Thus, the second leg of my journey was a flight from Istanbul to Bishkek.

Of course, *difference* is a relative concept. Somewhere can only be *different* in opposition to what you already know. I wanted somewhere beyond what the TV or glossy magazine images of the 'exotic' had made familiar even without going there.

For the West, the mysterious and exotic - that *difference* - has always been in the East. Indeed, Shangri-La itself was thought to be somewhere in the mountains of a distant and magical orient. However, then the Chinese government 'found it', and packaged it in plastic for the tourist hordes, foreign and domestic alike.

China is still *different,* but like everywhere else these differences are being expressed in increasingly homogenised and familiar forms. In some ways *difference* is dying out. Everywhere culture is commercialised and sanitised into a global gift shop of meaningless tat and superficial souvenir-soaked snap-shots.

The reason for this is not mysterious, nor, as many assume, is it the outcome of some 'natural' progression for which the human species was destined. As one scholar notes 'the economic, social and political system that prevails in the world today, with all its variations, including those of the Far East, is a European product and was spread through a combination of economic, military and political pressure known as imperialism… Europe has created a world after its own image, like it or not.'[1]

In less than a century China - arguably the epitome of the 'East' from a Western perspective - has been transformed from an imperial traditional civilisation to an atheist, communist country, and now, for a growing proportion of the population, to a consumer society no less capitalist (except in name) than America.

Writing over fifty years ago a wise man wrote 'for such civilisations it is only a matter of time before they find themselves at the same point as ourselves [in the West], knowing the same problems and the same phenomena of dissolution under the sign of "progress" and modernity.'

Today *they* and everybody else, with the possible exception of some peoples living in isolated areas, have reached that *point.* However, although the process is accelerating it remains far from uniform. This discrepancy is most commonly expressed in the terms of 'developed' and 'undeveloped' countries.

Kyrgyzstan and the other Central Asian nations are still labelled 'developing' countries. Of course, they have also been thoroughly subjected to the processes of imperialism and modernisation by Tsarist Russia and the Soviet Union. Communism as an ideology was materialist and utopian. Strange though it might seem, the same is true of capitalist liberal democracy. Both share a desire for global transformation and standardisation on a single template. Both are homogenising and destructive to traditional forms of living. Moreover, both have their origins in the European Enlightenment. It is a truism that all political forms that have dominated the modern world came from the West, whilst all world religions have their source in the East.

However, Kyrgyzstan was on the fringe of the communist world, a political and economic backwater where despite the immense change forced upon the people there, elements of a traditional way of life remained. I was under no illusions that Kyrgyzstan was some Shangri-la, untouched by the processes of modernity. Yet, in the rubble of communism's broken dreams and in the hills of the resilient nature it had sought to conquer, I hoped to soak up some essence, some trace of an older way of living. I wanted to do this before whatever the communists had left of 'tradition' was erased completely. As professor John Gray writes 'Free markets are the most potent solvents of tradition at work in the world today. They set a premium on novelty and a discount on the past.'[2] I was aware that I did not have long, on this short trip specifically, and in general. The Central Asian 'backwater' has already become the frontline in a resource war between surrounding 'great' powers. It is increasingly accessible to international visitors and business. The region is being drawn in and opened up to global systems that will change it, in some ways for the better, and in some ways for the worst, irrevocably. Eurasia's final frontier is fading out of obscurity.

Bishkek is the capital city of Kyrgyzstan. It is a country larger than Austria and Hungary combined, yet of the five former Soviet Central Asian republics, only Tajikistan is smaller. With 94% of its area mountainous and a third of that permanently under snow, Kyrgyzstan supports a population of just over five million. It is also a frog. On my first visit to the country in 2007 a local man told me how Kyrgyzstan resembles the shape of a frog. It's an image I've been unable to shake since. Kyrgyzstan is a frog in profile with no front legs. The Kyrgyz frog's eastern most point is its nose, which protrudes into Xinjiang. From its nose the Tian Shan Mountains run in a south westerly direction along the frog's throat and underbelly, marking the border with China. On top of the frog's head and westwards right along its back presses the border of big brother Kazakhstan. The frog's rear end pokes into Uzbekistan whilst its back leg kicks out into Tajikistan. However, what gives the Kyrgyz frog life is its prominent eye, the large elliptical Lake Issyk Kul.

The flight left late. I scanned the appearances of people assembled for it. With regards to 'Westerners', it seemed I was one of three. The other two were tall, powerfully built men. Their laid-back drawl identified them as Americans. Their 'high-and-tight' haircuts signalled military personnel destined for the large US base outside Bishkek. When it came to tourists, much as I dislike the term applied to myself, it appeared I was alone. Mid-winter was clearly not the season to visit this ex-Soviet republic, nine months out of a violent revolution, and seven months since savage ethnic clashes rocked the south of the country.

Russian, Kyrgyz, Turkish, and English floated over the crowd as it idled towards the gate. Oddly, they appeared mainly to be women. I guessed the girls to be on scholarships studying in Europe or working as nannies there. They were mostly dressed in the jeans and 'Western' fashion that is now ubiquitous globally. However, some of the older women wore the flowing patterned gowns and headscarves traditional to Central Asia.

The security lady spoke to me. When I didn't respond she shouted somewhat abruptly. Then recognition dawned on her tired features and she exclaimed in English this time "Aah, you're not Turkish. Take off your shoes please." I complied, pleased that even a Turk might think me Turkish, for I was relying on this fluke of appearance – I have no Turkish ancestry – to help me blend in down the road.

I was not anticipating any particular difficulties, but wanted to avoid looking obviously foreign and thus incurring the connotations of wealth and easy pickings, whether by guile or force, that can afflict one anywhere. However, I was also aware that this was not quite the same country that it had been on my previous visits. Peace had been restored, but the Foreign Office was still advising against all travel to some of the regions where I would certainly be heading.

Fortunately, as long as I kept my mouth shut, 'blending in' would not prove too difficult. This aesthetic subtlety would merely help me avoid unwanted hassle. However, for a long time travel in Central Asia by Westerners required full-blown disguise or some very nasty consequences.

Hungarian scholar Herman Vambery travelled through Central Asia before the Russian occupation disguised as a dervish. In 1837 British officer Eldred Pottinger entered Herat as a Muslim holy man. One element of his disguise was the use of dye to darken his skin. Another 'Great Game' player Arthur Conolly, who famously met his unfortunate end at Bukhara, had first tried to reach Khiva (in modern Uzbekistan) disguised as a merchant from India. He was warned how Turkmen slavers attacked caravans early in the morning. Killing anyone who resisted or who was old, they took the strong and beautiful to be sold in the slave markets of the Khanates. After a near miss that forced him to turn back from Khiva, Conolly headed to Kandahar in Afghanistan where he heard the slavers chopped off their captives ears believing it would make them too ashamed to escape.

Of course, even today travel in Afghanistan remains a dangerous enterprise for Westerners. Most that do visit will at least dress in local attire and, if of the right gender, grow a beard. Afghanistan is the only 'Stan' where such precautions are still necessary. However, when Afghanistan was a safe and accessible destination on the 'Hippy trail' to India in the 1960s and 70s, Soviet Central Asia remained strictly off limits. So too did Central Asia beyond the Tian Shan, once known as East Turkestan and now part of China. Even in 1989 intrepid student of the 'Silk Road' Christa Paula had to travel there in disguise – or as inconspicuous as a tall, blonde German could make herself.

The land of the Kyrgyz was similarly forbidden and very much restricted even to Soviet citizens. There is little record in English of Western travellers visiting the region, and those that did were surely under exceptional circumstances. We hear of British agent F.M. Bailey travelling with an armed group from Irkeshtan Pass (on the modern border between Kyrgyzstan and China) to Osh in 1918. He was on his way to Tashkent to gather intelligence on what was happening in Russian Central Asia amidst the chaos of the Bolshevik revolution, particularly with regard to the large number of German and Austrian prisoners of war the Tsarist regime had deposited there. Twenty years on, one such Austrian POW Gustav Krist, who had escaped, then chose to return in the name of adventure with false papers indentifying him as a mining expert. This was fine until the death of the real man whose papers he was under became front page news. In Central Asia Krist travelled with 'Qirghiz.' Indeed, he witnessed 'the last march of the free Qirghiz' before their subjugation by the Russians. His tale was published in English as *Alone Through the Forbidden Land: Journeys in disguise through Soviet Central Asia*. After that there seems to be little or no account of Westerners in Kirgizia until the end of the Soviet era many decades later.

The flight to Bishkek cut quietly through the night, most passengers getting the sleep my body clock would not allow. A hostess presented the same menu as the last flight so I chose option B this time. The in-flight entertainment was an animated movie about talking owls dubbed into Turkish. I opted instead for the vibratory silence of the fuselage. It was a clear night and the world flickered past below. Istanbul was a galaxy of light, but soaring east illumination seemed fading and sporadic. Through Anatolia, the

Caucuses, and into the desert and steppe of Central Asia, the lights of human habitation became increasingly sparse, scattered like pockets of distant stars in an empty cosmos. Again I became aware that, minus the 35,000ft altitude, I was vaguely retracing the route made by bicycle in 2009. Turkey, Georgia, Azerbaijan, Kazakhstan, Uzbekistan, Kyrgyzstan. The countries clicked by in reverse order of the way ridden, and six months in the saddle was subsumed into a five hour flight.

The pilot announced that we would soon be landing and that the temperature in Bishkek was -15°c. Due to be thrown to the inevitable taxi sharks I asked the girl sat behind me in faltering Russian what time I might expect the sun to rise. *Manas* airport is 30kms from the city and the advent of daylight would make the guaranteed hustle of taxi negotiation, coupled with navigation to half remembered addresses down unlit backstreets a less intimidating prospect. Unfortunately, the girl who was Kyrgyz and called Zarina did not know exactly. The reason for which being that she had spent the last three months in Qatar. She proudly explained that she had been the only Kyrgyz national in the whole country. She had a two year contract working in a hotel there. When I asked her if she liked it, her reply was that "Qatar's a closed country, where even the men wear long dresses, and they all pray five times a day." It was clear she had no affinity with the stauncher take on Islam she had witnessed. Her comments well illustrated that the Kyrgyz, although nominally Muslim, are generally moderate in their adoption of the faith. Indeed, with her jeans, jacket and make-up Zarina would not have looked out of place on any Western high street. It's also rare to see men in Kyrgyzstan wear a beard, skullcap, or any other instantly recognizable religious adornment.

When we landed no hint of dawn glimmered on the horizon of a still very black night. Leaving the plane I was enveloped by a piercing cold. Zarina shuddered in shock having just returned from the +30°c of a Qatari winter. I was surprised to see the surrounding airfield full with huge grey cargo planes of the U.S military. With predatory noses, and the slit black eyes of their cockpit windows, they lay on the icy runway like a shoal of beached and bloated sharks. A logistical fleet for America's 'War on Terror' running sorties south to Afghanistan. Somewhere I would be heading myself in the coming months.

The Americans have been in Kyrgyzstan since December 2001. Other countries that would have been suitable for bases, in a geographical sense, such as Pakistan or Saudi Arabia, were not politically appropriate places from which to wage war on Muslim Afghanistan. Central Asia proved a better option, and a base was set up in Uzbekistan[3] even before the one at Bishkek. Indeed, the fact that these secular post-Soviet states fear the rise of Islamic fundamentalism within their own borders meant that - on the surface at least – there was ideological convergence with the US, thereby justifying the presence of American bases on their soil. However, it was not a free pass, and impoverished Kyrgyzstan does very well financially out of the American presence. When the base opened the Kyrgyz government received $7000 for every American plane taking off and landing there.[4] No doubt this figure has since increased.

Of course, Russia views Kyrgyzstan as within her sphere of influence and was far from happy about this American encroachment. Indeed, beyond its role for supporting operations in Afghanistan, the base also conforms to a Neo-con policy of creating 'Lily pad' bases that enable American military might to be deployed quickly and easily anywhere in the world. American bases in Central Asia not only intrude on Russia's traditional stomping ground, but mean American forces now pincer both 'Rogue State' Iran and rising super-power China. Central Asia also happens to be home to some of the largest known reserves of hydrocarbons left on the planet.

However, the 'War on Terror' mantra meant Russia was free to pursue its own ends in Chechnya without negative feedback from the Western press. Plus, in 2002, the Russians set up their own airbase in Kyrgyzstan, at Kant, just thirty-five kilometres from the Americans. It was Russia's largest deployment to the region since the break-up of the Soviet Union.

The third big player in what has been aptly called 'The New Great Game' is China, and they were equally uneasy about America's arrival in their backyard. Still, like Russia they were quick to use the "War on Terror" rhetoric for domestic purposes. For China this meant an opportunity to clamp down on Uyghur separatism in Xinjiang province. An Islamic Turkic speaking people, the Uyghur share far more cultural continuity with their ethnic cousins in the 'Stans' than they do with the Han (the dominant ethnic group in China). China also signalled its presence in the region by holding joint military exercises with Kyrgyzstan. This was no small gesture because it was the first time in history that the People's Liberation Army had engaged in manoeuvres abroad.

At Bishkek's *Manas* airport the one terminal, small and bare, could not have been more of a contrast with the consumer extravaganza of Istanbul. Stocky Kyrgyz soldiers (perhaps they were just airport staff, but they wore camouflaged fatigues), male and female, with the iconic fur hats of their Soviet legacy, stamped their feet and exhaled clouds of breath into the bitter night. They instructed us to wait. Zarina complained how there was always some inexplicable delay when she returned to Kyrgyzstan.

I could see a handful of foreigners I'd missed in Istanbul. I learned they were American Peace Corps. Eventually we got instructions to move, Kyrgyz and foreign visitors dividing into separate immigration queues. Before we parted Zarina invited me to come and stay with her family in her home town of Naryn.

Kyrgyzstan is the only Central Asian country where you can get a visa on arrival, but only when you fly in. Obtaining it took most of my dollars, and with no local currency or signs of an ATM, I regretted not having planned a little better. Whilst I didn't have Turkmen slavers to worry about, there were taxi touts to contend with. My plan had been to wait until dawn for a *mashutka* (mini-bus) that allegedly ran to the city. However, I was soon forcibly ushered from the spartan terminal into the waiting phalanx of hyena-like taxi touts. Wading through their grabbing, and aggressive demands of 'Kouda?' (where?), I wondered how with barely enough cash to get a taxi, let alone a hotel, I was going to resolve the situation. The wee hours in unlit Bishkek was not the time or place I wanted to be hunting down a cash machine and then trawl the signpost-less gravel tracks of downtown for the old haunt I had in mind. That was before the problematic issue of making the owners aware of my presence from behind one of the sheet steel gates that protect all properties here.

Of course, most people would have arranged all these things before hand, or just dished out the cash for a taxi and a decent hotel the driver would be familiar with. However, such decadence challenged my thrifty budget as much as it compromised my conception of how one ought to travel in Central Asia. Getting a plane had been degrading enough for my Silk Road sensibilities, and

I resolved from that point on to rely on my wits alone. Unfortunately, this translated into me standing mute amongst the baying taxi-hyenas wondering how long it would take at -15°c for me to get frost bite on my nose and at what point I should consider walking along the unappetizingly dark road in the direction I hoped led to Bishkek.

Luckily, looking beyond the sea of cropped black-haired heads that were vying for my custom, I saw two European women heading towards the scattered array of decrepit vehicles that served as the taxi rank. Clearly I was far from the only Westerner coming to Kyrgyzstan mid-winter. Wasting no time I barged through the jostling touts and imposed myself upon the two who looked like they might be mother and daughter. They weren't. They were however being picked up by the owner of a budget guesthouse.

Their chauffeur immediately appeared. He was a middle-aged Kyrgyz man, dark and stocky, with the standard black crop and a mouth full of typically gold teeth. My inquiry if there was any more room at the inn was met with a smile that glowed in the moonlight, and a pleasing "sure, no problem."

Our awaiting chariot was an old Lada. With our baggage it barely accommodated us. The elder of the two women pointed disdainfully at my rucksack, asking in a manner that suggested it was a particularly offensive item, "is that yours?" I took the hint and hoisted it onto my lap so she could have two thirds of the backseat to herself. It turned out they were both from Sweden and had met at their delayed connection in Istanbul. The younger woman, blonde and with glasses, was called Helga. She was a student of something like Conflict Studies and had come to Kyrgyzstan for a month of investigation into the nation's recent traumas. The other lady worked for an 'international' organisation and had a six month contract in troubled Osh, "trying to get kids back to school" as she put it. How exactly she went about persuading the Uzbek, Kyrgyz or any of the many other nationalities living in the Osh region to go 'back to school', she did not elaborate upon. I tried to imagine a similar situation in the UK with well-meaning women of Central Asia coming to advise British mothers on the education of their children. It was difficult, yet in reverse it seemed normal to the point of being almost 'natural.' I did not doubt the noble intentions of the people involved or that such work had validity. However, the flow of aid from the West to the rest carries implicit assumptions of superiority;

that other people need saving from themselves, and that to be saved they need to become like us. It is very much a continuation of the Victorian Christian civilising mission. Such development is always in accordance with Western values because it is supported by and benefits the Western economic system. Moreover, it is ultimately backed by the kind of 'hard power' parked on the tarmac of *Manas* airport.

I turned to stare out of the window. Unfortunately, a thick crust of ice made this impossible, so I looked ahead through a windscreen that was at least partly clear. The road was narrow with no lights, lines, reservation or curb stones. It just fizzled out into frozen mud at its edges, and cut an ill-defined, pot-holed path into the slowly emerging dawn. At times it was flanked by an avenue of trees; the tall, thin Poplars that are so abundant in this part of the world. Behind them spread a flat featureless landscape. The mountains I knew were out there, lost in the darkness. Occasionally, I would see people emerge out of the murk. Presumably they were waiting for some sort of transport themselves. The thick fur hats, upturned collars, and plumes of heated air that escaped their lungs all testified to the stony cold. Nothing seemed to move. Everything in the vista was locked still. Even the people stood like ice statues.

As we approached the city, buildings began to loom from the darkness. Giant concrete blocks with boarded windows, peeling paintwork and tumble-down asbestos fencing. Yet they appeared infrequently, and one wondered if the city had yet started. There was no density to it. Mostly there were trees. It seemed like a great wood had reclaimed whatever city there once was. Now and then there was an isolated, flickering neon sign, indicating some seedy looking club or casino. Tokyo this was not. In fact, Bishkek's patchy attempts at glitz seemed only to highlight its general state of disrepair.

There were no streetlights. A road sweeper laboured in the gutter, veiled in the exhalations of his own exertion. More figures in fur hats started to appear, hunched over against the cold. For me those hats epitomise Russia, a country I've never even visited. They shout USSR and communism, and in brackets they whisper Stalin, Gulag, and the suffering of untold millions. Childhood indoctrination from James Bond films, and almost entirely negative stereotypes amassed from the Western media since, meant I could only see those hats as symbolising the goose-stepping, Kalashnikov-brandishing ranks of an ominous 'other' - not just the practical pieces of headwear they were for such frosty climes.

Yet the crumbling concrete, towering chimneys, and barely roadworthy wrecks of Soviet era vintage, did little to dispel bleak assumptions about grim decay in the old USSR. Someone once described the Soviet Union as a knight "dying inside his armour"[5], analogising the vast military spending that eventually strangled everything else. Looking at dishevelled Bishkek on that unflattering morning it seemed that with the knight long dead, now even his metaphorical armour was rusted and forlorn.

We stopped at a featureless but imposingly dark corner. The driver pointed and said to the older lady, "Your hotel down there." She was understandably apprehensive about getting out and wandering off alone into the frozen night. "Could you please drop me at it?" she inquired hopefully. He silently consented, pulling up outside an illuminated lobby, where apparent renovation had left it littered with dangling wires, step ladders and bits of plaster board. Seeing her safely inside, we continued down a maze of empty, black back roads before halting at an unmarked steel gate that was the entrance to our abode. I realised that I could never have found this place from the airport alone. It was utterly undifferentiated in a labyrinth of unsigned streets, breeze-block walls, and impenetrable metal gates. I learned later that this was because it wasn't legally registered. This was in order to escape the costs; bribes and the opaque bureaucracy that would accompany such an entrepreneurial venture. Inside we were led across a snow covered lawn to the one small room we would be sharing. It was the only option. The owner explained it was the only room they could effectively heat. A clunky mobile radiator hummed in its centre and vaguely imitated giving off warmth. The beds were small and ancient with sunken, stale mattresses. An exposed light bulb gave timid illumination. There were no curtains, only some ragged nets, and the outer door would not close shut properly. The adjacent bathroom offered a squat toilet and a shower fed by raw wires. It was accompanied by a handwritten sign warning, quite justifiably, 'DANGER.' On the plus side it was going to cost me less than £4 a night. Safe and secure, my body clock now began to take its revenge for transcontinental travel. I fell easily to sleep, glad to be in Kyrgyzstan, but quite unsure as to what I would do now I was there.

2

Place Below the Mountains

We awoke at dusk, hungry. I went to look for a shop and Helga decided to join me. The light was already fading and I hustled Helga along as she fiddled with her i-phone; a bold, if unintentional statement of wealth in a quite impoverished place. We stood out like sore thumbs and I felt eyes on us as we plodded over the fragmented pavement. Bishkek isn't a dangerous city, but it's also not a great place to look conspicuously foreign, and therefore wealthy, after dark. I had known a few tourists who had been mugged in Bishkek at night and did not intend to share the experience. Kyrgyzstan's recent instability made me particularly cautious. I needed to get a feel of the place again first.

The leafy, sun-kissed city I had known in previous summers, in winter took on a melancholy that bordered on the post-apocalyptic. Everything looked older and more decrepit than it already was. It was a colourless scene. The trees were stripped of their leaves. To the east a pair of giant chimneys spouted plumes of pale smoke which stayed static in the windless air. The dull grey sky was streaked with faint fingers of pastel luminosity. Everything seemed to merge together; the icy slush, the cracking asphalt, concrete, asbestos, shabby cars, and dirty white *mashutkas*. It was a cornucopia of grey. Only the sun was distinct in its colour; a small but glaring red disc hovering weakly on the western horizon. A foggy haze sat sticky in the air. The people trudged through it with short measured steps on account of the ice. Heads down, shoulders hunched, they compacted themselves against the cold, eyes permanently prowling the ground for stable footing.

At a corner, taxi drivers huddled together, muttering in low tones. They smoked and stamped their feet against the cold.

Unanimously dressed in dark clothes and black beanies or flat caps they blended seamlessly with the general drabness. Unfortunately we did not, as an outburst of "TAXI? TAXI?" testified. Blonde, light skinned Helga might have passed for Russian, except she had that plumpness and softness of skin so characteristic of over-indulgence and easy living in the West. It was an effect amplified by the 'outdoorsy' pocket-festooned trousers and synthetic hiking boots tourists feel required to wear even in cities; as if at any moment they might face a situation where only that extra pocket two thirds of the way down their calf, or the grip of their excessively expensive shoes ostensibly designed for mountaineering, could save them.

The drivers' dark, Asiatic faces regarded us curiously as we passed. There was a row of pokey shops with bars on the windows, and a dozen little kiosks set up outside selling the familiar knick-knacks of Kyrgyzstan: a multitude of cigarettes sold in packets and as singles, sunflower seeds, soft drinks, beer, chocolate, chewing gum, plus some more regionally unique items like *Kurut*, *Nasvai*, and seed powder. *Kurut* have the appearance of white gobstoppers, but are actually a rock-hard and rather sour dairy product. *Nasvai* is a tobacco derivative, normally in the form of small dark pellets which are placed under the tongue or the inside of the cheek. Such kiosks are found on any main street in Bishkek and were a considerable part of the economy after the Soviet collapse. Like all I've seen, these were 'manned' by Kyrgyz women. They sat bundled in clothes like so many Russian dolls, with round red-cheeked faces framed by hats and headscarves.

"Fog or pollution?" Helga queried with regard to the thick grey pall hanging in the air. "Both, I guess" was the best I could offer. In summer I had never noticed such a thing. "This place is so fucked up!" Helga lamented, before asking "are all Central Asian cities like this?"

"Yes and no" I replied. Bishkek was a world away from Kazakhstan's urbane Almaty, or the historical cities of Uzbekistan. Yet they were all Soviet constructions. As one commentator on the region put it 'The presence of the USSR can still be read more or less wherever you look, in the names of places, street-name signs that nobody has bothered to remove... the monuments to the dead, the statues of Lenin etc. It is, of course, a washed out USSR, with nobody bothering to repaint it.'[1]

I could understand Helga's feeling considering it was her first impression of Bishkek. Things seemed gritty and oppressive, not at all like the city of my memories. In the bitter cold it was hard to believe Bishkek lies at virtually the same latitude as Barcelona and Rome. However, unlike those Mediterranean hubs, it is subject to no oceanic influences, only a climate type known as 'extreme continental.' That winter 'extreme', along with the fact we were in one of Bishkek's less salubrious quarters, a city which had undergone a year of violent revolution and turmoil, probably explained the unaccommodating vibe.

On previous visits, I'd arrived overland after months of travelling through South or East Asia. In some ways Kyrgyzstan had then seemed a step closer to home. Footprints of Russia offered a more familiar civilisation and culture to contend with. After all, Russians look Western even if they aren't and Cyrillic is far easier to get on with than Urdu or Mandarin. However, flying straight in from the UK seemed to cast Kyrgyzstan in a different light.

We arrived at the supermarket, part of a chain called NARODNI, which in Russian means 'people', as in 'shop of the people' – a very communist name. It was small by Western standards, no more than you'd find attached to most petrol stations. Helga, scanning the aisles, commented that "maybe it will be hard to find something to eat here for a vegetarian." Undoubtedly, but I couldn't think of anywhere else locally – or in the country - where it would be any easier. Whilst we could buy vegetables we had nowhere to prepare them. The Kyrgyz and Central Asians in general tend to find vegetarianism a peculiar concept. The Kazakhs and Kyrgyz are traditionally pastoralists. The high altitude meadows and barren steppe they occupied are hardly suitable for agriculture. They were nomadic peoples, right up to the early 20thC in some cases. They lived off their herds, and meat remains the core of their diet today.

Still, they're not completely unsympathetic to the condition. I recalled a Kyrgyz man who I stayed with on my bike ride. Before he served dinner he asked "Do you like cutting animals?" Initially, I was bemused by this strange question, until I realised he was simply asking if I was a vegetarian. He had spent some time in the States, and clearly picked up his knowledge of curious western dietary habits there. He related nostalgically his American colleagues' astonishment at the ability of a few Kyrgyz to obtain a sheep in New York and devour the whole animal in one sitting.

Helga had to settle for bread and cheese. We scurried back to the hotel, Helga anxiously preoccupied with her i-phone the whole way. Back in the slightly less than sub-zero sanctuary of the room she looked at me lip quivering and promptly burst into tears. "Are you okay?" I asked awkwardly, clearly aware that she wasn't.

"I can't stay here!" she sobbed sorrowfully, "It's not what I expected. I think I've made a terrible mistake!" I tried to comfort her with such platitudes as "I'm sure things will seem better in the morning." However, she was adamant "I'm leaving tonight."

"Where will you go?" I asked. She said she would stay at the other Swedish lady's hotel tonight and find something more convivial in the morning. That explained all the frantic i-phone activity earlier. It was understandable. She had come here to work, and our current lodging was certainly not the place to do that. Fortunately, the owner was good enough to drive her to the other hotel.

And so I had the flickering light, inadequate radiator, and icy seclusion of the room, all to myself that night. Helga had left at the right time because about twenty minutes after her departure the power cut out, which was to become a recurring feature of my stay. With fourteen hours till sunrise and it being too cold to do anything but lie fully dressed in bed, I pondered on Bishkek.

Thousands of years ago when Turkic tribes, including the Kyrgyz, still inhabited southern Siberia, Central Asia was populated by Indo-European peoples. These were people who spoke Indo-European languages from which modern tongues as diverse as Hindi, Russian and English derive. Kyrgyz however belongs to a different linguistic heritage, the Turkic and Altaic language groups. These were brought to the region later with tribal migrations from the north east. Ethnically, the Indo-European peoples have generally been described as 'Iranian', differentiating them from the Turco-Mongolic characteristics dominant among the Kyrgyz. It was Iranian peoples who were the first nomads in Central Asia, and it was Iranian peoples who built the first cities there too.

The early civilisations of Central Asia were concentrated where oases could provide irrigation for agriculture, facilitating sedentary existence and the growth of towns. Thus, urban development was concentrated in the fertile Fergana Valley of ancient Sogdiana (now mostly within the territory of modern Uzbekistan), and around the Tarim Basin of what is now China's Xinjiang Province.

However, the routes between these urban centres, and the worlds of East and West beyond, went through what is now Kyrgyzstan. There are few places at which the natural barrier of the Tian Shan on Kyrgyzstan's eastern border can be breached. The Chuy Valley, where modern Bishkek is situated, offers one of the more accessible passages, leading to broad grasslands between the formidable Tian Shan and Altai ranges. It has been negotiated by merchants and armies from the earliest times, and thus has tended always to invite some form of settlement.

Somewhere under modern Bishkek is said to lie 'Jul', a trading centre that flourished between the 7th Century A.D. and the arrival of the Mongols in the 13th. The whole of the Chuy Valley was densely settled during this period, with towns such as Barkshan on the southern shore of Lake Issyk Kul acting as way-stations along the ancient trade route. The nomads also favoured the area for their winter pastures. However, no settlement around modern Bishkek seems to have been occupied continuously from these times until the present. Medieval traveller Tamim Ibn Bahr came across the ruins of such an ancient city near Lake Issyk Kul, but who had built it or why it had been abandoned was unknown to the local Turkic population.

Turkic peoples only really started infiltrating into Central Asia west of the Tian Shan in the middle of the first millennium A.D. Before their arrival, Iranian nomads known as Saka or Scythians had represented a single cultural complex that extended across the steppe from China to Europe. Since records began the nomads were regarded as having no settlements.* Herodotus described 'a people

---

* However, archaeology has shown that the Eurasian steppe, traditional home of the nomads, was far from always devoid of settlement. East of the Ural Mountains a fortified stronghold has been discovered. *Sintashta,* as it has been called, consisted of fifty or sixty houses and is one of twenty related settlements. The oldest carbon dates place it at nearly 5000 years old. That's before the Great Pyramids of Giza were built. It makes the people who lived there almost as remote in time from the Scythians as the Scythians are from us. It has been speculated that they were the original 'Aryans', ancestors of the people who invaded the Indian sub-continent and were immortalised in the Indian epic the *Rig-Veda.* Archaeologists have wondered

without fortified towns, living... in wagons which they take with them wherever they go.'[2] In the mid 6th Century B.C. Darius I of Persia, then the most powerful empire on Earth, led an army of 700,000 men into the steppe looking to crush the Scythians. The Scythians refused to join battle, so Darius pursued them further and further into a featureless landscape, but found there was no settled population to sustain his army. Moreover, the Scythians implemented a 'scorched earth' policy, depriving the Persians of water and pasture by blocking up wells and burning off the grass in their wake. By the time the Scythians chose to fight, the Persians were severely weakened and forced to retreat. They only narrowly escaped total destruction. The Chinese experienced similar tactics when attacking the nomads in the east. This strategy of retreat into the vastness of the steppe has been compared to Russia's actions during World War II; the German enemy deprived of supplies and demoralised by distances. As the Scythians sent those who could not fight safely north, the Russians transferred populations and industry east, with much of both ending up in Kyrgyzstan.

The ancient Iranian nomads that once ranged from Kyrgyzstan to the Ukraine had a definite relationship with settled people. Settlements provided the nomads with access to products like grain, salt, and luxury items which they were unable to produce on the Steppe. The military superiority of the nomads meant they could make settled agricultural communities their vassals and extract tribute from them. These Iranian nomads were in turn replaced by Turkic nomads. The Turkic nomads are also likely to have exercised some control over Central Asian urban centres, extracting tribute from settlements such as Jul in return for protecting the caravan routes.

Whilst 'Jul' actually means 'steppe-land' in ancient Turkic, the population was probably still overwhelmingly made up of ethnic Iranian people. However, the coming of the Turkic tribes created a far more pronounced ethnic and linguistic divide between the settled and nomadic peoples of Central Asia than existed previously. The Turkic

---

if it was the inhabitants of *Sintashta* who invented the chariot, and considering the settlement was so heavily fortified, have asked the enigmatic question; what were the people living there so afraid of? Anthony, *The Horse, The Wheel, And Language,* 371.

word for 'city' *Kend/Kent* is actually borrowed from Iranian (E.g. Samar*kand* or Penji*kent*). For a long time inhabitants of the cities of Central Asia were probably bilingual, speaking an Iranian and a Turkic tongue. This resembles the situation in Kyrgyzstan and Central Asia today; where a Russian *lingua-franca* overlays the Turkic languages of the indigenous peoples.

The Turkic nomads used the settled Iranian people for trading and administrative functions. Something illustrated by the medieval Turkic saying 'a Turk is never without a *Tat* [settled Iranian] like a cap is never without a head.'

Nomadic encampments also constituted settlements, but unlike their Iranian counterparts they were 'tent cities', so naturally little physical evidence of them remains. Linguistically however, the English word *horde* originates from the Turkic *ordu*' which meant 'camp of the ruler' and later 'army.' Similarly, linguistic clues from proto-Turkic, like words for 'agriculture', 'handicraft', and 'trade', seem indicative of not all Turkic peoples being nomadic.[3] The Yenisei River in Siberia, ancestral homeland of the Kyrgyz, was apparently also the site of an ancient settled civilisation, and during the 11th Century A.D. the ruler of the Kyrgyz was said to have been living in a town named *Kemijkath,* after the *Kem* (Yenisey) River.[4]

Between the end of the 10th Century A.D. and the middle of the 12th, the territory of Kyrgyzstan fell under the rule of a Turkic dynasty called the Karakhanids. The Karakhanids had two of their capitals in the Chuy Valley, Suyab and Balasaghun (near modern Tokmok). Another important Karakhanid urban centre was Ozgon. This is the modern Kyrgyz town Ozgon, just east of Osh. Whilst the Karakhanids were Turkic, they were only a ruling elite and did not have a significant effect on the still predominantly Iranian culture of settled Central Asia. The Mongol invasion of the 13th Century meant Jul, along with many other far grander settlements throughout Central Asia, was totally destroyed. For the next six hundred years caravans continued following the tracks of their predecessors through the Chuy Valley and past the dust of ancient Jul.

In the early 18th Century, the Kokand Khanate had a series of forts constructed to protect its trading interests through the Tian Shan. One of these was at the site of modern Bishkek. Like the Sogdians of yore, the Kokand Khanate was a regional power emanating from the Fergana Valley in present day Uzbekistan. These settled people, with no concept of nationality in the modern sense, were identified by Tsarist ethnographers as *sarts*. Just as in the days of Jul and Balasaghun, the population of Central Asia was split between sedentary and nomadic cultures. The nomads were still exclusively Turkic; Turkmen, Kazakh and Kyrgyz tribesmen, roughly concentrated in the regions which the Russians subsequently divided into their respective Republics (SSRs). However, the sedentary people denoted as *sarts*, unlike their Sogdian predecessors, were by now a mixture of the aboriginal Iranian stock and Turkic groups that had given up their nomadic ways and chosen to settle.

Despite their economic symbiosis, a gulf of distrust remained between the two ways of life. The only Kyrgyz residing at the fort of this proto-Bishkek were hostages donated by tribal chiefs as an insurance policy against their nomadic brethren. Indeed, the nomads still held sedentary people with contempt, raiding towns for booty as had been happening since the days of the Saka. The term *sart* became a derogatory word for 'trader', whilst townsmen could return the insult by calling the nomads 'Kazakhs!' This apparently carried connotations of 'vagabond' and even 'thief.' Indeed, 'kazakh' may derive from the Arabic 'qazac' which means 'outlaw.' The Kazakhs which we now associate with Kazakhstan preferred to call themselves 'Kyrgyz', whilst the Kyrgyz were known as the 'Kara-Kyrgyz' or 'black-Kyrgyz.'

The Kara-Kyrgyz first received real attention from the Russians in the 1850's when Kyrgyz bandits began raiding the new Russian towns that were slowly encroaching across the Kazakh steppe. However, the brutal winter of 1859-60 decimated the Kyrgyz flocks and obliged them to accept Russian 'protection' against enemy tribes. In 1862 Kyrgyz of the Solto and Sarybagush tribes attacked the fort belonging to the Kokand Khanate at the site of modern Bishkek. In need of assistance to close the assault they found the Russians only too ready to oblige, and the captured fort immediately fell under Russian control.

The town that grew out of the old *Sart* settlement and new Russian garrison was called 'Pishpek.' It is still debated whether this refers to an implement used to stir that Kyrgyz staple *koumiss* (fermented mare's milk), or if it derives from the old Sogdian word 'peshagakh' meaning 'place beneath the mountains.' In 1878 Pishpek became the Russian administrative centre for the region. Slavic settlers, Cossack, Russian and Ukrainian poured in, attracted by generous land grants ordered by the Tsar and provided with land stolen from the Kyrgyz. The burgeoning frontier town was divided along ethnic lines with separate quarters for the different Slavic nationalities, as well as for the Tartars, Sarts, and Dungans (ethnically Chinese). By the early 20th Century the population had reached 20,000 and was furnished with many modern amenities of the era. However, the Kyrgyz component of the town's population remained miniscule.

Pishpek in its Soviet incarnation became 'Frunze', named after the Russian general Mikael Frunze who was born there. The Bolsheviks deemed the town 'capital' of the newly created Kyrgyz SSR (Soviet Socialist republic). As with Almaty in Kazakhstan, and Dushanbe in Tajikistan, these new capitals provided an urban centre in parts of Central Asia which lacked the sedentary tradition of the oasis settlements in what became Uzbekistan and Turkmenistan. It was thought that all these new capitals would provide a focal point for the creation of new national identities transcending tribal allegiance and the old nomad/townsman dichotomy.

In 1991, upon the break-up of the Soviet Union, Frunze reverted to its old name Bishkek. Yet whilst the city and state were now officially Kyrgyz, Bishkek's population was still 70% Slavic. However, since independence the demographics of Kyrgyzstan have changed dramatically, particularly in the cities, where administrative, technical and professional jobs were held overwhelmingly by Russians. It had been Soviet policy to make all the Republics of the USSR utterly reliant on the central economy controlled from Moscow. With the break-up of the Union the Kyrgyz economy collapsed. The Russians have left in droves, feeling that their quality of life could only decline if they stayed in a Kyrgyzstan which belonged to the Kyrgyz, their favoured position usurped. Ultimately, it was economics that siphoned the Russians from Kyrgyzstan, just as the economic incentives of abundant raw materials had brought them to Central Asia and led to the political formation of Kyrgyzstan in the first place. Like all colonising powers they came to exploit what they found, putting that vast 'empty' space of Central Asia to the plough, and encouraging their own people (and others) to settle with economic incentives such as free land – a scenario reminiscent of European expansion across America.

The next morning was refreshingly crisp and clear. The fog was gone and the sun was shining, its warm glow radiating from every snow covered surface. The sky was pure blue, not a trace of cloud denting its azure complexion. It was still well below freezing, but the cold air seemed to bring a heightened acuteness to the senses. Everything looked more defined in its empty clarity, and sounds seemed to travel further without distortion. Chickens clucked and pecked noisily along the neighbours' wire fence. The white stacks of chimney smoke to the east remained unmoved, and were the only stain on the sky. The lack of cloud instead brought the epic backdrop of the Ala-Too Mountains into view. Their chipped and chiselled faces sparkling like cut diamonds in the sunlight. In places they rise to over 4000 metres, their natural splendour dominating the horizon.

Walking into town, the pavement bustled with people, mainly Kyrgyz, but also some Russians. A dress code of jeans, black jackets and beanie hats seemed to prevail. Those emphatically Russian fur hats were also common and I saw not a few older Kyrgyz men sporting the traditional Kyrgyz headwear; tall tri-corns, made of white felt and decorated with black spirals. The Kyrgyz *Al-kalpak* hat is elf-like and pleasantly at odds with the drabness of a post-Soviet city. They looked particularly incongruous on the heads of municipal road sweepers in combination with their modern luminous orange high-viz jackets. The *Al-kalpak* design has even been converted into a felt baseball cap format; an interesting blend of Kyrgyz tradition and global fashion often worn by the young men. The young women clattered along the icy pavements in high heels. Their clothes, again, usually dark in colour; figure hugging jeans, chic coats, accompanied by scarf and beret. They kept the Russian habit of always dressing to the nines. Casual didn't seem to be a concept they were familiar with, and there was nothing uniquely, even remotely Kyrgyz in their attire. Only some of the older women could still be seen wearing the traditional patterned dress and headscarf.

There was a large, red faced Russian, a fur coat to his ankles and a huge fur hat on his head. Then there was a man who might have been Korean. There are many Koreans in Kyrgyzstan as a result of Stalin's forced migrations. Today they're totally assimilated, having largely lost their own language and culture. Next was an old Kyrgyz man with the appearance of an aging Khan, bedecked in fur, bent over a cane, with a wispy white beard protruding from his chin. Then

I passed a young Kyrgyz chap in a dark jacket, with the Mongolian features characteristic of his race. Somewhat unusually he had a beard and wore the skullcap of a pious Muslim. Another young man followed with the felt baseball cap decorated in the style of his forefathers' *Kalpak*. A group of Kyrgyz men in black boots and bomber jackets pored over a car engine. One of them was singing; but rather than a half-hearted pop ditty one might expect from a mechanic, he produced a deep and serious note that seemed to carry a meaning all of its own, even without words. I was reminded what song had so recently been to the Kyrgyz; the medium by which their whole culture, the entire accumulated knowledge of their collective past, had been stored and transmitted.

Then I passed an Asiatic beauty, fur lined hood framing features that would look at home in Bishkek, Beijing or Bhutan. Kyrgyz primary school children toddled along the pavement in pairs, only rosy faces protruding from protective garments. There were some Slavic faces on the street too, mainly old, the ones who got left behind; a hard, wrinkled visage; a bloated drinker's face with a nose like a bulbous red sponge. An old Russian woman ambled past in thick woollen stockings, dragging a little trolley behind her. Occasionally there was a tall young Russian, a blonde girl lost in a sea of black hair.

Tower blocks loomed on my left, the architectural epitome of urban decay, whether in inner-city Britain or the old Soviet bloc. Still, it was hard to believe that flats had been sold here for as little as 1000$ after independence, even to foreigners. There was graffiti on the walls and laundry hung untidily from every balcony. I wondered how it would ever dry in such weather. The old one-story Russian houses are painted white, with doors and window frames picked out in sky blue. Plastic cellophane was pinned across glass panes as rudimentary double glazing. A hodgepodge of asbestos, wooden planks and wire served as fencing around these quaint but dilapidated dwellings.

Numerous gravel tracks branch off the main road, leading to residential areas beyond its northern boundary. At the junction of one such road hid a mosque, barely distinguishable from the sandy and off-white buildings surrounding it. Only a short, modest minaret and humble silver dome define its spiritual nature. The faith's public face remains mild and restrained, particularly in Bishkek. For Bishkek is a

Soviet city built on an ideology that had banned religion; a sharp contrast from cities of the Middle East where it was often Islamic law that moulded architectural forms, controlled space and created seclusion. However, in Bishkek Islam is still undoubtedly there, inextricably entwined with the culture.

Islam was first brought to Kyrgyzstan by the Arab armies that fought the Chinese in the west of the country in 751AD. However, internal rebellion meant the Arabs stay was fleeting and the mantle of converting the nomads fell to Sufi missionaries. Sufism's mystical take on Islam blended well with the individualistic spirituality of shamanism, the native faith of the Kyrgyz. Even today, threads from the ancient belief system remain rife. Similarly, the customary nomadic law of *adat* always took precedence over Islamic *Sharia*. Again, even today, *adat* or traditional law often overrides that of the fledgling secular state; for example in matters like polygamy and bride-knapping. Traditionally, the heaviest fine that could be imposed by Kyrgyz tribal law was five hundred sheep. This was according to a scale of value in which 'five sheep were worth one ox, two oxen one horse, five horse one wife, and two wives a gun.'[5]

Despite the received wisdom that religion would simply wither away under communism, the Soviets certainly did their best to help the process along. Of the 20,000 mosques that existed in the region in 1917 there were just 4000 left twelve years later. By 1941 Kyrgyzstan had only one functioning prayer house.[6] That Stalin particularly targeted Tajikistan and Uzbekistan testifies to the reality that Islamic practice was far more embedded there than in the formerly nomadic societies of the other 'Stans.' During World War Two Islam in Central Asia was given a brief reprieve. Russia wanted Muslim support for the war effort, and was well aware of the potential powder keg presented by millions of disgruntled Muslims residing along the Soviet Union's soft underbelly - something the Nazis were all too willing to ignite. Mosques and prayer houses were opened and registered. However, Russian victory in the West meant their war on superstition in the East could continue. During the following decades the number of Mosques went into decline. By the beginning of Gorbachev's era there were less than 250 Mosques in Central Asia,[7] and naturally they all adhered to the party line that tailored the version of Islam preached to the Soviet goal: That "Allah was using Marx and Engels to lead the faithful to socialism and communism."[8]

However, it was noted by a communist official in 1968, that Kyrgyzstan had ten unofficial mosques for every official one. The irony of the Soviet repression of Islam among the formerly nomadic Kyrgyz and Kazakhs was that Tsarist Russia had once actively promoted the faith in an attempt to influence these peoples. The Russian government had sent hundreds of Tartar Mullahs to the Kazakh and Kyrgyz tribes to propagate Islam, believing the faith to have a more powerful influence on them than it actually did at that time.

Adjacent to the mosque, *nan* bread, fresh from the oven was sold for the equivalent of about 10p. I purchased one through the metal railings that formed the counter. This round bread, when still warm and soft is perhaps one of the finest elements of Kyrgyz cuisine, which can at times seem rather repetitive. Despite being a staple on Kyrgyz tables today, this has only been the case since the Nineteenth Century.

Walking on, it was tragic to see a Russian pensioner rifling through a rubbish bin. That there could be anything she might want in the detritus – for this was not the throw-away society of the West where the still useful is nonchalantly discarded – only underlined the depth of her poverty.

It was bitterly ironic that immediately beyond this scene of impoverishment, where the vulnerable of society are forced to scavenge, a giant billboard had been erected over the central reservation. With the glamorous imagery conceived to tickle consumer desire, it advertised a brand of bottled water named "Tian Shan" (Heavenly Mountains) after the range that dominates Kyrgyzstan and defines its border with China. That water, people's most basic need, could be portrayed and sold as a semi-luxurious item in a country where most people earn barely enough money to satisfy their basic needs anyway, seemed ridiculous - especially when the pristine source of that water, the 'Heavenly Mountains' themselves, were in plain sight.

It is a sad feature of Bishkek to see many Russian pensioners reduced to begging. With staggeringly insufficient pensions, usually just a few dollars per month, and with their families presumably in Russia or non-existent, they have no other choice. A Kyrgyz teacher in Osh told me that "Russians do not care for their families" and many such destitute individuals were only able to survive thanks to the help of charitable Kyrgyz. In return the Kyrgyz family would often receive the old Russians' inheritance. Despite Soviet attempts to abolish loyalty to tribe, clan and joint family, the family ethic in Kyrgyz culture appears to remain far stronger than in Russia or the West. Indeed, I've never seen an elderly Kyrgyz person reduced to begging.

At the junction there was a Chinese supermarket, selling oddities such as vacuum-packed ready-to-eat chickens' feet. I turned left onto Soviet Street, the main artery on Bishkek's north-south axis. It had long since been renamed Abdurakhmanov, but the old name remained in use, and in my opinion at least, certainly rolled more easily off the tongue. 19th century military planning laid Bishkek out on a convenient grid. Indeed, the administration of Central Asia by the Russians was always essentially military. It has been said that the Soviet Union too was like a nomadic empire, where 'the military aspect dominated everything.' Something illustrated by Lenin's paraphrase of Clausewitz 'war is not only the continuation of politics. It is the epitome of politics.' The colonisation of Central Asia was underscored by a burning desire for revenge for the Mongol conquest of Russia between the 13th and 15th Centuries A.D. Both the Mongols and Soviets dominated Eurasia with military empires which incorporated many nations yet demanded subordination to a single leader, be it Genghis Khan or Stalin. Whilst Soviet ideology saw itself as a radical break with the past, in some ways it embodied a striking continuity with it. Napoleon once said 'scratch a Russian and you will see a Tartar.'

In my absence, I had forgotten the plight of the Russian pensioners, the way I forgot the unpleasant features of so many places I had visited; from habitual spitting in China, to the lepers and child beggars of India. Rather than these unfortunates, a rose-tinted view resided in my memory. To return was to be shocked. Yet it was a shock that the next day faded, and, in a disturbingly short time became so normal as to be unnoticed.

Certainly Bishkek had a grimness. Buildings had that look of dereliction which is a signature of the old Soviet world. Yet it had something else too; a fascinating story written in architecture both bleak but epic. Dirt roads and Slavic cottages of a provincial east colonised by Cossacks met monolithic concrete monstrosities made by anti-imperialist Soviet imperialism. With weeds left unchecked in every crack and curb-stone the grey slabs of past cultural glories emerged like abandoned temple complexes from the jungle. Except here the temples are a functioning theatre or museum. The jungle is tree-filled parks where a white winter haze slices down oak-lined avenues like the sun through slats on a blind. And everywhere in this jungle there are statues. Mysterious figures – soldiers and statesmen stern and impassive; immortalised in stone but forgotten all the same. Bishkek's charm is its decaying grandeur. How bold were these statements in stone, and look how quickly they have come to fade. Communist concrete covering a Kyrgyz plain; the Russians were bringing the future, but already it is history. Now they are largely gone, like the Arabs, Chinese, and Mongols before them. So the Kyrgyz re-occupy, living among the ruins of what was just another passing empire - a blip. Did the Ala-Too blink, did they move a millimetre up or down, did *Tengri* take notice or just float by in blue oblivion, unaware of man's conceit – no longer content to worship nature but set to conquer it.

Bishkek is a museum to faded might. Whatever oppression these rock face buildings once represented, they leave quite a dignified façade; geometrical simplicity, phalanxes of trees, soldierly socialist statuary. Among the parks and monumental architecture there is visual quiet. It is ironic how architectural forms designed to inspire conformity now seem more relaxing than the confused glass and steel of the new modernity. Maybe it is because those communist concrete giants are now just shells. The power that once resided inside them has gone. They leave just a dull elegance. Like the bleached bones of some once ferocious carnivore, they are perhaps only pleasant to walk amongst and study when the beast is already long dead. I wondered if this is how it will be when the other half of 'progress' fails too. Will people walk amongst the ruins of shopping malls and billboards baffled at the beliefs of their predecessors - where they paid for packaged water because a pretty picture told them to, and filled the sea up with the plastic their vanity left behind.

Among the cracking concrete cubes of communism rises the fledgling Kyrgyz capitalism. Behind rusting sheet-metal doors, rows of women chatted over clattering sewing machines, making clothes for the Russian market. Opposite sat a dozen polished limousines and even a pearly white Hummer, its bonnet lashed with red ribbons and a flowery bouquet. For the vehicles were to hire for wedding celebrations. An absolute must-have feature of Kyrgyz weddings is to drive through the streets in a noisy cavalcade of ostentatious vehicles, stopping for photos at all the city's landmarks.

Then I came to the circus, or 'СИРК', an entertainment staple of all Soviet capital cities. The giant disc-shaped building hovers on a chunky concrete pedestal of broad staircases ascending to the entrance. I'd never been to Bishkek circus before, but had visited the one at Tashkent (the capital of Uzbekistan and once the fourth largest city in the Soviet Union), which is housed in an identical building, as is the circus I would see in Dushanbe (capital of Tajikistan) many months later on this trip.

My memories of Tashkent circus harked back to something from the 19th Century. There were acrobats, a strong-man, performing dogs, plus elephants that swung on swings and stood one legged on tiny stools. Perhaps the most anachronistic - to say nothing of politically incorrect - act, was the four African men who came out wearing leopard skins, whilst juggling fire and limbo dancing to bongo drum music. A friend and I were waiting for onward visas and because our hotel was opposite the circus we saw a lot of the performers who spent their days off drinking at a row of bars on that street. Unfortunately, our continued presence ended up with us being labelled as spies and culminating in a nasty incident involving several clowns who were very angry that my associate had taken a photograph outside the circus and then refused to pay the extortionate sum they demanded. Indeed, the accusation of spy is not uncommon in the old Soviet World, where not too long ago every foreigner was regarded as a potential spy.[9] A few months before that I'd met a Russian speaking American who'd been attacked in Siberia on the accusation of being an Azerbaijani spy. The police had to keep him locked up overnight for his own safety. On my ride I met a Polish student of Turkic Studies whose Uzbek and Russian language skills brought the accusation of 'spy?' so regularly, that he had to stop using them.

The circus in Tashkent was a novel experience, but I have never been compelled to see something similar at any other such venue; my English convictions against animal cruelty holding fast. However, I heard that in 2009 the Russian State Circus came to Bishkek. Signs sprang up all over the city advertising the event and one of its star features; an ice-skating bear. Yes, a bear had been trained to ice-skate and even play ice-hockey. Incredibly, this is apparently a standard stunt for the Russian circus. Understandably the bear wasn't quite as enthused about being forced to perform as the expectant audience. This was ghoulishly illustrated during a 'rehearsal' when the bear, still wearing ice skates, attacked and gored to death the 25 year old circus director, nearly severing one of his legs and dragging him around the ice by the neck. An animal trainer who tried to rescue him was also critically injured. The bear was later shot at the scene by police. Shockingly this wasn't even the first fatal bear attack to take place in Bishkek. In 2002 a bear on loan from Russia to Bishkek City Zoo killed a small child who had reached out to pet it. The animal's aggression was blamed on chronic malnutrition. I was left wondering what kind of enclosure it was housed in if the child could get so lethally close. A tragic story, yet one with an obvious message.

Leaving the circus behind I proceeded to negotiate the icy pavement. It was interesting to see the young people make a kind of sport by sliding across it. Whenever the ice was smooth and unbroken, rather than attempt to walk they would push themselves with one foot then glide effortlessly for several paces at a time. Despite nearly everywhere being coated in this treacherous glaze, I only saw one person fall over all week. They were clearly used to it.

I came to the State Opera and Ballet Theatre, a picture of elegance. Fronted with white marble pillars rising to a triangular apex, it is a large neo-classical construction. Painted pastel pink in a city of grey, with white eves, edging and decorative raised relief, it looked to me like an ostentatious wedding cake. But instead of a plastic bride and groom perched on top, there were stone statues of revolutionary heroes. With some of the figures represented in traditional Kyrgyz dress, it was a very unsubtle piece of architectural propaganda; the colonised portrayed as happy partners in the culture of the Russian invaders.

Wooden boards lent against the columns advertising upcoming shows. Labouring through the Cyrillic, I read 'Rigoletto.' I had seen this same opera there in 2009. The inside of the Opera House was every bit as opulent as its exterior. There are grand staircases, chandeliers, and balcony seating encompassing the stage. What I remembered most was the domed ceiling, lavishly painted with figures from Kyrgyz history and myth; fair maidens and eagle hunters in traditional, medieval looking costume. The ticket had cost a mere

$2, yet the audience consisted of only a handful, mostly old ethnic Russians, perhaps reminiscing on the glory days of Soviet 'high' culture.

Approaching the city centre buildings rose up around me. No skyscrapers here, just an increase to several storeys. At the corner of Soviet and Chuy, Bishkek's two major thoroughfares, taxi and mashutka drivers stood in huddles and touted destinations. Stalls and kiosks sold the usual paraphernalia. Modest pyramids of oranges and clutches of bananas sat on single sheets of newspaper laid directly on the concrete paving slabs. Such colour and taste of the tropics seemed at odds with the bitter cold, and gloved fingers of customers. Opposite, a marble square held a large fountain, clock tower, the central post office and telephone exchange – now largely defunct in the age of the mobile.

I crossed the road via a subway. It was filled with a quadrangle of passageways occupied by dozens of small stalls. They all sold virtually the same thing, and that was stationery or toiletries. One after another I was presented with the same array of notebooks and pens. It was a fine illustration of an undiversified economy. It was surely just pot luck whether someone shopped at one stall or another. 'Unique selling point' or entrepreneurial initiative just didn't seem to be on the cards. I picked one, merely because it was the last and I remembered I needed something to write with. I was looking for a lined notepad but they only had squared pages like we use in the UK for mathematics. I went from stall to stall finding, unsurprisingly enough, that every pad in the subway was of squared paper. Clearly it was something I would have to get used to. Emerging on the other side the consumer 'diversity' continued; half a dozen money changers, internet cafes, and fast food joints selling the somewhat self explanatory *Gamburgers* and *Xotdogs*.

I walked the few hundred metres west to Ala-Too square, the symbolic heart of the city. On the way I passed one of the few ex-pat establishments in Bishkek. It was apparently owned by a Brit. Apart from the food and beer it also served as the United Kingdom's honorary consul in Kyrgyzstan. The UK actually has no embassy in the country. I couldn't quite get my head around the idea that if I were to be robbed, attacked or suffered some other misfortune that required official assistance as a British citizen, my first port of call would be the pub.

Chuy, named after the river on which the city resides, is a broad avenue accommodating four lanes of traffic. The monumental architecture begins with an arcade of marble arches, several storeys high, and topped with golden domes. These flank a vast concrete square filled with fountains. On summer evenings the fountains plume and crowds of people mingle or sit on the steps, accompanied by a 'sound and light' show synchronised with the jetting water. On that winter's morning it was deserted with the exception of a few hopeful Kyrgyz photographers waiting to snap any visitors to this national site in need of a souvenir. Every Kyrgyz person I've stayed with has a photo album with at least one photo of them with their family or their classmates at this place. Upon consideration this is quite understandable, as Ala-Too is probably the most picturesque spectacle in Bishkek. Unfortunately, the visual was somewhat spoiled on that day by the burnt-out shell of a government building on the street behind; testament to the violent coup that had rocked the city less than a year before.

The Ala-Too complex is divided by Chuy Prospektesi (road). The other side is a vast expanse of concrete. The scale is majestic, yet also cunning. It is a common theme of totalitarian architecture, be it Tiananmen Square in China, or the ludicrous scale of Hitler's fantasy capital 'Germania', that sheer size renders the individual utterly insignificant, almost invisible. Ala-Too (Formerly Lenin Square) followed suit in this respect. People are reduced to ants scuttling across its giant grey surface. Instead the eye is drawn to the square's three immense features: *Erkindik*, the monumental Kyrgyz flag, and the National Historical Museum.

The statue of *Erkindik* is a female personification of 'freedom' and Kyrgyz statehood. *Erkindik* is the Kyrgyz word for freedom. At twelve metres tall and weighing four tonnes in wrought copper, she is far from a subtle replacement to the previous tenant, Lenin. To make way for this 'Kyrgyz Statue of Liberty' Lenin was moved to a less prestigious location behind the national museum. The angelic winged lady is portrayed soaring upwards, a single arm outstretched and clasping the Kyrgyz heraldic symbol known as the *Tunduk*. The *Tunduk* is the circular smoke-hole found in the roof of a Kyrgyz yurt; the traditional movable home of this not so long settled, nomadic people. As such the *Tunduk* connotes hearth and home, and is a re-occurring feature in Kyrgyz symbolism. *Erkindik* starts her ascent skyward from a ball at the base of the sculpture. This sphere apparently symbolises 'all the people of the world dreaming of freedom and peace.' However, she has not always been found taking flight from this spot. Originally commissioned to mark the anniversary of Kyrgyz independence *Erkindik* began her career on a street that was to take the same name. There, with poignant positioning that emphasised her embodiment of liberty, *Erkindik* ousted the statue of Felix Derzhinsky, former head of the secret police.

Ala-Too square, along with the 'White House' and Philharmonia, were built during the 1970s and 1980s. Ala-Too refers to the Kyrgyz mountain range of the same name. Recently, some members of parliament have requested that the square be renamed again, this time after Manas, the legendary Kyrgyz hero. Since its construction during what have been termed 'The Golden Years of Stagnation' the square has become the focal point for public unrest and two full-scale revolutions.

In 1990 it witnessed large demonstrations in response to rumours that housing priority was being given to Armenian refugees, victims of the earthquake there. A shortage of housing was the crux of the issue, and this remains a problem in Bishkek to this day.

In 2005 fifteen thousand people assembled at the site in anti-government protests that would culminate in the so-called 'Tulip Revolution.' Two people were killed and over a hundred wounded as a result of clashes with government forces. The mob stormed the 'White House', the seat of Kyrgyz government, adjacent to the square. The country's first president, Askar Akayev, was forced to flee by helicopter, and later to resign.

In 2010, nine months prior to my arrival, events had unfolded with an eerie sense of repetition. I remember watching stunned as Kyrgyzstan, a place obscure to most people in the UK, suddenly became a news item - all be it a small one - on the BBC. The 'White House' was once more being stormed and the president, this time Bakiev, usurped. Whilst the monumental plaza may have been designed in a way that reduced people to apparent insignificance, things looked pretty significant on TV as an armoured car crashed through the 'White House' gates, and small-arms fire was exchanged between revolutionaries and the state security forces. Nearly one hundred people were killed.

The 'White House' is a large brick of a building faced with white marble. When hit by the sun it is far from unattractive. However, it lacks the 19th Century charm and curvature of its American counterpart. Instead, it is a rectangular mass, filled with sharp lines and row upon row of regularly spaced windows. This makes it look the very monolithic, bureaucratic apparatus of the state machine that it is. On the black railings of the perimeter fence now rests a small plaque bearing the names of those killed during the 2010 revolution.

I received an email from a Kyrgyz university lecturer in Bishkek at that time telling me how a friend had been shot in the shoulder, and how the men doing the shooting were mercenaries hired by Bakiev. He was alleged to have stolen the national budget when he escaped, leaving the state with a balance of just 16 million Som (about £360,000). Reports from Bishkek immediately after the revolution confirmed that there had indeed been six snipers, mercenaries from the Baltic States, who 'shot only at heads and groins'. At least one to be caught was apparently 'slit like a sheep.' It had been a manic time in Bishkek when gangs of armed marauders rode through the city in buses, and young men flooded in from the provinces to loot. In response local people banded together and started wearing coloured armbands; white for 'protecting our property' and red for 'public order squads.' At night groups of armed vigilantes even went 'marauder hunting.' Buildings were covered with posters saying 'Biz el menen' (we are with the people). The city services froze, and taxi drivers wanted $500 to take the risk of going to the centre.

Some fingers pointed to Russian involvement in initiating the coup, knowing Putin was not pleased about the American base in Kyrgyzstan. A *Guardian* article that day read 'Moscow still unfashionably insists on regarding this vast region [Central Asia] as falling within its sphere of influence.'[10] However, despite what may be deemed 'fashionable' geopolitical strategy, post-Soviet Kyrgyzstan is very much in Russia's sphere of influence, if only because remittances from migrant workers in Russia virtually sustain the economy of this new republic. Yet, whatever the cause of the coup, and doubtless there were many factors involved, the violence of less than a year ago was hard to reconcile with the tranquil scene I saw in front of me. With iced streets, white marble arches, and golden domes it was like strolling before some mysterious frozen palace.

On the western corner of Ala-Too square, just east of the 'White House', stands the monumental Kyrgyz flag. Two Kyrgyz soldiers in immaculate forest-green dress uniform are on ceremonial duty at its base every hour of the day. In the centre of this vibrant red flag there's a golden sun surrounded by forty flaming rays. The red is said to symbolise bravery and valour. A local man told me it represented sacrifice and the Kyrgyz blood that was spilt during his peoples' long journey to independent statehood. The sun's core is formed by a cross-hatched circle, the stylised icon of the Kyrgyz *Tunduk*. The forty flames encompassing it stand for the forty Kyrgyz tribes that were united by the legendary Kyrgyz hero, Manas. The flaming sun also speaks of the pre-Islamic religion of the Kyrgyz; shamanism and the sky worship of the nomads. The cult of the sun in nomadic tradition is testified by the images of sun chariots carved on rocks across Eurasia from Kirgizia to Scandinavia. It has been said that in nomadic tradition sun worship was used to justify the dynastic principle and the omnipotence of the ruler. It seemed an ironic thought in a country of such political instability.

However, despite the proportions of *Erkindik* and the flag, Ala-Too's dominant feature is the National Historical Museum. This imposing white marble-clad cube forms the square's striking centre piece. Impressive though it is, I could not help but think, what with its frontage of tinted glass, that it looked like a giant microwave. Perhaps this was fitting considering the atomic age ideology that built it.

3

Nazda

I sat in an expat bar on Chuy. There weren't many expats though. Mainly the place was frequented by young affluent Kyrgyz. The centrally placed, large flat-screen TV was always turned to Russian MTV, delivering a constant barrage of the youth targeted globalist drivel that defines our times. For example, shows like 'Russia's Next top Model' and several other inane reality TV programmes based on a Western template - the only difference being that the vacuous contenders spoke Russian instead of English. A thinker once went to Russia before the Revolution in search of people who 'had not been scribbled on by philosophers.' It seemed that now peoples and cultures everywhere are being corroded by MTV instead.

It seemed a little depressing how well such superficial dross travelled and translated throughout the world. Worse than that, it is venerated and desired. The four young Kyrgyz across the room seemed a good example of this; expensive phones, sunglasses, mp3 players, bags and other accoutrements were laid on the table. The two girls were even 'modern' enough to kill themselves slowly, smoking femininely thin cigarettes one after another. It was fairly obvious where they were taking their cues from. How sad I thought, if the American model of conspicuous consumption has become the greatest aspiration of people the world over; the only way of showing "I've made it." If people persist in being packaged so uniformly everywhere you go in the world, then travel for travel's sake is perhaps in its last decade, and certainly in its last century.

The 'American dream', or at least the material aspects of it (is there another side?), as perpetuated by the 'global' media seems potent to emerging 'elites' everywhere, even in the Islamic world. The four at the table looked as interchangeable with the cast of an

American sit-com as they did with four young people I remembered seeing at a similarly generic establishment in Islamabad, Pakistan, or the *nouveau riche* Kazakhs who spoke like Californians, that I had met in Almaty.

Currently, however, such a 'lifestyle' is only available to the 'privileged.' Also, I wondered - if it is merely a question of clothes, accoutrements and mannerisms - how much of a 'lifestyle' or cultural shift it even represented. After all, other than the superficial dressing, what substance did this universal brand contain, and how deeply could it really permeate. I recalled the fictional scenario proposed in Samuel P. Huntington's *Clash of Civilisations*: That 'Somewhere in the Middle East a half dozen young men could well be dressed in jeans, drinking Coke, and, between their bows to Mecca, putting together a bomb to blow up an American airliner.'[1] He goes onto point out that 'only naïve arrogance can lead Westerners to assume that non-Westerners will become "Westernised" by acquiring Western goods.'[2] There is a great deal of truth in this, but when those 'goods' carry lifestyle aspirations (as they are invariably branded to do) which are alien to where they're sold, and are supplemented by a 'global' media with the same message, then the potential for deeper change seems feasible, if not certain.

I recalled the just mentioned Kazakhs' outrage over the film *Borat*. This 'comedy' portrays Kazakhstan in an unfairly backward light. In fact, it offended the Kazakhs so much it has been banned there outright, and by Kyrgyzstan too as a symbol of solidarity. So, despite their 'mall rat' slang and manner, they showed they were still Kazakhs and proud of it. I tried suggesting that the film is actually far more about making fun of Americans than it is about belittling Kazakhstan, but they were resolute in their condemnation. Ironically, it is only really the film *Borat* that has awakened the concept of Kazakhstan in mainstream Western perception, albeit with an image far from approved of by the Kazakhs themselves.

That night I was to meet an old acquaintance and it became clear from her story that MTV and Western fashion far from equated with Kyrgyz culture's sublimation to the ways of the West. Two years previously I had arrived in Bishkek by bicycle, eight months after setting off from Korea. The nearest laundry to where I was staying occupied a typically run-down concrete building. Inside, there were no washing machines, just great vats of water and ten metre long metal tables on which clothes were pressed flat. The place was a maze of hanging sheets with enough steam in the air to impair vision and breathing. Burly washerwomen in aprons, rolled up sleeves, and sweat stained head-scarves, took our clothes and washed them for a pittance. Whilst admiring this Victorian set-up, I asked if I could pay one of the ladies to mend my jeans.

I had torn the seat of my jeans straight down the middle during a fifteen hour train journey from Wuhan to Shenzhen. I had needed to leave China immediately before my visa expired, and to get a new one from Hong Kong. Unfortunately it was Chinese New Year and the public transport system was strained to its utmost. I could only secure a standing ticket, and so stand I did, with about two dozen Chinese crammed into the small corridor separating carriages. After about nine hours of this torture I had attempted to crouch down to take the strain off my legs. Unfortunately the strain was just transferred to my jeans, and not being able to take it, they ripped wide open; leaving me with not the greatest outfit for negotiating immigration and navigating Hong Kong the next morning. A kindly Uyghur man in Urumqi had already repaired them once before, but unfortunately his good work hadn't lasted the intervening journey.

The washerwoman told me they wouldn't fix them there, but said I should try on the other side of the building. So, I went around the corner, through the battered metal door, and bare concrete corridor, following the sound of continual clattering made by massed ranks of sewing machines. I poked my head through the open door and found twenty women busily feeding fabric into twenty relentlessly chattering needles. With my appearance their industry momentarily stopped. I held up my jeans and asked if anyone would be kind enough to repair them. A young lady in the corner said that she would. That was Nazda.

I returned the next day to collect my laundry and my jeans. Nazda refused any payment, so I asked if she wanted to join me for something to eat instead. It was a warm summer's evening, a season when Bishkek really lives up to its former name 'Frunze', which apparently also means 'Green leaf.'* At that time of year Bishkek's

---

* Frunze, despite meaning 'green leaf', actually refers to Mikhail Frunze who was born in Pishpek, and became a great Bolshevik soldier, leading the attacks on Khiva

extensive parks and tree-lined avenues can make one feel like they're not in a city at all. We decided to eat at a *chaikhana* (tea house) called Jalal-abad. Finely carved wooden huts provided seating booths, like the style found in Uzbekistan. Named after Kyrgyzstan's third largest city located in the south of the country, it offered many examples of suitably southern cuisine. We chose *Plov*. *Plov* is actually the National dish of Uzbekistan. However, the strong Uzbek influence in Southern Kyrgyzstan has made it a staple there too. It consists essentially of rice with boiled meat (usually mutton) mixed with sliced carrots and onions. Cooked in a special cauldron called a *Kazan* it is also extremely oily. There is something like two-hundred varieties of *plov* in Uzbekistan, each region having its own, which the respective locals will always assure you is the best there is.

Nazda was then twenty-four with classic Kyrgyz looks; a moon face, small nose, dark Mongolian eyes, and cheeks permanently blushed pink from the strong sun and high altitude living. She was pretty and her black hair was cut in a bob. I had told her how I was cycling home after being an English teacher in South Korea, and was surprised to learn that she was an English teacher too; after all I'd just met her in a textile factory. I was stunned to learn this was an economic necessity, because by spending twelve hours a day, six days a week making clothes for the Russian market, she could earn four times as much as she would from teaching. This put her teacher's salary at something less than $50 a month, nowhere near enough to live in Bishkek. That she had spent five years at university and was now reduced to working in what looked like a sweatshop seemed absurd. She did however say that she was planning a return to teaching, this time at a university where she could expect a considerably better salary. Amazingly, her father was going to have to pay the university $500 in order for her get the job. $500 is a lot of money in Kyrgyzstan and I had trouble comprehending the idea of paying for a job. Of course it was an investment, offering better opportunities and a stable, liveable income. It was also my first insight into the curious – read 'corrupt' – way things sometimes operated in Kyrgyzstan.

---

and Burkhara in 1920. It has been noted that 'f' is not a sound in the Kyrgyz alphabet, highlighting how peripheral the Kyrgyz were in Russian considerations.

Nazda invited me to a *Tuy* (pronounced 'Toy') which is a traditional Kyrgyz celebration. On this occasion it served the purpose of house-warming party for one of her colleagues at the clothes factory. *Tuy's* are also arranged for other important stages in people's lives, although I was informed this did not include birthdays. We all met outside the factory at seven when their work finished. Nazda was the youngest, the other women being between thirty and forty, married and with their own families. The house was quite far from the centre so we had to catch a *mashutka*. These privately owned minibuses are numbered according to their route, of which there are many and that form a web of accessibility to all areas of the city.

The *mashutka* drove for a long time. Seats tend to fill up quickly, but there's apparently no limit to the number of people who can be squeezed in standing up as I soon found out. A feeble breeze came through the open window, barely penetrating the crush of bodies. Traditional Kyrgyz music blared from the tape deck. The further we went into the suburbs the less people remained on the *mashutka*. The asphalt changed to gravel and the houses generally rose no higher than one storey. It took so long I joked that we were going to Uzbekistan. Nazda said that actually she was kidnapping me. All the women laughed at this. Of course, it was a joke. However, men kidnapping women in Kyrgyzstan - 'bride-knapping' - is a cultural reality.

Eventually we stopped and exited the *mashutka*. The neighbourhood had that unkempt feel standard to Kyrgyzstan. The roads were just gravel tracks, the grass and bushes wild and uncut. A river ran between two areas of housing, and the utility pipes ran overland, bent into surreal 'n' shapes at junctions so vehicles could pass underneath. Curiously, pipes running over-ground rather than below it, is common across the former Soviet world. Surely this made them more vulnerable, and struck me as odd practice considering the paranoid Cold War regime that built them.

The houses were in the style of Slavic cottages, with wooden doors and window frames, usually surrounded with asbestos fencing. Things may have been a little ramshackle, but at sunset, with so much green around from surrounding trees, the effect was quite charming.

We made our way towards one such house, the crowd of people outside signalling that it was the venue for the *Tuy*. Everyone greeted each other, assumed I was American until I told them otherwise, and we went inside to what was the main living room. There were no chairs and the floor was covered by a huge blanket, absolutely heaped with food. There were many dishes containing all sorts of salads, sweets, snacks and bread. In between the bowls and plates the remaining space was filled with little diamond-shaped pieces of fried bread, a Kyrgyz speciality known as *borsoks*. I was directed where to sit and everyone else took their places round the edge of the blanket. Several people sat between me and Nazda. She was wearing a stylish Turkish dress. Her workmates wore jeans or dresses, whilst the older women were all in traditional Kyrgyz attire.

As we all sat on the floor in a ring circling the feast, the *chai* was served. The cups – which are like small bowls in Central Asia - were passed round, with the venerable old grandmother getting her tea first. She was nearly ninety and mother to eleven children. She sat opposite the door, at the head of the blanket. This is the traditional seating position for the eldest person in Kyrgyzstan as in a yurt it would have been the warmest place.

I was starving and expected everyone to just start eating. However, they only nibbled. Following suit, I reached for some tasty looking morsel, but was directed instead - to my dismay - to the salad, and told by Nazda 'There are rules.' Not wanting to disrupt the proper etiquette I had some salad and some *borsoks* and then watched what everyone else was doing. I was then asked by the man of the house 'Why aren't you eating?' Obviously, I hadn't want to seem rude as no-one else was really eating. However, now it seemed I was in danger of offending the host by not eating enough. For the rest of the evening I was always waiting for a hint as to when I should start eating something. Then I would always be asked if I liked it, and if I stopped eating for a moment, was then asked again 'Why aren't you eating?' It all seemed quite complicated.

We had many cups of tea, always with the grandmother getting hers first. Sitting immediately to her right I was served next, presumably due to my status of 'most unusual guest present'. However, despite everybody's constant nibbling we had barely made a dent in the ocean of food laid out on the spread. I asked Nazda about this. She said it was normal to prepare a huge amount of food like this for a *Tuy*, and that actually eating it wasn't really the point.

Looking around I noticed there was a sofa at the back of the room, and a dark wood chest of draws and wardrobe in the Russian style. Surrounded by the cuisine, dress and customs specific to the traditions of a Kyrgyz *Tuy,* it was somewhat incongruous to notice that on the chest of draws a TV was playing Britney Spears music videos.

After maybe an hour people started getting up. Nazda told me that "We will now go into another room to eat meat." I looked at the food we were leaving and virtually nothing had been touched. In the next room we sat like before around the edges of a blanket. A young male family member then came in with a basin, jug and towel. He walked round the circle to everyone in turn, pouring water over their hands so they could wash. The meat was then brought in. A sheep had been killed especially that day and everyone was handed a massive chunk of flesh, again with grandmother getting hers first. A huge platter of noodles was then served, which combined with the meat constitutes Kyrgyzstan's national dish *Beshbarmak.*

Beshbarmak means 'five fingers' and it was easy to see why as everyone scooped up great handfuls of noodles and ate it with chunks of meat torn from the bone without any cutlery being used. It was delicious, the meat tender and perfectly cooked. I suddenly understood why eating had been so restrained in the previous room. I hadn't realised that was just the warm-up. Now we had a whole sheep to get through. This time there was no holding back and everyone ate their fill.

Being encouraged to eat more every time I paused to swallow, I was soon stuffed. Fortunately, the other guests were having no problems consuming more than their share, and together made quick work of what had once been a whole sheep. When finished, the young man returned with the basin, jug and towel so everyone could wash their hands clean. Then, as if abiding some unspoken law, everyone got up and returned to the first room, although I clearly wasn't the only one having difficulty moving after such a gorging.

Once seated again, those who could manage it continued to nibble, and more *chai* was brought round. The man of the house regaled us with tales from his time in Moscow – where he had been a taxi driver. He told us how the children there were so urbanised and removed from traditional life that they believed bread grew on trees. Everyone found this hilarious.

The couple must have been in their forties. Previously they had lived in an apartment, crowded together with eight people from their extended family. Like many Kyrgyz men, he had gone to work in Russia in order to accumulate the wealth needed to afford a house in his own country. It seemed a ridiculous situation.

It was also interesting speaking to some of Nazda's colleagues from the clothes factory. I had arrogantly assumed that they would be uneducated and had always done such work, but again, I was wrong. Some of them formerly had much better jobs. One of them had even worked in America for a time, and another in Malaysia. I asked Nazda how she and her colleagues felt about having to work long repetitive days making clothes for Russian consumers, when they were often trained for, and had previously known, more satisfying careers. Weren't they in anyway bitter? They certainly didn't seem it, laughing and joking all the time. Nazda just responded by saying 'Life is life.' The ups and downs of it all were just stoically accepted. It was an attitude I had already encountered from the Kyrgyz. Things that I would have thought utterly devastating or traumatic were just met with a sigh, a shrug of the shoulders, and the notion that one cannot escape one's fate, so better just get on with it. It never failed to impress me. Perhaps they had the 'stiff upper lip' which was once attributed to the British people.

After kneeling or sitting crossed-legged on the floor for nearly two hours, I really needed to stretch my legs. Having drunk about twenty cups of tea I also felt like going to the toilet – not that anyone else seemed to feel the need. I was led to the outhouse at the end of the garden. It was almost dark, the last light of dusk dwindling away behind a thick grove of trees. However, the garden was busy with women hovering around smoking stoves, and I realised that everything we'd just eaten had been prepared outside.

Returning to the main room, the tea and chat continued for awhile. Then again at a moment I felt was adhering to a specific order, people began to get up. Throughout the evening there had been no-one drifting in or out, instead everyone seemed to follow a well-known pattern. Before we stood up we brought our hands over our faces in the Muslim gesture of thanks for the food we had received. This practice is called *Omin* and is common throughout Central Asia. Aside from after meals, it is also sometimes used when a vehicle is successfully repaired or when passing a cemetery.

Outside, night had enveloped the neighbourhood, and when there are no street lights this can seem quite a daunting environment.

Fortunately, taxis had been arranged to take us back to the city. Every guest was given the equivalent of a 'party bag' full of snacks and *borsocks* from the main spread to take with them, so it did not go to waste. I still had some *borsocks* a few days later. Seeing it lying on my bed, the Kyrgyz guesthouse owner seemed surprised, firstly that I had some, and secondly that I'd attended a real Kyrgyz *Tuy*.

That had been in 2009. I hadn't seen Nazda since, although we had exchanged sporadic emails. I was interested to hear about the revolution from someone who had been there and more about life in Kyrgyzstan in general. However, I ended up hearing a story that was far more interesting. That night we had arranged to meet outside Bishkek's main shopping precinct, Tsum. However, by then it would be closed and despite its central location there would be no lights. I was still not entirely clear how the security situation was since the coup. I decided to ask the young Kyrgyz waiter: 'Is it safe to walk by Tsum and the subway at night. For a foreigner I mean?' He smiled and replied with a confident 'Yes.' Well that's a relief I thought, until he continued with 'But watch yourself, many crazy guys there.' He made the gesture for 'crazy' twirling his finger at the side of his head. 'So it *is* dangerous then?' I persisted. 'No, it's safe,' he replied counter-intuitively. He then went on to tell me how he himself had been robbed there a couple of months previously, having his phone and money taken. It didn't sound particularly safe to me. Then, despite his insistence it was safe he finished with 'You know, my country has many problems at this moment. Now only safe to walk in daytime. Mostly.' *Okay* I thought, although delivered with some ambiguity, the message seemed to be that it was potentially risky to hang around outside Tsum after dark.

Later that day, after running a few errands I returned to my room. The electricity was out again so I didn't see much point hanging around. It was dark and bitterly cold. I decided to ask the owner for another opinion on street safety before I set off into the night. I told him I was to meet a friend at Tsum. 'Will I get robbed or attacked?' I asked, getting straight to the point. 'Sometimes', he replied, grinning broadly. That wasn't exactly the answer I'd been looking for, but then he said it would be better if he drove me there. I wasn't going to argue with that, and accepted his offer.

We pulled up outside Tsum at 8.00pm. It was pitch black and I had to wipe the already freezing condensation from the window in order to see outside. Tsum was shrouded in darkness with the shadows of youths grouped in knots by the entrance and around the adjacent benches. A few people, men and women, strode past on their own way. Really, it could have been a scene outside any building in Britain where young people congregate. Yet, the lack of street lights made it all seem that bit more threatening. I couldn't see Nazda and wondered if she would show. However, it was barely gone eight, and I recalled that punctuality wasn't exactly characteristic of people in Central Asia.

Then a girl did appear. I got out of the car and tried to make out the face hidden behind beret and scarf. However, she recognised me first and walked over. It was strange seeing her again after two years, but she hadn't changed, except for being well wrapped up against the bitter cold. We were just exchanging pleasantries when my driver decided to get out and join in too, starting a swift conversation in Kyrgyz with Nazda. He then turned around to me and said 'Okay, this girl is alright.'

'Thanks dad' was my initial thought, but it was nice of him to care. Perhaps he thought I was rendezvousing with a prostitute, temptress, or some other form of *femme fatale* who would lead me, the gullible foreigner, into harm's way, or at least seriously out of pocket. He then asked when he could expect me back. I told him before midnight. Presumably if I didn't show by then, he'd guess the black night of Bishkek had got the better of me, and, well, call the police or something, although I can't imagine what they would do about it.

Nazda and I set off along Chuy, negotiating the unlit subway without mishap. The streets weren't totally deserted, and people did their little sliding walk to negotiate the ice encrusted pavements. A large Christmas tree stood in Ala-Too square next to *Erkindik*. There were no fountains or music at this time of year, but some photographers were still hawking their services to passers-by, whilst children tried to sell roses to any couple they saw. Past the square there was virtually no one on the street. Punching machines seemed to stand at regular intervals along the pavement. They're the type you often see at fairgrounds, where the harder you punch the pad the more noise it makes and the greater score. On what is really Bishkek's main promenade, there were about six of them in half a mile. But no one was punching them in that weather.

It was not long before the cold became uncomfortable and we took shelter in a fast food diner, selling all the usual delights of gamburger, xotdog, even pizza. I noticed the man behind the counter looked South Asian, perhaps Indian or Pakistani. I asked Nazda, but she could only confirm he was from one of those countries, she did not know which, just saying "There are many here. They come and they set up their businesses and send their children to the Medical Institute because it is cheap."

We ordered pizza and chatted. Nazda's father had bought her position at the University where she taught English. It was a job she was perfectly qualified to do, but payment – which I could only understand in terms of a bribe – was still required to get it. However, she now earned much better money than she had done before, yet it still only equated with about $120 a month. As a result she also had to have a second job, again in a clothes factory, albeit a different one.

We continued this small talk, filling in the gaps of the past couple of years, but, at one point Nazda became hesitant, before saying "There is something about me I did not tell you before." My curiosity piqued, I asked her what it was.

She told me that she had a daughter and that she had been married. She told me that six years previously - when she was twenty - she had been kidnapped. She had been snatched in the street at a bus stop by four young men, and bundled into the back of a car. Incredible as it may seem the kidnapper was to be her future husband. Bride-knapping is said to be a Kyrgyz tradition, harking back to the old nomadic ways. Bride-knapping occurs elsewhere in Central Asia, and in the Caucuses. It exists in pockets and among certain peoples on nearly every continent. Even in modern Europe it is still known to be practised by the Romany gypsies and there have been cases in England and Ireland.

In Kyrgyzstan today it is increasing due to a number of factors, like the difficulty of affording the bride-price, and a re-assertion of traditions that were subdued in Soviet times. It has been estimated that up to half of Kyrgyz marriages are the result of kidnap or *Ala Kachuu* as its known. Yet, this includes a large proportion of consensual elopements. However, there is considerable debate over just how 'traditional' bride-knapping really is. Before Soviet times most marriages in Central Asia were arranged by the families (just as was common amongst the upper classes of Europe in the same period). For a girl to refuse the wishes of her parents was extremely disrespectful. Thus, during Soviet times girls would be 'abducted' by the man of their choice so as to make it look like they were not disobeying their parents, and thus preserve their modesty. That this was a practice disapproved of and repressed by the Soviets has led to its reassertion as something of a national 'tradition' in post-Soviet Kyrgyzstan, whether it actually ever was or not.

It was difficult to grasp that the independent young woman in front of me had been involved in such an occurrence. I could not escape the conclusion that what had happened to Nazda was wrong, and a terrible thing to befall any young woman. She had found herself being driven against her will to a village somewhere in Naryn Oblast, the real heartland of Kyrgyzstan. She realised that she had met her kidnapper once before. They had been introduced through a mutual friend some time prior to the event. However, she did not know him, or want a relationship with him. He on the other hand clearly had different ideas; targeting her for abduction to be his wife, and getting a few of his mates to help him do it. So Nazda was taken to the boy's home in rural Kyrgyzstan and kept prisoner. The boy's mother even slept in front of her door so she could not escape. It is a bizarre feature of this custom that the kidnapper's mother is often complicit in the action and sometimes even encourages her son to undertake it. This is because they want someone to help with the domestic chores, which in rural areas can be very demanding. In Kyrgyz culture the married woman will usually go and live with her husband's family, and there she will be expected to fulfil many duties in the running of the house.

In such a system, that extra pair of hands a daughter-in-law represents, can be very much desired by a Kyrgyz mother who usually has to do all the housework herself. Unfortunately, this can actively encourage bride-knapping. Once taken the kidnapper's family will then put pressure on the girl to marry their abductor. However, just the implications of the girl spending a night away from home in a culture where pre-marital virginity is very important, is often enough to compel her to accept marriage. I did not feel comfortable prying into Nazda's situation, but either way, she became the wife of her abductor.

At first the marriage was not official. However, when Nazda became pregnant it was then in the child's interests that they got proper certification. I asked if they had a ceremony or anything like that. She said they did not, so I asked how it was that they were "officially" married. She just said that 'Such things are easy to get in a village. You just go to the administrative building, sign the necessary forms, and...' she sighed, '...You are married.'

I asked what her family thought about her kidnapping and marriage. After all, she had been a recent graduate. Was it not a waste of her long education to suddenly be taken away to a rural backwater and become a housewife? She said her parents did not really approve of kidnapping but that they accepted that it had happened and that she was married. I knew Nazda had an older brother and asked why he had not felt obliged to round up a posse and go to rescue her. She replied that 'Yes if I was younger he probably would have... but I had finished university... I was over twenty. I think he thought "it was time."'

So Nazda was left to her fate, and it seems it was something she accepted. She worked as a teacher in the village and had a baby girl. The thing that struck me was that she would probably still be there now if it were not for the fact her husband became an abusive drunk. This happened gradually until it reached a point when Nazda would take it no more and escaped with her daughter back to her parent's house in a village in central Kyrgyzstan. She does not know if her husband came looking, but he never found her. Friends she had made back in the village said that he just got drunk every day, and had eventually gone to work in Russia where he had a brother. I was already aware of what a social problem the Russian legacy of vodka was in Central Asia, but wanted to know why it had become such a destructive force. Nazda said that in winter in the village there was just nothing to do, so the men drank. In the mountains, where it is often well below zero, I could appreciate that life would be pretty bleak. It seemed unlikely that a vibrant snowboarding scene, or anything like it, existed up there to distract the men with something more constructive to do than drinking to oblivion.

Now, Nazda's daughter lives with her parents in their village. They are pensioners so can devote all their time to raising her. Nazda on the other hand must work two jobs to support herself in Bishkek. I asked her how she felt about this whole dramatic episode. Again she seemed remarkably accepting of it, saying 'I regret the time I wasted with him [her husband] when he was drunk and a bad man. But still, I have my daughter, and that is good.' She then laughed, saying 'She can keep me company when I'm old.'

I then asked if there was any stigma attached to having been kidnapped. She was adamant there wasn't. She even told me of a friend of hers who had been kidnapped three times and had escaped on each occasion. I thought she must be a very attractive girl to command such attention, and of strong spirit to keep coming back from what must surely be a very traumatic experience. Yet, the fact that someone had been kidnapped three times and still wasn't married, that such an event could occur to the same individual repeatedly, was actually quite comic and Nazda laughed as she told the story.

I asked Nazda if her parents ever suggested potential husbands for her, and were eager to see her married again. She said that, yes, they would like her to marry again, but they do not suggest who she should marry; 'They know my character, and that I will only make my own choice.' So, I continued, 'Do you think you will you marry again?' She looked away, and seemed a little saddened. 'Maybe…' she said, '…but only for love this time.' This seemed a strange answer to me, as it would to most people brought up with the Western tradition of 'Romantic love.' After all, that one would marry only for 'love' seemed too obvious to bother stating.

However, it became clear that Nazda's desire to marry 'only for love' was not an ideal conceived purely for her own happiness. She stressed it was because her second marriage must not fail. She said she could not get divorced twice, and that this was for the sake of her parents. She did not use specific words like they would be 'shamed' or 'disappointed', but she was clear she would not risk a marriage where divorce seemed even remotely possible. For her this meant 'true love.'

Still, considering she had been taken against her will and forced into a marriage she did not want, it seemed a little unreasonable to count that union and subsequent divorce as, for want of a better word, 'real.' Nazda saw my point, but just said 'It is part of our culture.' Bride-knapping may have been made illegal by the modern state - if only to contend in the international system - but in the culture it remains a legitimate way of obtaining a wife. As such the marriages which result from abduction are indeed viewed as legitimate, by Nazda's parents, and by society as a whole.

'It is our culture.' Again I was struck by the attitude of total acceptance. I had obviously been a little surprised when Nazda dropped this revelation, but perhaps mainly for the reason that I would never have guessed it. That's not to say I'm blessed with some psychic intuition, but people's pasts, particularly if traumatic, have a way of revealing themselves in the present. If someone has had a hard time of it you can often read hints of that in their face or behaviour. Not so with Nazda. She was so youthful and 'normal' it seemed almost impossible to believe she had been abducted, and had a daughter as a result of this union. Yet, the whole tale of woe was delivered utterly matter-of-factly. There were no tears or breaking down. No indication that she even considered it that terrible. Sure, she regretted the time she had spent with the drunk and abusive man her husband became, but on the other hand, she had her daughter, and that was good. It was all recounted with the manner of something that happened in the distant past, with no signs of lingering trauma today.

Nazda had two brothers and a sister. Her older brother was 38 and made a living from going town to town selling sunflower seeds. Like the Chinese, the Kyrgyz are also quite fond of these little snacks. Somewhere, in both countries, there must be field after field of sunflowers, yet I've travelled widely in the region and never seen a single one. Apparently, he just bought his sunflower seeds en-masse in one place and then set off at his own pace, stopping where he liked to sell them. In a way, it sounded quite idyllic. He wasn't working for 'The man' selling 'Sunnyseeds. Ltd.' or whatever, with bosses, quotas and all the rest of it. He was working for himself, and despite sounding a humble profession, according to Nazda he did very well out of it. I asked where he went to sell the seeds. She said at the towns around the lake (Issyk Kul), and in Kochkor, Naryn, Chayek, and Kara-Balta. Essentially everywhere north of the great mountains that divide the country. "What about Osh and the south?" I asked, but she told me "No, never." Increasingly, I was learning of the strong north-south divide. They were almost like two different countries.

Her younger brother was a hunter, seasonally anyway. He was able to earn very good money taking Westerners - mainly Americans apparently - with more money than sense, to go and shoot some specimens of native wildlife for very high prices.

Nazda's sister worked in Russia, and in a very distant part of Russia at that. She lives on Sakhalin Island. This thin strip of land extends north from the Japanese Island of Hokkaido, beyond the eastern extremity of the Eurasian landmass. The Japanese claimed sovereignty over the island, which they called Karafuto, in the 19th C. However, Russian settlers were already established. For a time it was even partitioned between the two nations, but Russia occupied the lot at the end of WWII. The 400,000 Japanese there were deported back to Japan. Today Sakhalin is overwhelmingly Russian but with a sizable Korean minority. In fact, many of the Koreans that ended up in Kyrgyzstan were deported by Stalin from there. The island has a diverse and intriguing history. However, Nazda's sister has gone all that way, quite literally to the end of the earth, to work in a supermarket. There she earns $700 a month, which is mega bucks in Kyrgyzstan. She is illustrative of the vast numbers of Central Asians who go to Russia as migrant workers. They do menial jobs, but earn a wage it just simply isn't possible to obtain in their home countries. Indeed, these new nations very much rely on remittances sent back from relatives working in Russia. The Centre of Foreign Employment in Bishkek estimated the number of migrant workers going to Russia from Kyrgyzstan in 2010, at over half a million. That year the workers' remittances exceeded $1 billion, 40% of the government budget. Dependence on Russia clearly did not end with the collapse of the USSR.

Nazda had been invited by her sister to go to Russia too. However, Nazda did not particularly want to go to Russia. In Bishkek she taught at a university. She spoke Kyrgyz, Russian and English fluently. It seemed ridiculous that she could go to Russia and earn ten times more money for cleaning toilets. Even worse, was the fact that she was far from unusual. Genuine competence and ability is a poor substitute for being born in the right place. When it comes to making a living, Kyrgyzstan is not that place.

I asked, half jokingly, if her brothers had kidnapped their wives but she said they had not. Neither had her father kidnapped her mother, or sister been kidnapped by her husband. She was the only one in her family to fall victim to this 'tradition'.

We strolled on through the dark streets to keep warm, going to places I wouldn't even have ventured to in the daytime. Foot traffic was sparse, but at corners cars were often parked up with groups of men congregating around them. Uninviting apartment blocks set the city landscape. We walked past one building that looked derelict. Yet Nazda said inside there was a sewing factory she was thinking of working at, to subsidise her teaching. "Looks nice" I said, and Nazda laughed at the sarcasm. I had to admit, in comparison to the summer, I was finding Bishkek in winter a fairly grim prospect. The brutal cold and short daylight hours were totally restrictive. However, it remained fascinating; gaining insights to lives so different to mine. I wanted to learn and understand as much as I could.

Nazda was a great help in this quest. She readily broke down Kyrgyzstan the way she saw it, explaining it to me. Bishkek, her current lifestyle and expectations, she saw as being very much in vogue with Russian culture. In all of Kyrgyzstan, this was where she wanted to be. Bishkek and the Chuy Valley are the areas of Kyrgyzstan where the Russian population has always been concentrated, and thus where Russian influence has been greatest. Young people here are free to choose their spouses with little interference from their parents, and the traditional *kalym* (bride price) is the lowest in the country, approximately $400.

Traditionally the *kalym* was paid in livestock. Indeed, paying for a wife is common in pastoralist societies such as the Kyrgyz. It is also a feature found more frequently in patrilineal descent systems, i.e. where wealth and lineage is passed down through the father's line. The payment is part of a contract that shows the groom's family's intention to care for the wife and her children. Bride-price is not the same as dowry, which is when the wife's family must pay money to the husband's. Dowry is characteristic of agricultural societies with feudal economic relations and was once widespread throughout Europe and Asia. In essence it was essentially a pay-off to an out-marrying wife of her part in the family estate. Both bride-price and dowry traditionally served to establish links between the families of bride and groom. Despite the bride-price, Kyrgyz women will also come with a dowry, usually of household items. Whilst perhaps seeming 'old fashioned', this resembles the system in modern South Korea where the husband pays the bride-price and buys the house, whilst the wife's family furnish it.

The southern city of Osh, which Nazda had never visited, she seemed to regard as another world. She told how it was heavily imbued with Uzbek culture, illustrating the point by saying that 'To be a wife there means getting up at 5.00am every morning to sweep the floors and begin the household chores.' Clearly she did not view this as an enviable position to be in, and something different from the 'real' Kyrgyz way. It also indicated that she hadn't been used as such when she was a wife herself.

Interestingly, when I asked about the violence in the south, which had been far more prolific than in Bishkek, she had little opinion or interest in it; regarding it essentially as an Uzbek problem. For her the paramount event, and justifiably so, had been the violence and regime change in Bishkek. What the Uzbeks were doing in Uzbek influenced Osh Oblast, way down south, was of little concern.

She then spoke of Naryn and central Kyrgyzstan, which she regarded as the repository of 'true' Kyrgyz culture. Protected by a ring of mountains from the Russian-influenced north, Uzbek-influenced south, and the Chinese to the east, this part of Kyrgyzstan has remained in relative cultural isolation. On the other hand, Talas and the far north west of the country she described as being much closer to the culture of Kazakhstan. This is unsurprising considering the region directly abuts Kazakhstan, just as Osh and the Fergana Valley are a natural geographical extension of Uzbekistan, hence the cultural influence – a legacy of the erratic, jigsaw borders, by which the Soviets divided Central Asia. Nazda told me how in Talas a man must pay for his wife with horses and cows. Apparently this made women from there the most expensive wives in Kyrgyzstan. The Kazakh connection is also apparent in the way Kyrgyz is spoken there.

I met Nazda again a few days later. As I left the guesthouse, the little girl who seemed to run the place made an appearance. 'When do you go?' she demanded in her characteristically charming way. 'A couple of days' I replied, a little taken aback by her abruptness. I hadn't realised I was such an inconvenience; all I did was sleep in what was essentially the shed and give her money when she asked for it. I was probably paying for her future university fees. Perhaps she was just fed up with the extra chores a paying guest enlisted. Then again, I wondered if she thought I was a spy. However, in reality I suspect she was not disgruntled at all. Small talk and smiles do not seem to come easily to customer relations in this part of the world.

It was a clear blue day. Nazda and I went to the park along Chuy. It was also home to a funfair. These fairs are another example of the Soviet cultural legacy. Like the opera houses and circuses, every major city will have a funfair. Of course, they're not exactly Disneyland, and can come off looking pretty dilapidated. To this date I haven't felt the need to embark upon one of their rusting, creaking rides; there's usually a local in attendance who can recall – hopefully an urban myth - when a seat came flying off such-and-such a ride with grave repercussions for the occupant. There were dodgems and merry-go-rounds, plus an assortment of more adrenaline-fuelled attractions. Quite a few I could recognise as scaled down versions of those in theme parks in the UK. I would absently-minded make comments like 'mmm, that's like the 'Samuri' at Chesington' or 'Galleon', 'Detonator' or whatever ride it resembled. In reply Nazda would usually settle for the comment 'yes, that's very dangerous' and 'mmm, that one very dangerous too.' I never ascertained whether she meant they were just experiences for the serious thrill-seeker, or that things were liable to go badly wrong, much to the detriment of the passenger.

Still, it didn't seem to deter people. Their screams (of enjoyment – not terror as bolts came loose and they fell to their doom) were muted by the overly loud beats of modern dance music blaring from large speakers. There were also plenty of places to buy gamburgers, and if you felt the need, hit a punching machine or see how hard you could swing a hammer. Aside from that, there must have been about ten shooting galleries. 'Can you shoot?' asked Nazda as we passed about the fifth. 'I don't know' I replied, knowing that I could indeed fire a weapon, but just not having done it since my time as an army reservist some years before, wasn't sure how much skill I'd retained. For a small sum of Som we got a number of pellets and a pair of 2.2 rifles, in order to shoot cans and bottle tops placed on shelves about three metres away. It wasn't exactly sniper school, and in the context I proved I could shoot quite well. This was just as well, because the guy running the stall ambled freely around the range whilst people were shooting down it – which went against everything I'd ever learned about shooting, but hey, maybe they did it differently here.

Having successfully fired all my pellets without maiming the stall attendant, we sauntered from the park. I had noticed that in Kyrgyzstan I saw very few mixed couples, that is to say Russian and

Kyrgyz. I asked Nazda about this and she confirmed that it was indeed rare, the two groups infrequently intermarrying. However, she did say it was more common for Kyrgyz men to marry Russian women, than the other way round. She smiled as she recalled a story her grandmother had told her. She had told her that Nazda's own father, before he met her mother, was once set on marrying a Russian girl. However, for whatever reason it hadn't worked out, and funnily enough he had never mentioned it to his Kyrgyz wife or their children. Grandma, however, had passed the secret on to Nazda.

I queried why it was Kyrgyz men and not women who usually intermarried with Russians. She said Kyrgyz women marrying Russian men was discouraged, something to do with the mixing of the blood. This seemed a little odd, as surely the blood is just as mixed if the sexes are reversed.

Still, I suspected there were also more practical demographic reasons for this occurrence. The main point being that there are so many fewer Russian men than there are Russian women. This might be traced back to the mind-boggling 20 million soldiers they lost in WWII – which certainly puts into perspective all the memorials you see dotted around their former empire. Since then the balance has never been equalised, with social ills such as alcoholism seriously depleting the number of Russian men eligible for marriage. Indeed, the life expectancy for a Russian male is barely sixty, a figure incomparably low for a 'developed' country. Cardiovascular disease is responsible for four times as many deaths in Russia than in Western Europe, and the Russian murder rate is five times higher than the already far from modest US figures. Similarly, I had heard that along their border with China, increasing numbers of Russian women were now marrying Chinese men. That they are less likely to be alcoholics, and perceived to be wealthier and treat women better in general all contribute to this trend. Interestingly, this does not even seem to be a particularly modern phenomenon as a visitor to 19th Century Vladivostok recalled 'The Russian woman does not object to the Chinese as a husband.'[3]

Nazda mentioned another sister who lived in Bishkek. I thought she only had one sister and that she lived on Sakhalin Island, beyond Siberia. However, it turned out that the Kyrgyz refer to their cousins as brothers and sisters also. There is apparently no differentiation in the language. I asked if her family belonged to a tribe, but she didn't understand the word, which she pronounced as 'treeb.' She told me instead how all Kyrgyz trace their lineage back to their "seventh father", meaning seven generations back on their father's side. She knew the names of everyone of these fathers. This is called '*dzeti-ata*' or 'seven fathers' knowledge. Kyrgyzstan is a patrilineal society where descent is traced through the father's line, just as it is in the UK.

Nazda told me how anyone who traced their descent from the same "seventh father" was part of the same - she adopted the term "treeb" – and cannot intermarry.* It is something every Kyrgyz is aware of and one of the very first questions they will ask when meeting for the first time. Aside from determining whether someone is an eligible spouse, common ancestry brings certain obligations that influence all facets of life. For example, when providing a service for someone who shares an ancestor with you, it is culturally awkward to ask for payment. Obviously, such large webs of loyalty and obligation beyond the immediate family, have huge implications for the way society functions, and are often cited as a negative factor in national politics.

Nazda told me how traditionally this genealogy was recorded and passed down via the medium of song. Today, however, her father writes it down in a little book. She told me what she knew of her "treeb's" history. She told me how her tribe, the name of which meant 'fox', moved from their *jailoo* - the summer pastures where they grazed their herds - to the region of Chayek in Central Kyrgyzstan sometime in the 19th Century, and where her parents reside to this day. Before her "seventh father" she knew of the existence of one other man. She called him 'Siax' which she said meant something like 'traveller.' All she knew of him was that 'He came alone from another country' and that 'He was a good man', as our distant ancestors are invariably perceived to be.

I realised later, whilst reading on the subject, that Nazda was referring to the Sajak. The Sajak are one of the Kyrgyz clans - or *Sanjira* - of which there are about thirty today. The lineage of her 'seventh father' is a sub-group within the Sajak. The Sajak are the dominant clan in the central area of Kyrgyzstan, and this fitted with

---

* This contrasts with the Kyrgyz in Afghanistan, who prefer marriage to be between cousins.

Nazda's native region of Chayek. Indeed, she said that when people find out she is from Chayek 'They will know, and say "You are of Sajak people."' Being Sajak also brought with it certain connotations of character. I got nothing specific, only that "They are not shy people." I did however discover that the Sajak, living in the region they did, had retained an ethnic and cultural homogeneity which endows them with a status as the 'purest' Kyrgyz.

She went on to tell me that there are four or five sub-groups living in Chayek. She said that some could marry within their own group and others could not.

An interesting feature related to marriage in Kyrgyzstan is that polygamy still occurs. This is when a man takes more than one wife. Nazda said the wives live in different houses and that it is only an option for rich men. I told her about the tradition of polyandry – a much rarer occurrence in human cultures – in Tibet, where women sometimes take more than one husband.* She found this unbelievable, saying 'Impossible! Men are more jealous than women!' I asked if she would ever consider being a man's second wife, or remain the first wife if her husband got another. She laughed at the very idea, and said 'No, never! I am jealous too!'

By now we had walked quite a way and were close to the Philharmonic. I stopped to study the statue of Manas. He is the legendary hero and leader of the Kyrgyz people. The Epic recounts the adventures of Manas and his forty friends. This bodyguard or *comitatus* was a common feature of Eurasian nomadic societies; a war band of friends sworn to defend their heroic lord to the death. In the earliest times if the lord died first these warriors committed ritualised suicide and were buried '"armed to the teeth" for battle in the next world.'[4]

Looking at the statue I thought Manas was depicted battling a dragon, like the English St. George. In fact, it was revealed to be a snake, and they weren't fighting. The snake was helping him. He was flanked by statues of his wife and his uncle, key characters in the Kyrgyz epic. Like its Western counterparts, *The Odyssey* and *The*

---

* Among the Hephthalites or 'white Huns' (a nomadic people that lived to the East of Kyrgyzstan in the middle of the first millennium A.D.) brothers shared a common wife who placed horns in her headdress to show how many husbands she had.

Iliad, the story of *Manas* was transmitted down the ages orally by singing bards. The Kyrgyz bards were called *manaschi*. Remembering such a vast saga – far longer than the Western epics – was a considerable feat. Nazda told me that those who undertook the role were believed to have been chosen by God. The young apprentice would learn this was his destiny from a vision or dream in which Manas, or sometimes his wife, would appear and instruct them to choose the path of *manaschi*. I was interested that this message appeared in a dream as the prophetic aspect of dreaming is prevalent in other cultures too, such as among American Indians or Australian Aborigines. I asked Nazda if Kyrgyz people still had any belief that dreams could be prophetic. She told me that for many people they still had meaning, and gave examples of some common symbols and their apparent significance. She said that if one saw shoes in a dream, then it foretold that one (presumably this only applied to women) would soon find a husband. To see a knife anticipated that the dreamer was pregnant with a baby boy, and jewellery was indicative of a baby girl. If a cow appeared in your dream it was a premonition of sickness. To dream of raw meat warned that the death of a relative was close at hand.

I asked if Nazda believed in these omens. She looked at me, probably trying to gauge if I thought such an admittance would be silly, before saying, 'Yes, I do.' So naturally I then queried if she had any personal experience of 'dreams coming true.' Again, and I was more surprised this time, she said she had. She claimed that prior to the birth of her daughter she had dreamed of jewellery, and that she had dreamt of raw meat shortly before the death of her grandmother. Her grandmother had died at ninety-seven years old, spending most of her life as a widow, her husband having been killed in World War Two. However, they had already had five children.

Returning to more ancient history, I wanted to know if the Kyrgyz had any stories which pre-dated *Manas*. Nazda told me of one hero whose name and exploits survived down the ages. He was from a time when the Kyrgyz tribes lived far from present day Kyrgyzstan, their settlements still spread along the shores of the Yenisey River in Siberia. She also insisted that in those times the Kyrgyz were a tall, fair skinned people, with red hair and green eyes. She said that the great Manas had looked like this too. Indeed, medieval historical sources do attribute this appearance to the Kyrgyz, and this has led to a modern theory that the Kyrgyz were part of the Turkic Tahtyk culture, a mix of Asian and European peoples. It has also been suggested that a military aristocracy ruled over a people of different racial origins to themselves; a social system well evidenced throughout the history of Eurasia, for example the later Turco-Mongol domination of the 'Iranian' peoples in Central Asia.

'What's happened then?' I queried 'because the Kyrgyz don't look like that anymore.' We laughed at the blatant nature of this fact. 'The Mongols, they came, and they changed us, so now we look like Mongolian people' said Nazda. They had clearly done a very thorough job. Genetic studies seem to confirm this, revealing 8% of men living in the former Mongol empire carry Y-chromosomes that are almost identical. That translates to 0.5% of the modern world's male population. Some have gone as far to suggest that such progeny was the result of just Genghis and his male relatives. When one takes his whole army into account it is perhaps easy to see how the 'face' of the Kyrgyz people might have been changed so dramatically. However, somewhat contrary to this, we know that the Mongol invasions of Central Asia were carried out mainly by Turkic tribes recruited by Mongolian officers.

However, in the hills I had occasionally come across red-haired Kyrgyz with green or blue or grey eyes, and wondered at their origins. I thought of the 3000 year old red haired Caucasian mummies found next door in Xinjiang province China, and the challenge they caused to established ideas about the distribution of peoples in the past.

Whilst I had been quizzing Nazda on all things Kyrgyz, we were looking for a film to watch, or rather one that I could tolerate sitting through in Russian. There are three cinemas within walking distance along Chuy, and at the last there was a feature on within the next half hour that wasn't a rom-com or for kids. Many of the films were American – dubbed into Russian – and the others looked like Russian movies. Waiting in the 'queue', bundled around the ticket window I had time to peruse the price list which seemed incredibly complicated, with a different price for each showing, dependent on what time of the day it was. It was only the middle of the afternoon and prices were half what they'd be on a Saturday evening. I couldn't translate the Cyrillic title on the poster, but it looked sufficiently action-packed not to require an in-depth knowledge of the Russian language. Nazda translated it as 'something to do with witches.' It starred Nicholas Cage, and looked like a suitably ridiculous premise for some lowbrow entertainment. I brought some 'cold' drinks from the warm fridge behind the refreshments counter. I suppose there wasn't much call for cold drinks when it was -10°c outside. Inside, the auditorium was full, and warm, but everyone kept their coats on anyway.

In the film Nicholas Cage played a grizzled Crusader. A montage showed him fighting at numerous significant battles over many years, his features ageing accordingly. The fact that by default as a Crusader, he was waging war against Islam was apparently of no consequence to the Kyrgyz audience, who again by default, are overwhelmingly Muslim. Admittedly, this had nothing to do with the nature of the film. The Crusades just served as a dramatic stage where Cage's role as a great warrior could be attributed to him. The bulk of the film concerned him acting as an armed escort for a troublesome witch, from which point things got increasingly supernatural and unsophisticated. However, the Crusader pretext reminded me of a train ride from Bukhara to Tashkent in Uzbekistan. On board there had been a TV in the carriage. I had been surprised, to say the least, that it played back-to-back a Russian series about a war somewhere in the Caucasus – I presumed Chechnya. The whole thing was a war-fest in which heroic Russian soldiers consistently slaughtered the bearded Mujahidin who took every opportunity to attack and ambush them from the thickly forested Caucasus Mountains. It seemed a very strange programme to be playing to a train full of Uzbek Muslims. It was a bit like being on a British train where the TV (although lowly Uzbekistan seems to have superseded Great Britain in this respect, as there are no TVs on British trains) played a series where the plot consisted of brave and unyielding Taliban cutting down wave after wave of American soldiers. It would be odd to say the least. Yet, looking around, those Uzbeks watching it seemed entertained enough, and there was no hint they were dismayed at the blood-letting bestowed upon their Muslim brothers. However, the unpleasant nature of the regime in Uzbekistan probably has a great deal to do with what is on the TV in trains, and how exactly the populace choose to react to it.

Of course, Islam in Kyrgyzstan is its own expression of the faith. It overlays a far more venerable spirituality followed by the nomadic peoples from Siberia for long millennia. That was the religion of shamanism. I asked Nazda if the old religion still had its devotees in Kyrgyzstan. She denied that it did, but I had heard of many practices that were certainly not Islamic. I guess she meant that no one called themselves a shamanist anymore – and it is unlikely they ever did. Now they were Muslims who had some beliefs which pre-dated Islam, and that may even contradict it. She told me one example of how on a new moon the Kyrgyz will ask for health and other blessings, yet this is apparently something that is expressly forbidden in the Koran. Islam however is not the only faith in Kyrgyzstan. Nazda also spoke of 'Christians and Baptists.' I had always assumed Baptists were Christians, but even though they believed in God and prayed in a Church, Nazda was adamant they belonged to a totally different faith. She was no doubt differentiating between Russian Orthodox Christians and the new Christian churches that have come to post-Soviet Kyrgyzstan hoping to find followers in the spiritually deprived aftermath of communism. These include Baptists, Seventh Day Adventists, and Jehovah's Witnesses. The latter have apparently had the most success with the native population. American evangelists try to convert the Kyrgyz through late night television. Protestant missionaries from South Korea and elsewhere seek the willing by day.

To both the established Orthodox Church and the Muslim authorities in Kyrgyzstan these new arrivals are regarded with disdain, as disruptive and unwanted foreign elements. It is interesting that the relationship between the Orthodox Church and Kyrgyz Islam has been largely harmonious. By contrast the real source of friction and violence in the country has traditionally been ethnic and intra-Muslim. Kyrgyz and Uzbeks, the parties in question, are both of Sunni Islam too, so the issue cannot even be said to be sectarian. The number of Shiite Muslims in Kyrgyzstan is apparently as low as 1000.

There were Christian churches other than Russian Orthodoxy in Kyrgyzstan during Soviet times too. Protestantism and Roman Catholicism came to Kyrgyzstan with the forced migrants from Germany, Poland, Latvia and Lithuania. Roman Catholic missionaries also crossed to Kyrgyzstan from China in the Nineteenth, and early Twentieth Century. However, these denominations were followed only by the European and Slavic

minorities, and largely left with them during the exodus to their home countries after the collapse of the USSR. However, the new churches and missionaries in Kyrgyzstan have come to proselytise the Kyrgyz themselves. And it is not just a 'New Christianity', because a 'New Islam' has arrived in Kyrgyzstan too. As was explained earlier, the transmission of Islam to Kyrgyzstan by Sufi missionaries was a gentle compromise with the existing culture and belief system. Islam in Kyrgyzstan has been described as a 'cultural tradition and system that determines moral standards'[5] rather than a dogma that dictates every action in daily life. However, with the fall of the Soviet Union
     a 'New Islam' is being proselytised in Kyrgyzstan by foreign missionaries, who rather than adapt to local culture, seek a change within the culture itself. This was illustrated when I saw for the first time in Kyrgyzstan a young woman in Bishkek wearing a full black chador. Of course, she may have been foreign, but Nazda said some Kyryz women were now starting to adopt this way of dressing. This is undoubtedly the result of new Islamic missionaries coming to Kyrgyzstan from countries like Saudi Arabia, Iran and Pakistan. That Islam is increasingly linked with Kyrgyz identity and the rise of nationalist feeling no doubt aids these missionaries with their work, never mind that the version of Islam they preach is quite different from that which the Kyrgyz loosely acknowledged in pre-Soviet times. I recalled reading Colin Thubron's *The Lost Heart of Asia*, and how he was always asking the women he met in Central Asia if they were going to adopt the veil now the USSR had crumpled. Travelling through the same region nearly twenty years later, and having never seen a veiled woman, his asking such a question had seemed silly. However, since witnessing that chador-wearing woman in Bishkek, I began to reconsider and wondered how far the trend might continue.

     We walked back along Chuy, the immense red flag and bold marble buildings of Ala-Too square becoming very familiar. Nazda told me how the 'White House' was empty. The government was elsewhere, and it contained only representatives. No doubt they feared a counter-revolution. I tried to inquire about tribal politics and its influence on the new government, having read that leadership tended to originate from certain areas and certain Kyrgyz clans. However, Nazda insisted that the new government was made by
     people 'from everywhere.' Knowing nothing about it, I was in no position to argue otherwise.

That evening we went to a Chinese restaurant. I was taking the opportunity to stock up on some vitamin-loaded vegetables. It was therefore quite amusing to see that Nazda had ordered what was translated in English as 'A bowl of sinew.' Delicous as it sounded, if I still had any doubt remaining about the carnivorous nature of the Kyrgyz diet, her order put it to rest once and for all.

I mentioned how the Koreans and Chinese eat dogs, and Nazda replied that occasionally so will the Kyrgyz. She said that they eat it to treat typhoid. Snakes are also believed to have curative qualities, and people will eat the small ones found in villages when they are sick. This reminded me of an encounter I had in the Kyrgyz settlement of Toktogul. After a ride of several hours that had brought me down from the high plateau before the 3000m+ Ala-Bel Pass, I was taking a break at a roadside *chaikhana.* The strong midday sun slowly got the better of me and, after eating, I dozed off. I was shortly awoken by a Kyrgyz man waving a plastic bottle in front of my face. It took me a few seconds to register, but I finally noticed that he had a live snake wriggling around in there. He seemed very excited about this and mimed that he was going to have it chopped up, cooked, and then eat it. The reason being, he indicated, was that he had a bad leg.

At the time I hadn't known that snake-eating was considered a legitimate remedy in Kyrgyzstan, and had just assumed he was mad or hammered on vodka. However, it seems the benign quality of snakes is not universally accepted, because when he showed it to the woman in the kitchen and told her he wanted it cooked, she let out a blood curdling scream and ran around the other side of the building.

It was appropriate in the setting that talk turned to the Kyrgyz of China. Approximately 160,000 Kyrgyz live across the border, mostly in the Kyrgyz autonomous prefecture of Kizilsu in Xinjiang Province. According to their oral history, Kyrgyz people have been living there for nearly 700 years, since the time of Manas. Their presence is reflected in settlement names such as 'Manas City', 'Manas Lake' and 'Manas River.' Unfortunately, the Chinese government does not permit foreigners to visit many of these places. When the Chinese invaded the region in 1758, the local Uzbek, Kazakh, Uygur and Kyrgyz fought back (their respective nation states were yet to be created). Some Kyrgyz came from what today is Kyrgyzstan to support their lineages in the battle against the Chinese. Other Kyrgyz fled to the region - what has been called East Turkestan – when there was trouble in Russian Central Asia. During the 1916 uprising against the Russians, and their attempt to conscript Central Asians for the war effort, 120, 000 Kyrgyz were massacred and another 120,000 fled to China. Many of those fleeing froze or starved to death on the harsh journey. Later waves of Kyrgyz refugees reached China in response to the *Basmachi* Rebellion, the brutal settlement and collectivisation campaigns of the 1920s and 1930s, and again, during WWII. Nazda's own grandmother had fled there, only to return later. Nazda told me how the Kyrgyz Chinese are renowned for their archaic and pure form of the Kyrgyz language, uncorrupted by the Russian occupation. However, some of the Chinese Kyrgyz do not even speak Kyrgyz, using Kazak, Uygur or Tajik instead. Of course, they are obliged to learn Chinese at school, but its usage remains relatively low. She also said how they were much admired for their costume and dance. I asked about traditional Kyrgyz dances but Nazda insisted that the Kyrgyz had no such thing; they only sung and listened to their instruments. Conversely, the Kyrgyz of China apparently dance very well, and troupes come on tour to Kyrgyzstan to perform.

Although 80% of the Chinese Kyrgyz can be found in the Kizilsu prefecture, others live elsewhere in Xinjiang Province. A small number who came to China two hundred years ago can even be found in the far north east of the country, in Heilongjiang Province, Manchuria. The Kyrgyz from Tarbagatai in the Uyghur autonomous region of China are also worth mentioning. According to their oral tradition they came from Ala-Too in Kyrgyzstan some 300 years ago. In their new location they became subordinate to the Mongols who also lived there. The Mongols owned the land and rented it to the Kyrgyz. The Mongols also forced these Kyrgyz to convert to Buddhism. Of the three-hundred families recorded living there in the 19th Century only thirty remained Muslim. Unhappy with these abuses the Kyrgyz tried to achieve a more independent position with the help of the Chinese government. In 1833 a Kyrgyz representative went to Peking in order to obtain confirmation of Kyrgyz independence from the Mongols. He allegedly obtained this document, but unfortunately upon his return 'The Mongols... used his hobby in vodka drinking and made him drunk. From the document, they removed the seal, so the Kyrgyz dependence on the Mongols continued.'[6]

Interestingly, these Kyrgyz Buddhists of modern China venerate the *Panchen Lama*, and not the *Dalai Lama* like most followers of the faith. Homemade altars display photos of the 10th *Panchen Lama* who died in 1989, thereby avoiding the politically sensitive *Dalai Lama* and the proceeding incarnation of the *Panchen Lama* who the Chinese government abducted at the age of six and had replaced with their own.

I wondered where the most unchanged example of traditional Kyrgyz life existed. Was it even in Kyrgyzstan? In 2009 I had entered Kyrgyzstan from its remote eastern border with Kazakhstan at Kegen. There is no public transport connecting the two countries here, so bicycle is one of the few – inexpensive – ways of getting there. It is a region of vast pastures, and small, widely scattered settlements. What about there, I asked, that north eastern nothingness on the Kyrgyz Frog's snout, was that wild and authentic Kyrgyza? 'No' dismissed Nazda, 'that is not a wild place at all.' Instead, she told me that if I went south of Chayek, deeper and deeper into the land of Sajak, there I would find real 'wild places.' She spoke of places with no electricity or running water. She said this lack of amenities was not limited to when people took their herds to seasonal pastures and lived in yurts - as many Kyrgyz do - but always, all year round, even in the depths of winter. She said in such 'wild places' the people only ever ate meat. With that, she polished off the last bit from her bowl of sinew.

4

The Visa Debacle

I needed to get an onward visa. I wanted to head to China. However, I knew this might prove problematic. As far as internet travel forums were concerned Bishkek was not a good place to obtain a Chinese visa. Of course I should have got it in the UK, but departure had come upon me swiftly, and I didn't like the idea of being tied down with entry dates for a second destination before I'd even arrived at the first.

I had received Chinese visas before easily enough, in Tashkent, Islamabad, Bangkok, and Hong Kong. Having prior Chinese visas in your passport apparently greatly increased your chances of getting another – at least so the internet oracles claimed.

I set off early to the embassy so boldly marked in my guidebook. With me I had all the documents I thought I would need – passport, passport photos, photocopy of passport (the photo page) and the page with my Kyrgyz visa - hoping to pre-empt any tedious delays. Unfortunately, when I arrived at the location the embassy was supposed to be, I couldn't find it. I wandered back and forth up the street in confusion pausing to decipher Cyrillic street signs in the vague hope they might point me in the right direction. Eventually, I found it. It was abandoned.

The building was a rust flecked grey hulk that looked like it had been out of use for decades. Only the notice board outside, still home to vandalised magazine articles with titles like "Chinese sailors on exercise" and "Chinese Premier greets [this or that] world leader" gave any hint that this was ever the embassy at all. Even this small trace would soon be gone, lost under an encroaching jungle of ads for cars and apartments.

There was no indication of where the new embassy might be, or if there even was one. I wondered if like the British, China had simply decided they didn't need an embassy in Kyrgyzstan. This, however, I simply couldn't believe. I tried to ask a couple of passers-by, but they either looked at me non-plussed, or just pointed to the shambolic wreck that so evidently was no longer in operation. I had read somewhere or other that the embassy was only open Mondays, Wednesdays, and Fridays. Assuming there was a new embassy, and assuming it followed the same routine, I was eager to find it and get the ball rolling. Otherwise I would have to wait till Wednesday, which, even if all went well, would push processing time into the following week. I was in no rush as such, but didn't wish to spend an inordinate amount of time languishing around Bishkek. One could lose time and money with disturbing ease in the twilight zone that is the Central Asian visa chase.

I once spent four days outside the Uzbek embassy in Almaty, Kazakhstan. They even had a list which you signed on your arrival. This appeared to put the waiting rabble in an order, and seemed to be a great leap forward in the chaotic logistics of getting a visa in this part of the world. However, if the so called 'order' was adhered to, it was only in the very vaguest sense. I never understood how I could be fifth on the list and still wait all day without being seen, only to return the next day when there would be a new list and the whole charade would start over. Moreover, one was always fearful of leaving the crowd outside the embassy, even for refreshments or a call of nature, in case your name was called and you missed it – for rest assured there was no way you could use fair and reasoned argument with the stern faced guards to overlook your discrepancy. You would be received with a look of the greatest irritation that you had even dared to bother them, and if they talked to you at all, would simply say "zaftra" i.e. "Not my problem. Come back tomorrow."

The only conceivable positive to this ridiculous process is that you occasionally meet some interesting people waiting around in visa purgatory as well. One that particularly springs to mind was a young Afghan man. He needed an Uzbek visa to return overland to his home in the north of Afghanistan. He showed me a very large scar on his arm, allegedly from where he had been shot by the Taliban. He told me, in a surprisingly cheerful tone "my arm doesn't work anymore… but the doctor has told me to drink beer to make it better." I was guessing it was the beer that allowed him to chuckle as he said this. Either that or the handfuls of small black *Nasvai* pellets he kept putting in his mouth. He then introduced me to his companion. A thick set Mongolian looking chap, who was of a people called the Hazara that also live in Afghanistan. I hadn't heard of the Hazara at the time, but his Mongolian features turned out to be no surprise as the Hazara are actually a living legacy of Mongol expansion across Asia under Genghis Khan. The third largest ethnic group in Afghanistan, they occupy a remote region in the country's central mountains. Hazara are Shiite Muslims in a country where the overwhelming majority of people adhere to the Sunni side of the faith. The man who had been shot through the arm only said of the Hazara, with a huge smile on his face, that: "They hammer nails into the heads of their enemies."* However, he assured me that as long as you weren't their enemy they were very hospitable. Something verified by Rory Stewart's experiences of Hazarajat on his epic walk across Afghanistan.

Amazingly, getting an Uzbek visa in Almaty was considered relatively easy. In Bishkek due to the strained relations between the two countries, it is even more trying; among other things the embassy isn't open every day, you need a Russian speaker to book an appointment for you, and a letter of invitation that for some unknown reason takes a week or two to produce. However, these are minor inconveniences in comparison to Turkmenistan, where a three week application process only rewards you with a five day transit visa, and you only get that if you have an onward visa for Iran or Azerbaijan (which themselves, particularly in the case of the former, aren't always a breeze for a UK citizen to get anyway).

With these hassles in mind I rushed off to find an internet café, which fortunately are much easier to find in Bishkek than they are in Britain. Killing two birds with a single stone, I found one that was selling Samsa outside, which meant I had breakfast as well. Samsa – or Somsa in Uzbekistan – are no doubt familiar to the reader by the name of that famed Indian snack Samosa. However, they are actually believed to have originated in Central Asia many centuries prior to reaching the Subcontinent. In Central Asia, Samsa are made of baked

---

* When Kyrgyzstan was part of Moghulstan 'land of the Mongols' a horseshoe nail was driven into the head of any Moghul found to be not wearing a turban.

rather than fried pastry. They are usually filled with lamb and onion, although beef, chicken and potato varieties are also common. Sold on the street for about 20p they're a great snack on a frosty morning. Biting into one, hot oil squirted over my fingers. Fat is a facet of food in Central Asia and one has to get used to it. For example, with *Shashlik,* pieces of meat and pieces of fat will often be alternated on the skewer.

That glorious fount of knowledge, the World Wide Web, revealed that the Chinese embassy had indeed changed location, moving to somewhere a few kilometres out of town. Less encouraging was the long list of lamentations by fellow travellers who had unanimously failed to get a visa there. There was however, a glimmer of hope. It came in the form of a reference to a certain Mrs Cheng, who apparently could, if the money was right, procure a Chinese visa for you. By happy coincidence the address given was directly opposite the old embassy.

Speed walking back, I remained hopeful I could start proceedings that morning. I found the unassuming concrete block where her office was supposed to be easily enough, but there was nothing indicative of a Chinese presence. I wasn't looking for lanterns and dragons, but a few Mandarin characters, or at least a sign in Cyrillic with a reference to "Qitai" (China) might have been useful. The door was locked and the intercom had a list of names, none of which were Mrs Cheng. I wondered if perhaps she had moved with the new embassy too. I shimmied back along the icy pavements to the internet café, this time to use a phone. I rang the number. Someone answered. I said "Hello." It roused no response. I tried my fledgling Russian. Again, there was confused silence. Then came a barrage of Russian I could not interpret. Then she, for it was a woman's voice, hung up. However, I had detected the twang of a Chinese accent, so it seemed all was not lost.

But I was. What should I do next? I decided I would just walk back to what was hopefully her office, and that *hopefully*, something favourable would occur.

It did. There was a man outside. I asked in Russian if he spoke English. "Nyet" he replied. So I jumbled together "Qitai visa zdyies?" (China visa here?) which got a more favourable response. He smiled and bucked his head in indication to follow him. He buzzed me through the locked door and led me through a dark wood-panelled corridor. It seemed to be as cold inside as it was outside. He then pointed to an open door at the end. Thanking him, I approached the office. Inside I was relieved to see two Chinese ladies, which I felt considerably narrowed the chances that I was in the right place.

The office was small and cluttered, fitted out circa 1970. The women I estimated to be about forty. The one sitting behind the desk had long black hair and glasses, and was wrapped up in coat, scarf and jacket. I smiled and was just about to say something, when she erupted in a barrage of Russian directed towards me. I didn't have a hope of deciphering it and just stood there, no doubt looking fairly moronic, before I managed to respond with "Ya eez Anglia."

"English?" she replied, somewhat surprised. There was a momentary pause whilst she processed this information, before barraging me again with an unnecessarily loud torrent of words, this time in English. She spoke so quickly it seemed she was even in too much of a hurry to converse, missing out words that might slow delivery of the essential message "I VERY BUSY! I VERY BUSY! COME BACK ONE HOUR!"

"I want to apply for a visa" I persisted, looking for confirmation that I was not barking up the wrong tree. "YES, YES!" she roared "COME BACK ONE HOUR!"

The other Chinese lady apparently found this exchange mildly amusing, her face set in quizzical smile that seemed to suggest a more sympathetic ear. So I smiled back and confirmed that I would indeed return in one hour.

One hour later, having done nothing but trawl the icy streets to kill time, I returned. I was not surprised to find that Mrs Cheng wasn't there, and that the office door was locked. However, I was determined to get this thing moving today, and sat down prepared for a long wait. I tried to look on the bright side. I was inside, there were seats, and I was the only person present which presumably meant I would be first in line for the visa application. I had even had the foresight to bring a book to read. I had certainly been in worse embassy wait-outs.

One hour passed; then two. The office door remained locked and Mrs Cheng elusive. After another hour two extremely Russian looking men arrived. Both large, one wore a fur lined coat and fur hat, had a full deck of gold teeth, steely grey eyes, and skin (not stubble) you could light a match off. His companion was squatter, darker and younger, but had a heavy brow and set, with a covering of hair wherever there was exposed skin.

They spoke no English but seemed quite pleased to meet an Englishman. I managed to convey that I was there for a Chinese visa. I gave them Mrs Cheng's card, which they phoned to no avail. They then returned the card, smiled cheerily and left. I flopped back into the chair, bored of my book, and let another hour crawl by. Then, at 3.00pm she returned, bustling through the door in what I was beginning to accept as her permanent state of frantic agitation. However, me sitting there actually managed to momentarily pause the whirlwind. She even looked a little shocked, saying "You wait all this time?"

I nodded gravely in reply, hoping any sympathy I could elicit might work in my favour for the visa process. "Come" she instructed, leading me through to her office. With her ¾ length coat flapping, hands occupied with bag and papers, and beret-clad head bowed against the cold, she looked every inch the "VERY BUSY" woman that she claimed to be.

Her office was very cramped, stacked with piles of forms, and vines of loose wires dangling from the walls. The odd mix of furniture and fitting made it look like a very messy jumble sale. There was no flat screen PC or minimalist work station. However, it was easy to perceive as Cheng navigated the clutter that this was a place of great industry and diligent application.

I looked round for clues of Mrs Cheng being Chinese (except for the fact she looked Chinese). On the wall behind her desk were two rolls of rice paper adorned with elegant Chinese calligraphy. Balancing on the wall's chest-high partition was a plastic crab and ladybird. Such trinkets, that to the Western eye might look cheap and tacky, must have rather different connotations for the Chinese. Clearly they had been put on display there because somebody liked them, and indeed they did give the room some much needed colour. The plastic tat theme continued behind me on the windowsill with a 'Gollywog' doll. Above the computer there was a calendar of "The ethnic peoples of Russia" composed of pretty girls dressed in their various traditional attire, and striking a pose from their native dance. I could see from the writing that it had been produced in China. It had that typical, somewhat colonial representation the Chinese used to portray minority peoples within the PRC. They have a rather patronising way of reducing the public face of minority peoples to jolly simpletons who wear colourful clothes, enjoy dancing and make interesting cuisine; essentially, their entertainment value being the only thing of interest to the Han majority. Of course, there is great crossover between Russia and China demographically; Mongols, Tartars, Kyrgyz and Kazakhs for example being ethnic groups in both countries. In China the Russians are also counted as a minority people, one of their 56. They are known as *Russ* and a Chinese publication I have which is written in a similar vein to Cheng's calendar condescendingly observes that 'Thanks to the [Chinese] policy of equality among nationalities, various undertakings of Russ have been developing moderately.'[1]

On the opposite wall there was a Russian map of the world, something that would prove a great source of entertainment the following day.

Mrs Cheng, after some minutes shuffling papers, proceeded to give me the application form, or forms. I was surprised, remembering the Chinese visa application usually to be just a double page. Here I was given three sheets, two of them double-sided. The writing and boxes were all very condensed. Filling it out was clearly going to be a lengthy endeavour. I scanned through, disturbed by the detail required. 'Employment?' well, none, but I probably shouldn't put that. 'Purpose of visit?' well, possibly seeking employment, but probably shouldn't put that either as it will require a work visa, which would probably require having a job in the first place. 'Inviting party?' that was easy – none. 'Contact telephone?' nope, don't have one of those. 'Contact details of employer' nope, sorry. 'Place of entry?' that will be near Kashgar, but don't want to put that as it's in the politically sensitive Xinjiang province, and a sound reason to refuse me a visa. 'Method of entry?' best make that a flight. 'Places to be visited?' anywhere on the tourist trail and far, far away from Xinjiang and Tibet. An itinerary like Beijing, Shanghai, Xi'an, Hong Kong, should be innocuous enough to do the trick. 'Name and contact numbers of hotels to be stayed' No idea.

It seemed I might have to stretch the truth a little bit, and possibly make some stuff up. I started getting paranoid, wondering if they would check the details. What would I do if they refused me? I didn't have a plan B. I wondered if my name would flag up my cycling blog on their system. After a long day in the saddle I knew I sometimes had a bit of a rant. I racked my brains trying to remember if I had written anything that could possibly warrant a visa refusal. It may sound far-fetched but I know of people who have had their blogs blocked in China, and been refused visa extensions because of what they had published. From 2007 two cyber policemen began appearing on computer screens in the internet cafes of China to warn users they were being monitored. Filters scan for content unfavourable to the Party, and huge numbers of human monitors help censor the internet, constituting what has been called the "Great firewall of China."

Whilst cycling through China I was asked by the authorities to leave the Kazakh autonomous region in Xinjiang province, as well as a "Tibetan area" in Gansu province. The reason given was simply "tourists aren't supposed to be here." However, I thought it unlikely that those events had been documented, at least not in a way that would be immediately accessible to whoever processed my visa. Even if they were, it's not like I had done anything wrong. However, such things bothered me as I mulled over anything that could be detrimental to my visa request. It was crazy really, considering one could get a Chinese visa in a day from Bangkok or Hong Kong, yet here they had decided to be restrictive and difficult. It was like the embassy had automatically become imbued with the Central Asian – i.e. Soviet – way of doing things, just because it was in Central Asia. However, the difference was understandable in a way, as there were certain threats the Chinese perceived and feared from this region that simply didn't exist in Hong Kong or South East Asia.

I muddled through the form leaving too many sections blank because I didn't have the information to fill them. Mrs Cheng asked for my passport, which contained only my Kyrgyz visa. It was a new frequent traveller passport and considerably larger than regular passports, which I seemed to burn through with frustrating regularity; often needing a replacement with half-a-dozen countries between me and home.

As she flicked through the bare pages I felt somewhat embarrassed by its nudity. She asked if I had been to China before. I presented her with my old passport that had four Chinese visas in it. She told me to get them all photocopied. She sternly instructed me that the photocopies must show two passport pages on a single sheet. Then, with the mannerism of a headmistress addressing a naughty schoolboy, she pointed to the "Ethnic peoples of Russia calendar" and commanded "Tomorrow 11th Free time!" Her finger then moved to the 12th "Here 9.00am!" she stressed, before moving onto the 13th "Thursday, free time! Friday, embassy, passport!" meaning that only on Friday I would be able to actually hand my passport into the embassy. Her finger then traced its way across a vast stretch of numbered boxes (days) and several species of minority peoples before finally stopping at the following Friday. "Collect visa!" she announced.

Wow! I thought. It's going to take two weeks, and even then there's no guarantee I'll actually get it. What was I going to do in Bishkek for two weeks? How could I leave the city without a passport? Even if I could, where would I go? It wasn't exactly trekking season. However, the process was at least started. The wheels were turning, and the first barrier of bureaucracy broken. For that I was very grateful. I thanked Mrs Cheng and left. It was 5.00pm and getting dark. It had taken me all day just to fill out a form.

It took me another hour to slide back to my room on the outskirts of the city. It was to be a very long night. The electricity was out again and the temperature plummeted. As darkness closed in I could see my own breath when I exhaled. With no light, I could not read or write except by torch light. I went to the main house to ask for a candle. I hadn't seen the owner for days. Only a little girl occasionally made an appearance to clean the bathroom and ask for my rent. Unsurprisingly it was the little girl who answered the door. She eyed me suspiciously, as if there was some taboo against interaction with guests. I asked for a candle and she disappeared back inside. I was glad when she returned with one, handing it over in stony-faced silence. I thanked her in the most cheerful and exuberant voice I could muster, determined to see her crack a smile. The corner of her mouth lifted in a bemused expression, which I had to consider a success. I then retreated to my cocoon. The outer door was still incapable of shutting properly and let the deathly cold of night slice into the interior. I put on all my clothes, took the blankets from both beds and tried to sleep.

January in Bishkek means darkness from between 5.00pm and 6.00pm until nearly 9.00 in the morning. It was far too long just to sleep, but without electricity there wasn't much else to do. Outside was the same black sky. Night after night the same distant window flickered blue from late night TV somewhere where they had power.

If there was power at least the radiator worked and it was warm. I started to query the owner on the rare occasions I saw him and ask why there was no power. Always he just hunched his shoulders only saying "Yes, itz problem" offering no further explanation. The little girl too, always had the same line "Yes, itz problem" before quickly hurrying off in case I asked something else. Of course, it was nothing to do with them. As I was to learn, intermittent power cuts are just the norm in Kyrgyzstan.

Sleep. Wake. Sleep. I stared endlessly at the curtain-less window imagining I could see the faint fingers of dawn caressing the horizon. I willed the sun to rise, but it never did under my vigil. Having eventually succumbed to sleep I would just wake up to daylight. Ironically, when I least needed it, this was when the radiator would undergo a creaking resurrection. With the electricity back on, the room became an environmentalist's nightmare. I left the radiator on permanently just to create a bubble of tepid warmth. Yet the large window acted as a very permeable membrane through which all accumulated heat rapidly disappeared. The same was true of the outer door. Even the wall next to my bed radiated an icy cold that would chill any exposed skin within ten inches of it. Perhaps most ludicrous of all was the light, the switch jammed permanently in the 'on' position. I had to tape it 'off' with masking tape just to wake up and find it had peeled away during the night. With no electricity, even going to the external squat toilet became an expedition. As for having a shower – a trickling, cold, exposed-wire death-trap – I didn't even consider it for nearly a week, preferring to strip wash the old fashioned way instead. All this could have been avoided by upgrading to a better hotel, which Bishkek certainly has, but like I said before I prefer to pay less, travel longer. Paying for all the soft touches one has at home has always seemed counter-intuitive to my vision of travel.

Two days later I returned to Cheng's office. She had left me with the uncomfortable impression that I was to be cross-examined by the Chinese embassy about my reasons for visiting China. Could getting a visa here really be that much of an issue?

Cheng went through my application form minutely, addressing each of the many glaring omissions. One that immediately caught her eye, and which I hadn't even thought applicable to me was "NAME IN ETHNIC SCRIPT." I had never thought of English as an ethnic script, but of course to the Chinese, and anyone who doesn't use the Roman alphabet, it is, so I dutifully filled it in. Next was the requirement for all the hotel names and addresses of my whole stay. Of course, I had no idea, and just jotted down half remembered hostels in major cities. Cheng graciously came forward with a name for a hotel in Urumqi. She revealed she owned a tourist company based there, handing me a brochure filled with pretty Xinjiang scenes and Cyrillic script. Clearly it targeted the holidaying wealthy of the old Soviet Union. Write "Hotel Binguang" she instructed. "And make sure you remember it. If the ambassador asks you where you're staying say this hotel." She then told me I must remember the half dozen other hotels I was allegedly staying at – in order. I began to feel like I was trying to gain access to North Korea, not China, the world's third most visited country and which received over 55 million foreign tourists in 2010 alone.

Eventually, satisfied that every minuscule detail was in order, and would stand whatever rigours awaited at the embassy, I thought we might possibly get there today. However, four Kyrgyz men then arrived and bundled into the tiny office. They were applying for visas for themselves and their families. So the whole process began again as Cheng laboriously proofread every form, occasionally giving an order in Russian, which resulted in one or other of the men dashing off to photocopy something else. In the confined space, with a surprisingly effective heater blasting out hot air, it began to get swelteringly hot. However, I noticed no-one took their coats or even their hats off. It's sort of received wisdom in the UK that you remove your outer garments indoors, not least because if you leave them on you'll only feel the cold more when returning outside. It was a strange thing to notice, but from then on I noticed it all the time; people sitting in restaurants, cinemas, their own houses, and wearing coats even when it wasn't that cold. There was probably an anthropological study in there somewhere: 'Coat wearing etiquette as environmental protection vs. social habit, indoors and outdoors across Middle Asia.'

With the small office now positively overloaded with people, I tried to edge my way between the Kyrgyz and the wall, hoping to find enough space to at least remove a layer of clothing. Unfortunately, during my graceful shuffle I failed to notice a stray cable extending across the room about six inches from the floor. I walked straight through it with a loud snap as the plug, along with the socket itself were ripped out of the wall, sending splinters of plastic everywhere. The computer where Cheng was typing away vigorously, immediately shut down and the light went out, leaving us in semi-darkness. Oops!

Suddenly there was space as everyone made way to stare at the destruction. Cheng was straight on the case, picking up the two pronged plug she proceeded to ram it into the hole in the plaster where the socket – now shattered into pieces - had once been. Blue sparks of electricity began dancing across the dented metal pins of the plug. "Er... Be careful" I offered meekly as Cheng unperturbed by the shower of raw electricity continued bare-handed to make the connection. If she electrocutes herself, I thought, I'll never get my visa. Fortunately her persistence, Chinese people's apparent inability to conduct electricity though their bodies, and the adhesive qualities of sticky-tape, combined to ensure power was restored.

Crisis averted, the Kyrgyz had whatever paperwork they needed assessed and with it apparently being all in order, they left. This was good, as I reasoned Cheng could now focus on me, and we might be able to cut down that ridiculous proposed fortnight of processing time. Just then her son arrived, a schoolboy of about 14. He went straight over to the computer and began diligently going through visa forms, putting the details into the computer, effortlessly switching between Russian and Chinese. Despite seeming a little young to be playing his part in the Chinese immigration process, it was clearly a job, or chore, he was used to. Unless he was just earning pocket money, I assumed he was being groomed for his future stake in Cheng's operation. However, all his apparent efficiency counted for nothing when the printer suddenly stopped working. Cheng went berserk, loudly berating him until he went cherry red, bowing his head in acquiescence. I actually began to feel quite sorry for him. I thought of "face", a Chinese concept in some ways similar to pride, but which is also linked to the maintenance of harmonious relations between individuals. The Chinese will under normal circumstances always strive to preserve "face", and also the "face" of others, because by extension if you cause someone else to lose "face" it reflects badly upon you, and you lose "face" too. Clearly that didn't apply here, as the lad had strips publically torn off him. Maybe this was the Confucian family hierarchy at work instead. Or more likely, it was just a stressed out business woman angry with her son for disrupting her busy schedule – not that I thought the printer not working was really his fault. Fortunately for him, Cheng's phone rang and she began shouting at the poor soul on the other end instead.

There's a curious feature of the Chinese language and its tonal nature which can make conversation sound to the Western ear far more charged and aggressive than it actually is. This characteristic of the Chinese tends to fly in the face of a generic Western stereotype that all 'Orientals' are taciturn and submissive. The Chinese are actually quite a loud and garrulous people. What is often normal conversation pitch can, to the uninitiated, sound like a heated argument on the verge of coming to blows.

Cheng stood there shouting down the phone in what was perhaps a perfectly benign exchange with a fellow Chinese. As she did this she made constant spitting motions with her lips, no doubt a mannerism picked up in her home village from that favourite Chinese habit of sunflower seed consumption. The Chinese devour these in huge quantities, and anywhere this happens can quickly become awash with spat out seed casings.* She hung up and continued chastising her son, whilst they repeatedly fed the same piece of paper through the printer that evidently wasn't doing what they wanted.

Some light relief then entered the room in the form of Quba. Quba, short for Qubanesh, as he quickly informed me, was a large jovial Kyrgyz with a permanent showbiz smile of pearly whites that pressed his eyes into permanent slits. He was smartly dressed and had a thick wave of jet black hair which he proudly told me "was like the Sex Pistols!" He had a wrinkle-less round face that seemed unreasonably youthful for his thirty-four years. Clearly he hadn't spent all his life exposed to the extreme continental climate that often seems to weather and age the men of Central Asia prematurely, by Western conceptions at least. Why he was in Cheng's office I never ascertained, but he definitely lightened the mood as I could see him doing everywhere he went. It turned out he and Cheng were old classmates, who studied Foreign Affairs together at Peking University. Quba had used his degree to work at the Kyrgyz Foreign Ministry before starting his own company. Discovering I was English

---

* The Chinese government has gone to considerable effort, with success, to change this habit from dirtying modern transport links throughout the country.

clearly caused him to reflect on the English he had met whilst at university. He said after a thought-filled pause "English and American very different."

"Yes, they often are" I confirmed, pleased that for once a non-native English speaker or European had acknowledged this reality. It can become rather irritating to be constantly and wrongly assumed to be American just because you're white. Quite often the first question or statement I'll get will be "You are from America (?), and I'll hear 'Americanitz' (in Central Asia) and 'Meiguo' (in China) when there's clearly no other foreigner around they could be referring to. A favourite response of mine in China is then to ask if the person addressing me is Japanese. If they are Kyrgyz I will ask if they are Uzbek, and vary this strategy depending on what country I'm in. It always goes down like a lead balloon, but I think I make my point.

Quba then recalled how at his university he observed the English and Australians had stuck together, whilst the Americans were relatively sidelined. He told how a daughter of someone in the Bush administration had been particularly shunned by her non-American Anglophone classmates. This seemed a little unfair on her, but I could believe it. Anyway, with that little anecdote Quba got up and left with his permanent grin. Shaking my hand and promising next time I was in town to call him and "we will drink real Guinness."

The printer debacle was still in full swing but I wasn't left alone for long as a middle-aged Kyrgyz man arrived shortly, shaking hands with Cheng and her son. He was quickly followed by an unreasonably large and somewhat oafish looking Chinese man. Yet despite the latter's rather simple appearance, he had in fact come to fix the computer and printer. Now Cheng, ever the whirlwind, muttered something about "embassy" before sending me and the other hapless souls awry with her eddy as she blew out of the building. "Wait here" she ordered. I assumed she was going to the embassy. The Kyrgyz man went with her complaining about the chaotic nature of obtaining a Chinese visa. "Always problem" he lamented with cheerful fatalism.

With that I was resigned to wait again. I sat down to study the world map. The son and the oaf continued puzzling over the computer – coats still on, naturally. I noticed the son's school bag next to my chair and admired its 'Chinglish' branding "Personality and Handsome" decorated its main pocket. "Guangzhou best make" it announced on the label. As the oaf struggled with his delicate work, the son and I fell into conversation. He was originally from Urumqi, which is located in the north west of desolate Xinjiang province and is the closest Chinese city – with the exception of Kashgar – to Soviet Central Asia. I had already uncovered that his mother hailed from a village called Taklimakan, on the edge of the desert of the same name. The Taklimakan Desert dominates Xinjiang province, appearing like a giant empty eye on the map. Incidentally, its name means "If you go there, you will not return."[2] I had already skirted it twice via the northern road but was intent on going back, and this time along the more intrepid southern route.

He said he didn't like Bishkek. I asked him why? He said he didn't like the Kyrgyz. I asked him 'why?' again, but he just shrugged. "What about the Russians?" I asked. "Russians are okay" he conceded. I can't say I was particularly surprised by his opinions. I was well aware of the esteem in which the Chinese held their 'barbarian' neighbours, and indeed those within their own borders. The funny thing to me was that some Chinese could actually pass as Kyrgyz, and vice-versa. Of course, my observation and reaction earlier to Westerners outside the West constantly being labelled as Americans proves that skin colour or general appearance is irrelevant when it comes to identity. Call a Welshman or Scotsman English and this soon becomes very apparent.

Of course the Kyrgyz and other formerly nomadic peoples, who encircle China's border, have throughout her history been the 'other' to which settled China was opposed. The ancient Chinese conception of the world followed a cosmographical plan known as the 'Five Quarters.' The last two 'quarters' or zones were those furthest from the imperial centre and inhabited by what the Chinese considered to be "Steppe people and savages." The last zone was simply known as *huangfu* or the 'submissive wastes' Indeed, nomadic tribes from the *huangfu* for a long time presented a very real threat to the Chinese, and were a source of great fear, that, mingled with contempt, remains embedded in the Chinese psyche to the present day.

Of course, the Chinese need no longer worry about merciless hordes of mounted warriors bearing down upon them. Instead they see a more subtle threat of Islamic or Pan-Turkic solidarity catalysing and sustaining discontent among the Turkic Muslims of China's

Xinjiang province. Stability in this troubled, but oil rich province, is of critical concern to the Chinese authorities.

However, if his judgements were just a product of history, then it was interesting that the Russians did so well in the boy's estimations. For at the turn of the Twentieth Century it wasn't nomads of the steppe terrorising China, but an alliance of 'Western' powers which included Russia and Japan. After putting down the Boxer Rebellion this international expeditionary force ran amok in Beijing, and Russian troops were complicit in the ensuing atrocities; a humiliation which every Chinese schoolchild is made well aware of. At the same time Russian forces were expanding into Manchuria and Qing dynasty territory. In July 1900 'Between 3000 and 5000 Chinese were drowned at Blagoveshchensk when they were forced by whip-wielding Cossacks and local Russian police to swim across the wide and fast flowing Amur to the Chinese side. No boats were provided and those that resisted or refused to get in the water were shot or cut down with sabres.'[3]

Thus, it seemed strange that the Russians escaped – to say nothing of me, considering the behaviour of my predecessors in China - the disdain he reserved for inhabitants of this fairly innocuous mountain nation.

We studied the map together. He said he wanted to go to America or England to learn English (although we were actually speaking in English at the time). "But much money" he complained, with which I could only agree. India and Pakistan were cheaper options he said. It had never occurred to me that people would go to the Sub-continent to learn English, but I supposed it made perfect sense. In India at least, English is widely spoken. The 'English industry' I mused. I knew from my time in it, as an English teacher in Korea, that many Koreans went to the Philippines for intensive English study.

I smiled at the thought of all the young Chinese returning from their language courses and speaking English with an Indian accent. The boy was equally amused to find out that British people had to have a visa to enter India and Pakistan. "But Britain once owned them?" he questioned with wide-eyed astonishment. "Yes, and that might have something to do with it" I replied.

I asked him if he had thought about studying in the Philippines. He turned his nose up in apparent disgust. Clearly that was a "No."

"Many black faces there!" was the justification he gave. I was surprised he found this a legitimate reason, especially in light of the fact he was probably going to India anyway. However, the colours traditionally attributed by the Chinese to non-Han peoples, were often as much symbolic as they were related to true pigmentation. It was a way of ordering the world and the Han's place in it. For minority groups within China this symbolic separation meant that the name of each group was given an animal radical, which by definition made them less than human. This system of categorisation existed until the 1930's.[4] A degree of ethnocentrism is common to all cultures, and the sense of identity it fosters is, arguably, a key component of being human. To the Nineteenth Century Chinese, Philippinos' were "Black devils"[5] Contemporary attitudes in Europe were similarly xenophobic. Even the 'modern' Western doctrine of 'tolerance' embodies notions of moral superiority about what it means to be 'civilised.'

The opinions of this young Chinese made clear that even in a globalised world, entrenched beliefs remained. However, historically racial stereotypes have changed as the situation required, highlighting their largely symbolic quality. When fighting the Americans in 1898, the Chinese suddenly started portraying the Philippinos as the 'spearhead of the yellow race's fight against the white race.'[6]

I asked if he disliked "black faces" so much, why then did he want to go to America, as there are many "black faces" there too. This seemed to throw him a bit, before he countered with "Hip-hop, R&B, NBA!!" accompanied by an enthusiastic 'thumbs-up' sign. Evidently, to his mind "black faces" were okay when associated with these things; i.e. 21st Century Hip-hop with its mantra of 'bling', vacuous materialism, conspicuous consumption and a bad attitude that are all now inextricably linked with youth culture globally. Such an empty message seemed apt in the now ultra capitalist climate of 'communist' China. I was reminded of the lyric by 'Public Enemy' (participants in a nobler age of Hip-hop) commenting on people "Thinking [basket] ball and rap is the greatest thing from blacks!"[7] It was undoubtedly written as a rebuff directed against 'White' America, but unfortunately now seemed just as applicable to attitudes in 'Yellow' China.

Finding the opinions of this little chap intriguing, and surprised by the strength of his conviction, I moved across the map and pointed to Thailand. He said he didn't like Thailand but couldn't explain why. So presumably this opinion had been installed in him by the Chinese state media, his parents, schooling, or by a combination of all of them. I then queried him on Korea and he just shook his head in dismay. "Korean people not like Chinese people" he said, but he did differentiate between the North and South, conceding that North Korea was "Okay." I remembered my young students in Korea and who when asked about China, usually said "China dirty", which indeed it can be in comparison to South Korea. Then again, they were a fastidious bunch; if I happened to distractedly put the end of my pen in my mouth whilst thinking something over, the whole class would be in uproar chorusing "TEACHER DIRTY!!!"

He didn't like Japan. The wrong doings of the Japanese against the Chinese during the war is so impressed upon the public it was hardly worth asking him. Flick through the TV channels in China any time of the day and you're bound to stumble across at least one historical melodrama glorifying Chinese resistance to the Japanese aggressors. Such programs are overloaded with gushing music, long drawn out scenes of heroic Chinese self-sacrifice, and the atrocious cruelty – not exactly misplaced – of the Japanese. With constant exposure to this propaganda - which really serves to legitimise the Chinese communist regime - it's not surprising that many Chinese remain quite negative about the Japanese.

Moving West I pointed to Mongolia and got the surprising response, almost shouted, "THAT NOT MONGOLIA!" I re-read the Cyrillic and told him that it was definitely Mongolia, but he wouldn't have it, instead identifying the Chinese province of Inner Mongolia and informing me "THIS IS MONGOLIA!" Confused, I asked him why "Mongolia was not actually Mongolia?" He muttered resentfully something about "STALIN TAKE IT!!" and left it at that. He then became increasingly animated and with his finger encircled China, Korea, Manchuria, Mongolia, Kazakhstan, Kyrgyzstan, Tajikistan, and a fair bit of South East Asia, "THIS ALL CHINA! THIS ALL CHINA!" He exclaimed.

Of course Chinese troops had previously been stationed as far West as the Fergana Valley in Uzbekistan. Yet any thought of real expansion was put to an end when they were defeated by the Arabs in one of the most significant battles in Eurasian history at Talas, (modern day Kyrgyzstan), in the year 751AD. As for the other claims of 'This all China' they were places that had at one time or another in the past, been incorporated in the Middle Kingdom, or in the case of parts of South East Asia, acted as vassal states who paid tribute to the Chinese Emperor.

Having staked his claim to a greater China, the lad sat down, sighed, and changed the subject. "Do you have wiff?" he asked. Well, I thought, considering I hadn't showered for a while, I probably did. "What's a wiff?" I replied. He seemed perplexed, and then re-iterated "You know, wiff, a woman."

"Oh, you mean a wife. No I'm not married." This seemed to confuse him further. "Why not?" He queried. "Well, I'm only twenty-eight for a start" I responded. This struck him as thoroughly unsatisfactory "Twenty-eight!" he replied, incredulous, "You should be married!" Not being married by your mid-twenties was always inexplicable to most people in Central Asia, but I hadn't expected quite such a response from this young Chinese. I rattled off the usual excuses about a wife meaning a more settled existence; house, career, car, and certain responsibilities I wasn't quite ready to commit to. Oh, that and the prescient fact I hadn't met anyone who I wanted to spend the rest of my life with yet. He shrugged at my answer with amused puzzlement.

By this time some hours had passed since Cheng's departure, but she finally breezed back in at 12.00pm, greeting me with a surprised look. She had apparently forgotten her order to "Wait here." It even looked like she felt a little bit guilty about it. However, it was now lunchtime, a potentially drawn out affair in Chinese circles, and she said with her usual clipped manner "Here Three o'clock." For more waiting I presumed. But then she picked up her favourite prop, the calendar, and pointed to the coming Friday, and said "we get visa this Friday." I was delighted, the process had been brought forward a week without me saying a thing.

So I left, looking to waste a couple of hours, but very content that the cogs of bureaucracy were slowly turning in my favour. Returning at 3.00pm, Cheng was all business again. "Sit down" she instructed and passed me the computer keyboard to balance on my lap. "Write China plan" she told me. By this she meant she wanted me to write my itinerary. So I reeled off some half truths and flowery elaborations about places I had already been, and wasn't really intending to visit again. I've already stated that I wanted to pursue the Southern Silk Road, which beyond Hotan was not really frequented by tourists. It was still off the beaten track and authorities showed no sign of opening it up to tourism the way they had on the northern route. I would witness good reasons for this later. For now, it was not something I was going to mention, as snaking close to Tibet through Uyghur-populated southern Xinjiang, both pebbles in the proverbial Chinese state shoe, was probably not going to get me awarded a visa.

So I wrote of Urumqi, to see the famed Taklimakan mummies; Dunhuang with its Buddhist frescoes; the Qaraz irrigation and ancient Jiaohe near Turfan; before moving out of Xinjiang to more prestigious tourist attractions like the Terracotta Warriors of Xi'an. I had just finished this finely composed statement when Cheng intervened, instructing she wanted the format to run "Number one: Urumqi. Number two: Turfan." So I had to abolish my intricately woven prose with which I hoped to blind the embassy, and revert to bullet points.

That done it seemed all my documents were finally in order and we might proceed to the embassy. At this point Cheng mentioned a Frenchman who was going to join us and that we would have to wait for him. He too was after a visa, but thanks to Sarkozy's fling with the Dali Lama, this had become even more arduous for French nationals than I was finding it myself. I wondered if Sarkozy had known when he aligned himself with Buddhist Tibet, that the Chinese had actually once thought France was a Buddhist country too.[8] That was in the early Nineteenth Century when confusion regarding European geography remained considerable in China. Later opinion was that France was Catholic, but that it was also the same country as Portugal. Still, this seems a minor error compared to the observations of a Chinese traveller to France in the same era who noted how "Many [French] women have long beards and moustaches."[9]

I asked Cheng why obtaining a visa had become so longwinded, saying how I had received three month tourist visas in 2007 from Chinese embassies in Islamabad and Tashkent. "After Olympics, not easy" she said. Indeed, I remembered the requirements when I tried to apply in Korea in 2008. They wanted flight tickets in and out, and hotel reservations for every step of the way – a logistical and financial impossibility when you're planning to traverse China by bike. Fortunately, things had considerably relaxed by the time I reached Bangkok four months later, where I secured a one month tourist visa with ease.

However, I had to consider myself fortunate, as the Frenchman still needed to provide air tickets and hotel bookings for his whole trip. She phoned him to find out where he was. There was a brief conversation and she hung up. "French lost!" she exclaimed, looking at me and giggling. "Aah, French" she continued, shaking her head. It seemed she took his being lost as a natural display of Gallic incompetence, and a joke to be shared. I laughed accordingly.

About twenty minutes later a man appeared at the window, Cheng confirmed it was "French." However, after five minutes, he still hadn't materialised in the office, apparently failing to navigate the thirty second walk down the corridor. "AAH, FRENCH!!" Cheng tutted again with a mix of irritation and amusement at what she took to be the antics of a complete buffoon.

Having eventually found the office he revealed himself to be a man in his late forties, dark eyes, with the tan and wrinkles borne of healthy outdoor living. He was a successful businessman, and rather unusually, had just opened a cheese factory in Kyrgyzstan. He had just spent the weekend skiing in the mountains near Issyk Kul, and was a former ski instructor himself. He said he would take us to the embassy in his chauffeur driven car. The car was a large black saloon. Its driver was a young Kyrgyz, wearing what seemed to be the winter uniform of the Kyrgyz male; black Adidas jacket and black beanie hat. He looked like a member of Run-DMC. The fur-lined interior and blacked-out windows of his pimped-up ride added to the Hip-hop affiliations – adopted style of angry young men everywhere. We set off on the short drive out of town to the Chinese embassy.

The Frenchman despite his success was very down to earth and constantly laughing. He talked of his many visits to China, and the incredible changes he had witnessed there since 1992. I could well believe it.

As we drove through town Cheng tried to direct the driver in her characteristically brusque manner. I could tell from the tone of his retort that he neither agreed with her directions, nor appreciated being directed. She tried again but he spat back "ZNEYE-OO" (I know) accompanied with a scornful look. He clearly didn't like her, and I couldn't help wondering if it was because she was Chinese. I had heard a lot of anecdotal evidence – and would hear a lot more – that the Kyrgyz generally didn't favour their Chinese neighbours. When in Bishkek in the summer of 2009 there were several incidents of young Japanese being attacked and quite seriously injured near to where I was staying. It seemed strange that only Japanese were targeted when the guesthouse was used by plenty of Europeans also. The owner informed me that "The Kyrgyz, they don't like Chinese people. They think these Japanese are Chinese, that's why they attack them." I wasn't entirely convinced by this explanation, but there did seem to be some animosity.

Historically, the Chinese were the settled 'other' to the Kyrgyz nomads long before the Russians arrived. In the Kyrgyz epic *Manas,* all 'out' groups were described with a derogatory stock phrase; 'the Russians with hairy mouths'; 'the Sarts who love their asses as if they were horses'; and 'the jabbering Chinese whose language no one understands.'[10] Manas himself was mortally wounded during a raid against Beijing by the treacherous Chinese prince Kongurbai. On the other hand, China has often been a place of refuge for Kyrgyz escaping the excesses of the Russians. The two peoples share a long interlocking history. Perhaps the powerful China of today is easy for some Kyrgyz to resent.

For example, I had heard one Kyrgyz complain that there were already too many Chinese people in Bishkek. That "They come here to study because it's cheap" and that "the products the Chinese sell in Kyrgyzstan are very poor quality and always break." Some of this prejudice no doubt harks back to the Soviet propaganda against the "Yellow Peril" that was pushed after the Sino-Soviet split of the 1950's, and which was 'fed by an old fear of China's desire for living space in the West.'[11]

However, the evidence of increasing numbers of Chinese in Bishkek is plain to see; to quote a teacher interviewed by a Bishkek based reporter "The number of Chinese students grows yearly. Our university even founded a Confucian institute. We have flights to Urumqi every day. We have Chinese restaurants on every corner and the number of Chinese medical centres is huge."[12] All this helps fuel rumours that the Chinese are trying to take over the country through immigration. Yet prior to the arrival of the Russians, Central Asians are thought to have held China in greater esteem than they did Persia or Afghanistan. Historically at least, Chinese products were also very well regarded among the nomads. However, in recent times it has been observed that 'the Central Asian peoples have always tended to accord prestige and admiration more readily to Russia than to China.'[13]

Rising China is indeed an ominous proposition to have on your doorstep, its bulging population a huge contrast to what has always been a very sparsely populated Central Asia. This is a natural product of harsh ecosystems not suitable for hydraulic agriculture. A landscape traditionally used by nomadic pastoralists, like Kyrgyzstan and much else of Central Asia, sustains and requires far fewer people than the irrigated rice cultivation of China. Historically, constant warfare, and possibly even a loss of fecundity resulting from a life spent in the saddle and extreme cold, might also have contributed to the region's low population density. Of course, it is only relatively recently that populous Han China really came eyeball-to-eyeball with Soviet Central Asia. When Xinjiang – culturally and linguistically contiguous with 'Central Asia' – was officially annexed by the PRC in 1949, there were only 300,000 ethnic Chinese living there. By 2006 there were 7.5 million. Today the Chinese population in Xinjiang is greater than that of the indigenous Turkic speaking Uyghur.

There are already thousands of Chinese farmers in Kazakhstan working the land. In 2009 there were public demonstrations in Almaty – something normally banned in Kazakhstan – against "Chinese expansionism" when plans were announced to rent a million hectares of land to China for the Chinese to farm. In 1995 the Kazakh capital was moved from Almaty, which is close to the Chinese border, to a desolate location on the northern steppe, site of a provincial town called Akmola, which in Kazakh means "White grave." Various reasons have been given for this strange move, such as its more 'central' location, or to secure the heavily Russian populated north against separatism. However, it has also been suggested that the location of newly built 'Astana' (capital) was influenced by a fear of China.

I asked the Frenchman if he thought the Kyrgyz liked the Chinese. He just laughed and said "They are scared that one day they will wake up and they will all be Chinese." I had a feeling this wasn't too far from the truth.

Indeed the Frenchman's comment seemed hard to dispute as, after a long poplar-lined road out of Bishkek, we turned into the new Chinese embassy. It was an architectural symbol of power if ever I saw one. I had been unjust with my judgement of the Kyrgyz 'White House' earlier. If Darth Vader was to rule his Galactic dystopia from anywhere, it would be here. It was huge, constructed in that oddly 'LEGO' looking style of New China's architecture; i.e. cold, blocky, plastic and impersonal. The place was built like a fortress with a huge perimeter wall that was spiked. There were very few gates, all firmly shut. Beyond the wall sat the huge central building, highly comparable to a Keep. The Chinese flag flew proudly from its centre, its bright red the only colour on the building, every square inch of which was faced in white.

I was surprised a host country would allow such a domineering foreign structure within its borders. At that moment it looked like it might be the biggest building in Kyrgyzstan. Its audaciousness seemed analogous to Ancient Egypt's impenetrable fortified towns in Nubia, or the Norman castles of England: simply put it struck me as a brazen display of foreign power inside another country's borders. The effect was heightened when one studied its surroundings; half-finished low-rise housing in bare concrete, the rusty blue trailers/caravans so archetypal of rural Kyrgyzstan, and a few grubby runny-nosed Kyrgyz children playing in the assorted debris. It looked like a refugee camp outside the walls of Babylon.

We pulled up outside this windowless exterior and Cheng, business as usual, clicked over to the red steel gate and spoke into a letter-box sized slit in the wall. Then, a person-sized gate-within-a-gate was unbolted and swung open. Cheng beckoned for me and the Frenchman to join her. As we crossed the threshold the Frenchman smirked, "Welcome to China." I laughed, and mused on the truthfulness of his observation. 'Welcome to the official version of China' at any rate, I thought. The dusty wasteland outside was gone, and we entered an interior of spotless cream polished floors, decorative Ming vases, and dragon-filled frescoes. A large screen to one side was tuned to a Chinese shopping channel, showing a lengthy infomercial demonstrating some bizarre kind of ear cleaning product. Whilst grinning actors had strange devices vigorously plunged into their ears, a hail of Chinese characters scrolled up the screen, no doubt telling you what a good deal this thing was. 'Welcome to China' indeed, I thought.

Apart from that the place had the standard visa section windows, seats and queuing barriers. Oh, but it was completely empty except for us and a couple of Chinese staff. The Frenchman was up first receiving his passport in a flash, whilst I waited there tensely. Cheng went to another window with all the Kyrgyz passports she had accumulated that morning. She then indicated for me to come over. I approached the window and sat opposite a very weary looking official. He nodded in greeting, his eyes reduced to cracks by the fleshy bags of fatigue hanging beneath them. My presence seemed pretty ancillary as the conversation raged between him and Cheng. It sounded like a desperate struggle and the fate of my visa rested on its outcome. Cheng was pointing at my previous Chinese visas, hopefully saying something like 'look, he's been to China lots before and hasn't caused any trouble. I think you should give him a visa.' The official looked unimpressed, shrugging his shoulders as if this was irrelevant, before taking issue with something else on my passport. Cheng countered, and I gazed on in complete incomprehension, but hoping none the less.

After some minutes the storm calmed, Cheng fell silent, and for the first time in a while the official looked at me and asked "So, you did not go to China last year?"

"No" I replied honestly. "Okay" He said, tapping my passport on the desk, and saying "Good Luck!"

"Chez Cher" I said gratefully. "Chez cher" he repeated with a chuckle, clearly amused at the 'long-nose round eyes' attempt at civilised speech. He then got up and left with my passport. Cheng called me away.

"How did it go?" asked the Frenchman. "I don't know. He just said good luck and took my passport" I replied. The Frenchman maintained his grin. I guess he assumed everything would work out fine. With that we left the white fortress and drove back to Bishkek. The Frenchman dropped us back at Cheng's building, before vowing to be back for another Chinese visa another time. Then he was gone. "Aaah French" chided Cheng absently as we walked into her office. Inside she hit me with the bill, so I guess that meant I was going to get my visa. $120 for my passport to be returned next Friday. $150 for it to be returned this Friday. A cunning ploy I thought as anybody would surely pay the extra $30 to get their visa seven days quicker. I told her I would take the second option. "Okay, back here Friday 4.30. Tomorrow free time" she instructed, ending by breaking into a friendly smile.

Another day had disappeared on the visa chase and we left the office together. The sky was descending to a darker shade of grey and the freezing air bit sharply at my face. "Now I go to other job" said Cheng. Wow, I thought, she really is a busy lady. Turned out her other job was for her tourism company. She even walked fast, commenting "Bishkek danger. There was war here. At night people want take your dollar. Bishkek danger!" I wondered what had brought Cheng to Kyrgyzstan in the first place.

We had cut through an estate of concrete apartment blocks and when we emerged back on a main road I had lost my bearings. "Where's Chuy?" I asked. Cheng looked about herself, seemingly lost too for a minute. She made a strange gesture with her hand, then pointed and said "Philharmonic." Oh, I understood, she was indicating the Philharmonic on Chuy by pretending to blow a trumpet or something. I thanked her, told her I'd see her Friday, and began the icy walk home. On the way I passed two Russian teenagers whose fair skin and blonde hair, already relatively uncommon in modern Bishkek, was pronounced by their many facial piercings, tattoos and distinctly Punk dress code. They were wearing vests and ripped jeans in about -10°c. In a city of dark jacketed and hat-wearing Kyrgyz, they really struck a pose.

"Free time" Thursday came and went. On Friday I returned to Cheng's office. Turning into Manas Propektesi, amongst the other ordinary pedestrians, the students and office workers, skipped a little Russian girl of about nine. She was alone, in human terms anyway, but accompanied by at least eight dogs. The largest, a grey beast, missing one of its forelegs, was a head taller than her. Still, in spite of its disability, it remained an intimidating looking animal, and led the pack. The other dogs surrounded the girl as if in formation, like she was the flagship of a fleet to be protected by this canine convoy. Smaller dogs trotted along on the flanks, and another wolf brought up the rear. They moved in silent complicity that surely meant they were used to travelling in this company, knowing to stop at the roadside and automatically falling in around their human charge. It was an enchanted sight, an inverted 'Little Red Riding Hood.' I wondered at the story behind it; the little girl who feeds the feral dogs of Bishkek. In return they follow her loyally and give protection as she walks the streets commanding her own wolf pack.

Arriving at Cheng's, the middle-aged Kyrgyz man who I had seen there the other day was waiting outside. It was easy to guess what he was doing outside, and a short walk to the locked door confirmed what I suspected, Cheng was late. I fell into conversation with him. He had no English so it tested my limited Russian. Interestingly he had spent a large part of his career working as an engineer at the Minsk Institute in Belarus. He looked back on this with some nostalgia and the opportunities once afforded by the old Soviet Union. He asked if I had been there, but I told him a visa to Belarus was probably harder than getting a Chinese visa in Bishkek. He laughed in agreement. I asked him if he spoke Chinese. He said he didn't. How, then, I asked would he speak to people if he spoke no Chinese (not that I spoke Mandarin myself, but English can afford some understanding there, sometimes). He whispered "Uyghurstan" (Literally 'Land of the Uyghur'), and I instantly realised my mistake. As I've already mentioned, Xinjiang Province is the home of the Uyghur people and they speak a Turkic language just like the Kyrgyz. He could of course communicate with the Uyghur people due to the mutual intelligibility that exists, to varying degrees, between tongues of the Turkic language family. He reeled off a fascinating list of regions where Turkic languages were spoken. Indeed, there are many, stretching from Siberia to Europe and the Middle East. Mostly, Turkic peoples do not occupy their own states, but exist within larger political entities, like the Uyghur of China. Indeed, the same was true of the Turkmen, Uzbeks, Kazakhs, and Kyrgyz until twenty years ago. For the preceding seventy years they had been enveloped in the Soviet Union. Other than those already mentioned, Turkic speaking peoples include the Azeris, Chuvash, Tartars, Bashkirs, Qashqai, Yakuts, Gagauzs, Crimean Kariates, Krymchaks, Karakalpaks, Karachays, and Nogais. Some names, like the Kazakhs or Tartars will receive only the vaguest recognition to many in the West. Most of the rest remain totally unheard of except to specialists.

He asked me how I was getting to China. I told him I didn't know yet. I had told Cheng I was flying to Urumqi. Talk of overland travel to Kashgar and the Uyghur heartland of southern Xinjiang might not have been conducive to my visa application.

Kyrgyzstan has two borders with China, the Torugat Pass, and another at Irkeshtam in the south east of the country. I was counting on crossing at Irkeshtam, and believed there was a weekly bus from Osh (Kyrgyzstan's second largest city) to Kashgar, China. I had completed the same journey in 2007. However, the Kyrgyz man said that I could also get a bus from Bishkek and that it travelled to Naryn, in Central Kyrgyzstan, and over the Torugat Pass into China. This was news to me. The Torugat crossing still holds a certain mystique among travellers as a breathtaking high altitude journey through the Tien Shan (the border is at nearly 4000m). However, ludicrous amounts of bureaucratic red tape make it a logistically difficult and expensive option. Also, in winter I assumed the pass would be closed, but not according to this man. He even told me I could buy a ticket for $70.

I was on the brink of asking where, when Cheng made her timely arrival. The Kyrgyz took his visa, shook my hand and was gone. I handed Cheng two crisp $100 bills and watched her face drop. Please tell me you have change I thought. I mean, you've been collecting money all day, how can you not have change? Then again, this was the Central Asian visa chase, and a final piece of tedium seemed fitting. Luckily she remembered that she did indeed have change after all and swiftly dealt me out a $50. She then seemed to get quite excited, offering a rare smile, and saying "Tomorrow you go to mountains, yes?" I grinned back, chuffed to have got my visa, "Yes, tomorrow I go to mountains." She then gave me one final instruction "Next time you must apply for visa in your own country." "Of course" I replied. I then thanked her wholeheartedly and shook her hand, or rather took her hand in mine and moved it up and down, as she failed to reciprocate the gesture, which obviously bemused her. "Thanks Mrs Cheng, farewell!"

5

Heartland

Kyrgyzstan is a country of few roads, which to my mind is one of its strong points. Kyrgyzstan has considerably less roads than Burma, North Korea, Mozambique or Tajikistan. Looking at the map I could see I had taken many of the major routes before. This made choosing my next destination simple. I would travel to the enticing blank spot in the middle Kyrgyzstan I had yet to explore; the country's heartland. I would go south past the great lake of Issyk Kul and its little sister Song-Kul, and head to the town of Naryn, the largest settlement in central Kyrgyzstan. There were some historical sites in that area I was intrigued to reach; something I expected to be both more challenging and more rewarding in the depth of winter. Afterwards, if the road was open, I would attempt to cross the central mountains and break through to Jalalabad and the Fergana Valley in the south of the country.

"NARYN?!" exclaimed the guest house owner. "Naryn very cold! Naryn veeery cold!" He clasped his hands and sucked in his breath in exaggeration of the point. "How cold?" I asked. "VERY COLD! More cold than Bishkek. Maybe -25°c or -30°c!" Okay, pretty cold I thought. I'd never experienced that kind of cold before. Still, I'd survived in Bishkek with no electricity at 15°c below and was getting used to it.

The next morning I procured a seat in a shared taxi; Bishkek to Naryn in six hours for 400 Som, or about £5. The driver was a short stocky Kyrgyz with baby fresh cheeks. I guessed he was in his early twenties. What struck me most about him was that he was wearing merely a flat cap, jeans and sweatshirt. He seemed a little under-dressed for Bishkek, but for a trip to the mountains where it regularly ducked below -30c, it seemed foolhardy to say the least. The boot, into which I chucked my rucksack, revealed no stash of furs or survival gear; just a spare tyre and a flask of petrol. I took this lack of provision as a good sign; he clearly believed we would get there without complication.

The car itself was an old, white Volkswagen that had probably seen its best days on the Autobahn circa 1980. However, like so many of its German-made brethren it had ended up plying the roads of Kyrgyza into the second decade of the Twenty-first Century. I was the last of four passengers, meaning we could leave immediately. The man immediately next to me slept, and the girl on his far side stared out of the window. In the front passenger seat slouched a tall, young man. He didn't glance my way, concentrating instead on his cigarette, which he smoked with considerable passion.

There were no seatbelt fittings in the back, so I exiled from my mind any associated risks of icy roads, obscure mountain passes, and the prevalence of drunk driving in these parts. Instead I resigned myself to fate and as mere observer to the moving image that flickered past my window. The first part was a repeat; just the slush and grey of waking Bishkek I had seen so much of recently. However, leaving Bishkek to the east, we entered a winter wonderland. Everything was covered in a carpet of white. Snow lined every branch, gutter, and exposed edge. The mundane transformed by an icy coating that glimmered golden under the highlighting rays of the morning sun. Slavic cottages flanked the road. Occasionally they were finely decorated, looking jewelled and fantastical like abodes from a fairy tale. All were painted white, with window frames, eves, and doors picked out in sky blue or grass green. They were fronted by loosely woven picket fences painted in the same primary colours.

I could see no housing estates, for we had left the city and its suburbs far behind. Instead the cottages were strung along the roadside one deep, like beads on an icy chain, with a rustic, rural aesthetic. Less attractive features like the asbestos fencing, rusty wire and concrete walls, largely lost behind a veil of snow, left a vista of ramshackle beauty. It was a scene set at eye level, with nothing man-made reaching beyond a single storey, except for the regularly spaced telegraph poles. They leaned at wayward angles and appeared to hang from their wires like emaciated puppets on jangled strings. Behind the cottages stretched an empty white that eventually merged with jagged mountains, guardians of the Chuy Valley. It is nature that reaches closest to the heavens here. The road was often lined with poplars, which stood like upturned broomsticks marching off into the distance.

In the flicker of sunshine through iced-up windows, country turned to town and fairy tale to formulaic; a supermarket, a garage, a rotten apartment block. As if in recognition of this transition the driver changed the radio station; traditional strings swapped for Russian Hip-hop. There was a mosque, its dome like a chrome coriander upturned on the standard concrete cube of communist architecture. But as quickly as the town begins, it ends, fizzling out as undramatically as it appeared. For this is generally the way with Kyrgyz towns, low-level and sparse.

Signs for settlements called 'Luxemburg', 'Kant', and 'Rotterfront', tell of the significant German minority that once lived throughout the Chuy Valley. There had been German communities living in western Russia since the 18th Century, but in 1941, fearful that they would collaborate with the invading Nazis, Stalin had the entire population sent east. In Kyrgyzstan they joined other ethnic Germans, descendants of those invited to settle Russia's new territories at the end of the 19th Century. A third wave of Germans arrived in Kyrgyzstan shortly after the second in the form of prisoners of war. Central Asia had long been a dumping ground for those the Russians wanted out of the way. During World War One 40,000 Austrian, Hungarian and German prisoners were sent there. Even when Russia had exited the conflict because of the Bolshevik Revolution, for a long time these men remained. They were free, but trapped by sheer geographical isolation. Whilst some stayed in their old camps others went to live and work in the surrounding settlements. Such a large number of trained men in this location caused great consternation to the British who feared they might be mobilised for an attack on British India. That didn't happen, but it seems these former prisoners were instrumental in helping the Bolsheviks hold onto Tashkent.

Stalin's paranoia in the Great Patriotic War meant that it was not only the nationalities of combatant countries that found themselves exiled to Middle Asia. Over half a million Koreans also ended up there, as Stalin believed they might otherwise assist Japanese expansion on Russia's eastern flank. Fitzroy Maclean, on his unauthorised journey east in the 1930s, witnessed something of this forced migration when 'we stopped for several hours while a number of cattle trucks were hitched onto our train. These were filled with people who, at first sight, seemed to be Chinese. They turned out to be Koreans, who with their families and their belongings were on their way from the Far East to Central Asia where they were being sent to work on the cotton plantations. They had no idea why they were being deported, but all grinned incessantly and I gathered from the few words I could exchange with some of their number that they were pleased to have left the Far Eastern territories where conditions were terrible and to be going to Central Asia of which they had evidently been given enthusiastic accounts.'[1] I had the pleasure of staying with some of their descendants at the border settlement of Qaraqalpaghistan when cycling between the Republic of the same name and the desolation of Western Kazakhstan.

Today, as a result of this mass deportation, there are around 20,000 ethnic Koreans living in Kyrgyzstan. However, most of Stalin's migrants were sent to the considerably more sizable Kazakhstan. In 1944 the entire population of Chechnya and Ingushetia were deported there where they suffered greatly. The survivors were not allowed to return home until 1957. Stalin even intended to deport Azerbaijan's entire population to Central Asia, but the Allied opening of a second front in the West negated the 'need.' Somewhat ironically, in 2002 thousands of Chechen refugees from the war with Russia sought safety in Kazakhstan by asking the Kazakh government for asylum.

Whilst the scale of Stalin's forced migrations is staggering, this was not the first example of relocation at the whim of a Eurasian superpower. The Mongols forcibly resettled large numbers of Iranian and Chinese craftsmen to Mongolia and Siberia. They were made to mine metals and manufacture tools and weapons. 13th Century missionary William Rubruck even came across a goldsmith from Paris who had been captured in Hungary and was working at the Mongol court.

We drove on into emptiness, nature only occasionally disrupted by sporadic skeletons of industry – operational or not, it was hard to tell – and the overland pipes so curious to the former Soviet Union. We passed clusters of homesteads where people congregated around clanking metal hand pumps in the street. The pumps, painted sky blue, spurted water. People filled metal barrels and loaded them onto sledges and wheelbarrows to transport back home. Beyond such settlements nothing hindered one's eye until the mountains; just a few A-frame pylons, scattered out in the white waste like the stragglers of a routed army.

At the road's edge black crows pecked and a black dog padded along on its own mysterious mission. On both sides the mountains rose to mould the valley. To the north they delineate the border with Kazakhstan. To the south they form the buffer to Kyrgyza's rugged interior. The mountains stood with blinding definition against the clear blue sky. They seemed to crash down in a violent surf, with foaming foothills, upon the cold white beach of the valley floor.

Outside each settlement a cemetery lay silent in the snow. The cemeteries of Kyrgyzstan are like cemeteries everywhere; a glimpse back in time. For where the dead rest the concrete of the communist townscapes gives way to far older traditions, and those that were in Central Asia long before the Russians. For all the rhetoric there was about creating *Homo Sovieticus,*[*] the Russians and Kyrgyz remain as separate in death as they were in life; with different burial grounds according to their different religions and cultural traditions. Mud-brick structures, weather-beaten to indefinable age, with arches and domes, stand in the snow. These are the tombs of once well-off and respected people. Amongst them sat shelters made of metal rods, reminiscent of an old fashioned bird cage. It took me a while to realise they were representations of yurts. That people should mark their final resting place with a symbolic yurt, says much about the significance of this traditional abode in Kyrgyz life. As one Kyrgyz local is quoted as saying: 'Death is the only point at which a Kyrgyz stops being a nomad and must stay in a "house."'[2]

Often the tombs are surmounted with metal crescents symbolic of Islam, whilst a great many others are decorated with antlers and horns – representative of the pastoralist, hunter and nomad at the core of Kyrgyz identity.

Amongst these grand tombs are humbler gravestones. Instead of being squared or rounded like the headstones of the West, the top is cut at an angle, and the front often bears an engraved portrait of the deceased.

---

[*] The Russian goal in Central Asia was *sblizhenie* (bringing together) and ultimately *sliianie* ('melding together') into a new 'Soviet Person.'

A memorial strictly of the modern age can often be seen at the roadside; a steering wheel and a bunch of flowers leaving no doubt as to how someone met their end. I thought these memorials a bit strange, like leaving cigarettes where someone had died of lung cancer, or a knife where someone had been stabbed to death. Were these steering wheels trophy-like, and was dying in a car accident somehow its own perverse honour. Maybe I was reading too much into it, but wondered with their nomadic heritage whether the car had become an extension of the Kyrgyz's horse-bound life-blood, a symbol of masculinity, as well as an obvious sign of prosperity in an impoverished nation. Men from mounted warrior societies down the ages have often been buried with their horses, were these steering-wheel memorials just the modern equivalent.

Just out of Bishkek we had passed a severely mangled car mounted on a stone pedestal, a clear warning to drivers. Not that it seemed to have made any impression on ours. At the first stretch of road where dark asphalt was visible, and not just a layer of ice, he unleashed. I searched again for a seatbelt, but to no avail. I told myself I should just be grateful he had waited for an ice-free stretch of road. But what about black ice I thought, and then there was the overtaking on blind bends, which is never a good idea.

We whizzed through Tokmok, greeted on the outskirts by an old jet fighter. Another cliché I've noticed in the old communist bloc – military hardware as decorative items, but now just rusting lumps of metal.

There was a sign for the town, then nothing, such is the somewhat ethereal nature of these old Soviet settlements. Afterwards appeared an incongruous mix of several yurts and a huge billboard advertising a mobile phone network. The centre was an uninspiring crossroad with a supermarket, a mosque and little else.

By contrast, when Chinese traveller Hiun Tsang passed the plain of Tokmok in 630 A.D. he found a colourful and extravagant scene among the ancient nomads; there were tents 'ornamented with flowers of gold so bright they dazzled the eyes', officers 'clad in glittering habits', 'cavalry mounted on camels or on horses, dressed in furs or fine wool and bearing long lances, banners and tall bows. So vast was their multitude, they stretched far out of sight.'[3] Tokmok was also visited by European monks during the 12th Century and even became 'the seat of a Nestorian archbishopric.'[4] Surprising as it may seem 'by the dawn of the Mongol period Christianity was certainly the most visible religion amongst the steppe people'[5], with some tribes apparently even having portable tent chapels. However, in practical terms this probably only meant Christianised forms of traditional practice; *Tengri* was easily equated with the Christian or Islamic God, and priests were simply perceived as shamans.

The turning south at the crossroads led to Burana Tower. This mysterious structure is virtually all that is left of the old Karakhanid capital which was destroyed by the Mongols. Around it lies a field of waist-high anthropomorphic stone figures depicting Turkic warriors. Their flat, stylised faces staring impassively from behind sunken eyelids and drooping moustaches. It is a tradition which originates with the Turkic nomads in southern Siberia, and travelled with them. Leaning at precarious angles, like stolid toy soldiers which time had tried to knock down but failed, their blank, enigmatic gazes hide from our view the world of thoughts they once inhabited. It was a world they surely prospered in, to have left such durable reminders of their existence. They mark the graves of dead heroes. They are commonly known as *balbals* but this term actually refers to the smaller uncarved stones which surrounded a warrior's grave and were used to identify the number of enemy he had slain.

We continued east. We passed the statue of a mounted hero and left Tokmok behind. The mountains to the north crept closer, like the frosted scales of some giant lizard half submerged along the length of the valley floor. Wrapped in furs, babushkas waddled like penguins at the road's edge.

We enter the *Boomskoe ushchelie* or 'Shoestring Gorge.' The road, which is prone to avalanches, rises in a wall of rock on one side, and drops dramatically to the river on the other. The concrete blocks that pose as barriers are disturbingly irregular, and the abyss waits with open mouth for an inattentive driver.

Black goats clung precariously to the snow flecked precipices, whilst statues of a deer and a man with a bow guard this gateway to Lake Issyk Kul. Perhaps they were built to recount some illustrious saga from history. Now they are only crumbling relics, with paint stripped away by the weather.

The road threaded through the gorge in tumultuous fashion and our car bounced along as the driver seemed determined to catch some 'air' at every oscillation. It was in the tight confines of the gorge that

I first noticed a huge white Chinese container lorry. Heading in the opposite direction, clues to its Chinese provenance were provided by the large black Mandarin characters adorning its flanks. It was the first of many I was to see, forming an endless baggage train that streamed on bad roads and through bitter conditions across the five mountain ranges between Bishkek and the Middle Kingdom. Being 3600kms from the nearest open seaport, Kyrgyzstan is the second most remote of all landlocked countries. In fact more than 70% of Kyrgyzstan's imports come overland from China, yet less than 5% of Kyrgyzstan's exports go the other way. Bilateral trade between the two countries in 2008 amounted to nearly 10 billion dollars, with China clearly as the main beneficiary. However, trade has since slowed due to the global financial crisis, and also on account of the violence that rocked Kyrgyzstan in 2010. China, ever fearful of insurrection in volatile Xinjiang province among the indigenous Uyghur, temporarily closed its borders and evacuated 1,200 of its nationals. Approximately 50,000 Uyghur live in Kyrgyzstan, mainly in Bishkek and Osh, where the trouble was centred. A few months after this visit, in the summer of 2011, *The China Daily* reported China's president Hu Jintao's meeting with his new Kyrgyz counterpart Roza Otunbayeva and their agreement to 'deepen co-operation in trade, infrastructure and security'[6] and pledge to combat the 'three evil forces' of terrorism, extremism and separatism. China plans to further increase trade with its smaller neighbour (and to accelerate development of China's western regions) by opening a free trade zone around the bordering Chinese city of Kashgar.

Leaving the gorge the road opened up, and so did our driver. Brown mountains, shielded from the snow, had giant words I could not fathom written with white stones on their slopes. We pulled into a rest area. The café had a dingy interior, with a décor that can't have been redone since the Soviets left. A couple of serving girls sat unsmiling behind the counter. I bought some somsa and lingered in the dusty car park outside, enjoying the sunlight and view. I chucked scraps of my lunch to a couple of stray dogs. They flinched, cowed by my every move, testifying to the rocky relationship they must have had with man.

Leaving, we accelerated into the broad expanse that marks the Issyk Kul Basin, the driver taking the racing line as always. Strangely, after the white, winter world prior to the gorge, we found ourselves in a landscape more akin to the American Badlands. I was surrounded by orange cliffs and sandy desert scrub. Only higher up was the snowline realised, sitting in fat white pillows that split ground from sky. We turned south, off the main road. I had expected this, having done the same by bike. It was a short cut, bypassing Lake Issyk Kul.

If one recalls the image of Kyrgyzstan as a frog in profile, then Issyk kul is its prominent, placid, blue eye - and this eye has seen much. Cave paintings, simple tools, and other evidence of primordial human habitation have been found in the region around the lake. On the northern shore lie the burial mounds and petroglyphs of the ancient Scythians. On those rocks I had seen tangled images of fading men and beasts, portraits of ibex and other local fauna. Most impressive was the scene of the hunt, depicting the hunter's use of eagles and tame snow leopards in their pursuit of their prey. As nomads and mounted warriors (also with a penchant for mare's milk), the Scythians shared much cultural continuity with the later Kyrgyz. The socket of Issyk kul's eye, sunk as it is in the northern arm of the Tien Shan Mountains, has served as a natural corridor for traders and armies ever since. Legend tells of two children - the only survivors of a massacre in which all the other Kyrgyz were killed - who were brought to Issyk Kul by a cow whose calves had been slain by humans. At the lake she raised them until they were old enough to marry. The resulting sons were the founders of two Kyrgyz tribes. This story resembles the origin myth for the Turks who founded the first Turkish Empire on the Orkhon River in the 6th Century A.D. Before the migration west of both peoples, the Kyrgyz lived to the north of the Turks in southern Siberia. Their languages were very close (perhaps indistinguishable) and hence the Kyrgyz are described as a Turkic people. In the origin myth of these ancient Turks, enemies killed all their tribe, the Ashina, except for a ten year old boy whose feet they cut off. This boy was raised by a she-wolf who fed him meat. When the boy grew up he mated with the she-wolf and their ten sons founded new Turk tribes. According to this myth the Turks worked for several generations as ironsmiths for another people called the Rouran. Likewise, in historical sources we hear of the Kyrgyz collecting iron ore after the rains to make high quality weapons with, which they then 'delivered to the Turks.'[7] However, a Chinese emperor of the 6th Century A.D. remarked 'that the Kyrgyz were waiting with gnashing teeth for their chance to attack the Turks.[8]

The Kyrgyz did not come to Issyk Kul until later. Some seventy mountain streams flow into the lake but none flow out. Due to thermal activity and its high salt content it never freezes, its very name meaning 'hot lake.' For the same reason the Mongols called it 'Iron Lake' and maybe this was why the Kyrgyz once refused to swim in its waters. Or perhaps it was because of the water taboo of nomadic tradition. Water reflected the heavens and *Tengri* the supreme Turco-Mongol god. To wash in rivers or even to eat snow was to defile the sacred. The ancient nomads apparently did not let water near their bodies at all. Instead, they ritually cleansed themselves with steam baths which were made by throwing water and hemp seed onto hot stones, with intoxicating effect. Public saunas or *banyas* - without the hemp - remain common throughout Central Asia today.

Such was the prime pasture the lake afforded, some Kyrgyz even gave up their nomadic ways; opting instead for village life, growing vegetables, and short-haul seasonal rotation to feed their flocks and herds. The lake is 182kms long and up to 70kms across. At 1608 metres above sea level it is the second largest Alpine lake in the world. Although Issyk Kul's official depth is 700 metres, some believe it is bottomless and that it reaches down to the hot centre of the earth. Folk stories record memories of cities now sunk beneath the piercing blue of its rippling waters. At the Lake's eastern end the ruins of 2200 year old *Chegu* ('Red Valley') city reveal artefacts that give some truth to these tales. More than two millennia later Russian settlers arrived at the Lake to relieve the Kyrgyz of their best land. On the wave of the 1916 rebellion the Kyrgyz took their revenge, slaughtering two thousand of the newcomers. Tsarist colonial forces repaid the Kyrgyz in kind, and with interest, putting them to flight and burning their villages to the ground.

In Soviet times Issyk Kul, like much of the rest of Kyrgyzstan was sealed off from foreigners by the military. Secret mining towns appeared in remote valleys to harvest uranium for atomic warheads, whilst the Lake was used for naval weapons development and a shadowy research complex.

However, I would not so much as see Issyk Kul on this journey. Instead, we turned south, cutting through the mountains. We passed another eatery; a polished, plastic version, far more globalist in the cut of its jib. I had been there before and knew it definitely had cleaner facilities and its interior was light and airy. Yet I could not help but resent it. Was this to be the new face of Kyrgyzstan I wondered? At least communism only managed to pour concrete over half the world – What we have now is bent on taking the lot, giving it all the same plastic veneer. I knew that inside, the wall mounted plasma screen played MTV and Russian hip-hop videos with their empty message of the new world religion that material success surpasses all else. Next to this shiny café, in ridiculous juxtaposition, stood a yurt: setting a striking contrast between the pre-communist nomadic ways, and the new incursions of capitalism's generic global look.

The road was in disrepair, and we climbed to the Pass in a cloud of dust. Out of this brown haze came the shadows of more Chinese monsters, lorry, after lorry, after lorry. They clunked by like prehistoric beasts in a primeval mist. After a long, bumpy climb the dust dissipated and Orto-Tokoy reservoir came into view below us. It was frozen white in a landscape still and empty. We descended to join the road skirting its southern shore, which would lead us to Kochkor and eventually Naryn.

After a corridor of cliffs we entered a great plain. Yellow pastures accommodated herds of cows, plus flocks of sheep and goats. They appeared like swarming ants against the scale of the landscape. Hay strewn hamlets littered the barley plain, where rivulets of icy slush provided water for the animals. Kyrgyz cowboys minded them from horseback, and in the distance smoke rose sleepily from isolated roof tops. From 1941 to 1991 the number of sheep and goats in Kyrgyzstan quadrupled to ten million. One of the first guidebooks to the country, published in the mid-Nineties reported that the Kyrgyz were outnumbered three to one by their animals. However, the Nineties for newly independent Kyrgyzstan was an extremely lean time economically, something exacerbated by the rapid transition from state collectives to a system of private ownership. By the end of the century the number of sheep and goats had dropped by more than half to a figure of 3.8 million. Much of this decline was due to animals being slaughtered for food, so dire was the situation.

Today the figure has stabilised to approximately 6 million. However, the move to private ownership and the capitalist economy has left myriad individual herders who simply cannot afford the costs of infrastructure and logistics that would have previously been undertaken by the collective. This in turn has led to the overgrazing and erosion of local pastures, whilst the often prohibitive cost of reaching the traditional high pastures, or *Jailoos,* has left them under-grazed and vulnerable to invasions of foreign flora.

As we rattled along, the plain soon gave way to mountains once more. The gravel road wound between these great interlocking mounds of rock. We passed through Sary Bulak, a town which looks more like a train abandoned at the foot of a cliff. This is due to the crescent of a dozen or so trailers – quite indistinguishable from train carriages – that line the road through it. They sell a limited supply of refreshments, each one stocking the same as the next. Shortly beyond this a road turns west to the lake of Song Kul, which sits pretty at 3000m.

I recalled how I had ridden that way in 2009. Even in May it had been frozen and we had abandoned our bikes to climb the snow-capped final ascent. We watched in horror as a shepherd, eager to be the first to get his herds to the lake, drove his horses with a whip and curses, neck-deep into the snow. Eventually they panicked and routed down the mountainside. Their bodies cut black trails in the snow as they fell, and their terrified neighs sliced through the air. I couldn't quite believe what I was seeing. The scene was so dramatic it was like watching a Hollywood rendition of Hannibal crossing the Alps. The horses became lodged in the snow several hundred metres down the slope. Incredibly they had all survived and had to await rescue from their shepherd. A huge Kyrgyz, forever taking nasvai, he was, if nothing else, a determined man. Where his horses had failed he sent up the cows, kicking and spitting at them the whole way. They traversed the last perilous shelf of snow - and it was avalanche season – making it safely to the plateau on which the Lake rests. Remi and I were free to follow in the slush of their tracks, hopeful that if a hundred or so cows hadn't caused an avalanche, then we shouldn't either – although we were enlisted by the shepherd to assist him pull free animals wedged helplessly in the snow.

The memory faded as we passed the turning. Instead our car climbed into snowfields that seemed to stretch on forever. My ears popped with the change in altitude, and my eyes winced from the relentless white glare. I could hardly see and had to refocus on the car's dark interior. I remembered hearing how when the Kyrgyz ride in winter they stare at the back of their horse's head, something dark, to stop them from going snow-blind. I noticed no-one in the car had sunglasses to guard against this. In fact I didn't recall seeing anyone wearing shades since I had arrived in the country. The driver's eyes just narrowed to the point of barely looking open at all.

The road zigzagged up through the mountains until we crossed the Dolon Pass (3038m). We descended into a steep valley where dense coniferous forest swept the slopes. We passed the occasional horseman, using ropes to tow logs for firewood behind them. There was no doubting that it was still a wild land, sparse in people and the clutter of 'civilisation.' Yet, coming to a high-altitude plateau, a mosaic of snow-topped roofs gave evidence of habitation. Black dots in the distance told of herds on the plain.

Whilst Naryn to Bishkek is not that far, the distance of the journey is magnified multiple times by poor roads and obstructive terrain. We entered Naryn through a dramatic gorge of orange rock, seemingly impervious to the snow which laid so thick on the landscape before it. Indeed, Naryn seemed to be subject to two climatic conditions depending on which way you looked. To the south the view was truly alpine, thick with snow and frosted conifers. Looking north I was greeted by naked rock and the terracotta coloured terrain of the Wild West. Indeed, with bare blue sky and cowboys tending their herds at the base of sand-shaded cliffs, it was a sight stolen from Westerns watched in childhood, not my expectations of winter in high-Asia.

The reason for this double edged panorama is that winter sweeps in from the north, leaving the mountain's southern face snow free. By this point it was only me and the driver left, the others having got out and traipsed off into the snow at various inhospitable looking points along the way. I told him the hotel I wanted to stay at and he duly delivered me. I was frustrated with my basic Russian. I could get where I wanted to go and bumble through simple conversations, but my vocabulary dried up well short of what I needed for an exchange which was anything beyond the elemental. As it was, after covering the bases of name, age, profession, marital status, where I was from and where I was going, the driver was limited to expressing his admiration for the weight of my rucksack, before shaking my hand and seeing me trudge towards the spectacularly dismal looking hotel. To be honest it looked abandoned, and I wondered if it was. The adjacent 'restaurant', identified by a rusty sign, was just a shell of broken windows. Its Soviet wreckage a striking contrast to the majesty of the nature in which it was set.

The foyer was a dark, unwelcoming cavern, something explained by bare wires dangling from the light sockets. It was a typical Soviet behemoth, the marble floor testifying to a not inexpensive construction. However, its best days were clearly far behind it.

The reception 'desk' was just a small window with a gap at the bottom through which money and keys could be passed. It was very much the entrance to an institution. However the gaoler was not present, so I loitered until the text-book gold-teethed babushka made her appearance.

There were three accommodation options available. The cheapest, with communal bathroom was about £2.50; the next one up, with a toilet in the room was about £4.00; the 'lux' which had a shower was £15.00 a night. Ever the bargain hunter, it was an easy choice. 'The poor nomad is the pure nomad' after all.

The babushka was visibly disappointed. She repeatedly stressed that if I took the £4.00 option I would have a TV, but couldn't quite grasp the fact that if I couldn't really understand it, her major selling point became somewhat irrelevant.

I was shown to my room. Two narrow beds, a sink, a cupboard with dried blood on the door, no curtains – don't these people know anything about insulation? – and the smell of stale vodka saturating everything. Apart from the charming "NCEH LOVE YOU SHNKA" etched into the wall, that was it. It would do. I just wondered if the dubious output of the archaic portable radiator would suffice for heating when the temperature plummeted that night.

Getting settled, which in those conditions meant putting on another couple of layers of clothing and leaving immediately, I went to investigate Naryn. Outside a young man on his mobile greeted me with a nod. Fifty metres down the road, a middle-aged man nodded at me too. Well, isn't this pleasant I thought, I'd never been greeted by strangers in Bishkek, such is the anonymity of city life. The second man was even wearing sunglasses. Perhaps I could get some here too, rather than just walking around with a permanent squint and in a state of semi-blindness. Naryn actually means 'sunny' in Mongolian, and despite the bitter cold, the place seemed to be aptly named.

Having reached this relatively remote mountain town the first thing I did, the irony of which was not lost on me, was look for an internet café and re-connection with the wider world. Naryn stretches for fifteen kilometres along the Naryn River Valley. Dominated by a backdrop of craggy peaks, the town was still and snowbound, ivory pretty. Only the clatter of a solitary trolley bus trawling Lenina Street gave life to the icy quiet. Long Lenina Street is the spine of Naryn, the trolley bus its slow but predictable nerve. Understandably, the cold kept people inside. Yet the Pacific-blue sky and piercing sun seemed to deny the true temperature. My face tingled and tightened but I was unsure whether the sensation was burning or freezing. Naryn is known as the coldest town in Kyrgyzstan, and I had arrived in January, its coldest month, when temperatures could drop as low as minus 40°c.

I stopped in a shop to inquire "Izvinitiye Pazhsalsta, goodzya internet?" Directions led me to another derelict looking building, something of an architectural theme in Central Asia. But appearances can be deceiving here, where ruins of the old regime now serve the needs of the new. Cement stairs and windowless walls led me to a room with half-a-dozen computers and double that number of teenagers. They stared at me blankly in unison. On the ash-grey walls hung three giant paintings depicting Kyrgyzstan as it is romantically recalled in popular imagination; a chain-mailed army amassed on sturdy steeds under flapping pendants; a field of yurts, white like fallen petals on green meadows that flow forth from epic mountains. But only these historical Kyrgyz, perhaps supposed to be Manas and his kin, need the artist to give them form. The nature here however, remains as idyllic, if not more so, than a creative's brushstrokes can render. Kyrgyzstan may have been colonised - indeed created in a political sense - but it has yet to be totally tamed. Other places have mountains and nature too, but man is compelled to blight it with good roads and easy accessibility, to stamp order and regimentation on nature itself - to turn wilderness into a playground - to make it safe and boring. Finding it is no longer satisfying, he will go somewhere else and, whether driven by 'good' intentions to 'develop', or bad intentions to exploit, will invariably destroy (or at the very least detract from) what attracted him there in the first place. To say that this is human nature is to deny what most people have been doing for most of human existence. That it is the folly of modern man's rapacious recent 'developments' is a certainty.

The teenagers seemed surprised by my presence. The word 'Americanitz' buzzed between them. Clearly my elaborate disguise had been foiled. After huddling for a couple of minutes, a girl turned around and said in slow and deliberate English "Please wait a minute." So I did, watching as the other users attended to what looked like college work and CVs on their screens. It was a striking contrast to the smoke filled, 'World of Warcraft'-dominated *Wambas* that constituted every 'internet café' across the mountains, in China.

I searched the historical sites in the area I wanted to see. Traced travel forums for information on winter logistics; looked to see if roads were closed, routes through China or Tajikistan open. I had searched before, but never found anything useful; just a few blogs from travellers in fairer weather, home-page pitches by 'adventure' travel companies, and the exaggeration of advice giving gurus. There was only the scantiest information on where I wanted to go, with winter just being written off as 'roads closed.' Nothing that was remotely relevant had been posted since the violence of the preceding summer. This could only be a good thing. Maybe it wasn't possible, but I wanted to try. I jotted down the number Zarina had emailed me, the girl I had met on the plane into Bishkek and who lived in Naryn.

I left to find the light fading fast and the temperature also. I couldn't see any cafes and the streets were nearly empty. It seemed I would be eating in. So I returned to the shop where I'd asked for directions and purchased some bread, tinned fish, and some biscuits, before hustling back to the hotel to escape the searing chill. There, upon devouring my three course meal, I had little alternative than to put on all my clothes and bury myself under the blankets of both beds. The radiator didn't do a bad job, and in my arctic hat I actually achieved a reasonable level of cosiness.

Lying in bed my room seemed perfectly positioned acoustically to collect all sound from the hotel's capacious interior. For the first half an hour I was subjected to the sound of someone in the room opposite having inhuman difficulty locking their door. The key clattered in the lock for what seemed like an eternity with the door slamming back and forth as they went through the process again and again. If it wasn't so cold I might have considered going to assist, but as it was I preferred to remain cocooned in relative warmth and silently curse the noise-maker for their incompetence.

No sooner had they finished, and the drunks came rolling in; shouting, stumbling, and throwing up in a continuous cacophony that carried down the corridor. It turned out that the defunct restaurant I had seen on my way in was used for just this purpose; a place to get very drunk before sleeping it off in the adjacent hotel. I can't remember if it fell silent before I fell asleep, but when I awoke the next morning, the drunks were sleeping it off as the lovers got it on.

Despite this, I hadn't slept too badly and went off in search of the communal bathroom. It was worse than I expected. It's one thing to find such squalor on an Indian train, or in a rural Chinese trench toilet, but that it could exist in a hotel just a few feet away from where people slept in furnished rooms was a little surprising.

It was a squat toilet, with which I have no issue, but it had to be accessed by a stable door, upon which one was forced to carefully tip-toe around copious previous human ejections - from both ends, and that had largely missed the hole they were supposed to go down – and then attempt to find a secure enough position to take care of one's own business. Unfortunately this was impossible because all the badly aimed urine had frozen into a layer of yellow ice across the tiled floor. Even worse, a water leak halfway up the wall had frozen into a kind of glacier that extended in an icy pyramid down to its base next to the toilet. Somehow, and I couldn't even conceive the mechanics of this, a turd had become fossilised half way up this impromptu ice sculpture. Well, I had seen enough and decided to abort until I upgraded rooms to one with a loo. On the way out I passed one of the cheerless babushka floor ladies. She exuded the stony-faced misery a lifetime of cleaning such toilets was bound to inflict. 'You poor woman' I thought, as I suddenly understood their characteristic unsmiling demeanour.

I left the hotel and walked to Naryn's inconsequential centre. I ambled up and down looking for something to draw my attention but failed. After a while I went to the telephone exchange and rang Zarina. She said that she worked close by and that she would come and meet me. I waited outside and she appeared about five minutes later. She was wearing jeans, high heels, and a long black jacket with a fur lined hood. She was smiling and full of energy. Right away she asked if I wanted to get my stuff and move in with her family. This took me a bit by surprise, and I didn't really feel comfortable with imposing myself on the family of someone I'd really only just met. However, this seems to be the nature of hospitality in Kyrgyzstan. It harks back to nomadic tradition. In the sparsely populated and harsh environment of Central Asia, such generosity to strangers emerged as a survival tool, not merely a cultural nicety, among nomads and settled people alike. Add to this the Islamic obligation to welcome guests (particularly when they are foreigners with no friends or family in the country), and such overt hospitality makes sense. It's wonderful, and humbling. However, it can also be exhausting as you become the main attraction in that household for the duration of your stay. Indeed, whilst you are spoilt as the guest, you are also an object of great interest and entertainment for the host family.

I told Zarina that I'd already paid for that night in my hotel, so maybe I could meet her family first, and then if it was okay with them, perhaps come and stay tomorrow. She relented for the moment, and phoned her friend Almas to drive us to her house. Almas arrived shortly, driving an old Audi. He was a couple of years younger than me, but spoke no English, which limited the depth of our conversation to my Russian. Zarina's home was just a short distance away, and fronted by the standard sky blue metal gate that completely obscured the house behind. Entering, I saw that it was a house built in an appropriately Alpine style, with the mountains rising directly behind it. The yard was bare and snow covered, the wooden outhouse in one corner and a scraggy old dog with cataracts called Rex in the other. He rushed joyously to meet Zarina who greeted him with a "Hello Rex" but looked bemused when I stroked him. The cat seemed semi-feral, living outside in such harsh conditions.

Inside I was welcomed to a house of carpets, or *Shyrdaks* as they're known in Kyrgyzstan. They covered the floors and nearly all available wall space. After the sparseness of Gostinitsa Ala-Too, it was an incredibly comfortable environment in which to find oneself. And it was roasting hot too. I was down from seven layers to one in minutes. A low central table dominated the lounge, with rugs and cushions spread around it where the family sat. *Nan*, honey, salami, sweets, and a seed-based snack were already laid out, presumably from breakfast. They lay alongside the more familiar items of Coca-cola and Nescafe. In the corner a TV was on, tuned to a Russian channel. It would be the natural focus for anyone sitting at the table, and underlined the universality of the TV dinner. Against the back wall was a hefty pile of comfortable looking blankets, stacked up in accordance with their traditional place in a yurt. Called the *Juk,* the height of the pile used to be indicative of a family's wealth. At night these were laid out, and this is where Zarina's mother and father slept. There was also one chair standing in the back corner, but I was never to see anyone use it. I recalled the native woman in George Orwell's 'Burmese Days' and her comment "Look at those English chairs – I have never sat in one of them in my life. But I am very proud to look at them and think that I own them."[9]

A hatch-sized metal door in the wall near the table emitted a strong heat. The house was heated by coal, or *oogal* from a furnace in the basement. I would become used to the sound of Zarina's father poking around down there, the sound echoing through the house, as he loaded the *oogal* like the engine room of a 'steam age' locomotive or ocean liner.

On the wall were a number of decorations. There was a calendar with a large image of Mecca on it. Somewhat conversely, hanging next to it was a large picture of Santa Claus. Zarina told me she had returned to a house full of decorations and a small tree. For this Muslim, Kyrgyz family celebrated Christmas and certainly the New Year, but not the birth of Christ. There were two more calendars in the room. These depicted rabbits wearing sunglasses, jewellery and general 'bling' – a kind of Bugs Bunny endorsement of capitalism and conspicuous consumption.

At that moment Zarina's brother and sister returned from school. Her sister was called Sarah. Obviously, this wasn't her real name, but they insisted I wouldn't be able to pronounce that, so I should just call her Sarah. I didn't argue. Her brother was maybe twelve and called Abai. What ensued was a three way English, Russian, Kyrgyz lesson, with Zarina as linguistic overlord. They were all very impressed that I could read Cyrillic, even though most of the time I had no idea what it actually meant.

Literally the first question Sarah asked me was if I could ski. I realised later that she had probably asked because it is possible to ski on the slopes above Naryn. I told her 'not really' explaining there wasn't that much opportunity for it in England as it's not as cold as Kyrgyzstan. She shook her head as if remembering the obvious. Soon afterwards Zarina's father arrived as well. He was quite a short man, but broad across the shoulders. His eyes were round like a European, but his skin was so dark that in a different setting I might easily have mistaken him for Indian. However, this may also have had something to do with his greying moustache, something rarely worn by Kyrgyz. He had a head full of black hair, peppered with grey streaks.

Zarina's siblings disappeared to do chores and homework, whilst I, Zarina and her father sat around the table. Zarina served as translator as her father asked me question after question about life in England. He was particularly interested in the economic side of things. He asked about wages in the UK and was impressed by what are simply astronomical figures in this part of the world. However, when I started to elaborate on the cost of living, he became increasingly disenchanted. He seemed amazed when I told him that in the UK land for building was so expensive it was virtually impossible for the average individual to buy it. The concept of a mortgage – although I'm sure similar things must exist in Kyrgyzstan – also surprised him. By contrast, he had purchased land at a reasonable price (even by Kyrgyz standards) and built the very house I was sitting in. After many more questions, he sighed, smiled, and concluded that upon reflection it was probably better to live in Kyrgyzstan than in Britain - certainly more affordable at any rate.

Zarina was twenty-six, two years younger than myself, but had already spent a year studying in Turkey, set up and run her own NGO in Naryn, had a degree in Law, and just returned from working in Qatar. She spoke four languages fluently, and had mutual intelligibility in the surrounding Turkic tongues. This was a varied and accomplished life for anyone, but for a girl from provincial Kyrgyzstan it was exceptional. She said her friends were always impressed by her ability to achieve whatever she put her mind to. I could well believe it.

I asked her what her plan was now. She said that although she had signed a two year contract, she would not be returning to Qatar. I asked why not, and she went off on a long litany of complaints about the country. Firstly, she objected to what she viewed as obsessive religious practice; the praying five times a day, the strict dress codes, and the treatment of women. To her mind there was no need for such dogma "as long as you are good in your own heart." Something she did not feel was true for most Qataris; she saw them going through the motions and rituals of Islam with mechanical adherence but then acting in a totally hypocritical fashion. She described Qatari men as covetous and sleazy, always trying it on with young girls, whilst regarding their actual wives as domestic slaves and baby-making machines.

She had also discovered that it was not just wives who were treated as slaves, as the eight hour working days described in her contract, upon her arrival, doubled to sixteen. She had tried to complain and even to leave but was bullied to comply. They threatened that she would not be paid if she breached her contract, whilst knowing full well that outbound flights were too expensive for her to escape independently. Thus, as is the fate of most guest workers in the Gulf States, she effectively became a prisoner and a slave for a low financial return. She described her two months there as a nightmare, just an endless cycle of work and sleep, constant hassle from men, and a life that became so stressful her hair even started to fall out. It was easy to reflect on how Turkic peoples from Central Asia had historically often been used as slaves by the Arabs. In fact many Turkic nomads first encountered Islam as the targets of slave raids. Turkic nomads were revered as good soldiers and were enslaved to serve such ends. They provided men of a hardiness that could not be easily found among the soft, sedentary populations of the powers they served. Today, Zarina and girls like her are being imported to the Gulf States because they provide a pretty face to the public services of such a state's 'international' façade. However, like the Turkic slave soldiers of the past, they do something the host populace cannot, or not as well. In the modern example, it is the cultural restrictions on activities of Qatari women in public in Qatari society that prevent them fulfilling the public service roles Zarina and other outsiders are being employed to do.[*]

However, Zarina was not your average 'guest worker' or slave, and with her law training was able to formulate a case and get it to a

---

[*] Gulf States now constitute what have been called 'ethnocracies', with citizenship being defined in opposition to foreign guest workers who make up the bulk of the population. The host population lives off the imported labour of foreign nationals, often racially, culturally and linguistically different from themselves. In some ways this two tier society can be paralleled with past societies of the Eurasian steppe where nomadic:settled and aristocratic:agricultural divisions of labour existed along similar ethnic/cultural dichotomies.

high ranking official. She caused a bit of a fuss and it became clear to her employers that she could not be bullied into submission. They suddenly began to fear her insubordination could spread to other guest workers and then they would have a full blown rebellion on their hands. Thus, they discreetly paid Zarina for her work, along with a $3,500 flight ticket back to Kyrgyzstan. So she had managed to escape, but had been left with some very negative views on Qatar and on some of the other guest workers 'who would do anything for money.'

After the chat over many cups of *chai* the tour of the house continued. Her father showed me a large pen outside where the family kept about a dozen sheep. Most people in Kyrgyzstan, despite their now settled existence, will still keep some animals, even in towns and cities. One of the lambs came and pawed at my legs like a puppy. He proudly showed me a mother ewe and her new born, kept separately, the placenta still lying on the hay strewn floor. I was then led to the garage where he kept his pristinely polished 1992 registration Mercedes, and the *oogal* furnace from which a network of pipes heated the whole house.

Zarina then took me to her bedroom, where there was a small double bed, the only bed in the house. On the walls were posters of Turkish pop stars. She told me "You will sleep here" and that she would sleep in the other upstairs room on the floor with her siblings. I tried to protest, her cultural values of hospitality starting to conflict with my own ideas of proper behaviour. But again, Kyrgyz hospitality proved unrelenting, and she insisted "don't be silly, you are a guest, you must."

We returned to the lounge for another long round of *Chai* and snacks. On the TV a Russian version of 'Jerry Springer' was showing. That evening her father drove Zarina, her brother, sister and me to a local café. It was only five hundred metres down the road, but in the brutal cold, the drive was deemed necessary. However, the café was cold and empty and not to Zarina's liking, so we checked several more until we found one warm and with enough people that Zarina decided it would do. The owner, who spoke German, welcomed us joyously. The waitresses however were cut from that miserable mould strangely common to the old Soviet world. A traveller to the region some two decades before made a similar observation and wrote "never did a closet service addict crave so ardently a false smile and a well trained 'Can I help you?'"[10] It was interesting that Zarina was the one who actually commented on the sour quality of table service. Having travelled perhaps she could appreciate the irony of such an inhospitable manner in the 'hospitality industry.' When your wage depends on how much the people you are serving spend it makes little sense to be a miserable and unhelpful waitress. However, she could offer no insight as to why it was this way. I suspected it was the residue of communism and a time when there was no ideological correlation between wages and service.

The menu offered the standard Central Asian fare, and Zarina ordered me two dishes to ensure I didn't go hungry. Having been snacking all afternoon at her house there was no danger of that, but again, she insisted. I struggled to finish, and when I did, was absolutely stuffed. Whilst we were eating my attention was drawn to Sarah. There was something different about her I hadn't noticed earlier. I was a little bit alarmed about how attractive I was finding Zarina's sixteen year old younger sister, but I evidently wasn't the only one, as male heads turned around the restaurant.

When the bill came Zarina fingered through a thick wad of 500 com (about £6) notes (more money than I usually had on me) to pay. Initially I offered to pay for everyone myself, so grateful for the hospitality already shown me, but of course it was futile.

Zarina told me she earned $350 a week, working in an office one week on, one week off. Her father was the boss so I guess that helped, but it was still an extremely good salary for Kyrgyzstan.

Naryn *Oblast* (province) is the poorest in the country, and the majority of its population lives in what the UN classes as 'extreme poverty.' However, in Soviet times, mountainous areas such as Naryn received 'hardship salaries' that were 40% higher than the lowlands.

Before we left the restaurant she said she would phone her boyfriend to pick us up. This mention of a boyfriend was actually something of a relief. The hospitality I had been shown had been wonderful but also a little overwhelming. In a quite traditional society such as Kyrgyzstan's, the opening lines of *Pride and Prejudice,* 'it is a truth universally acknowledged, that a single man in possession of a good fortune, must be in want of a wife' retain a certain validity. I was not eager to fall into that category – although not being in 'possession of a good fortune' probably discounted me automatically anyway.

However, I was a little surprised when Zarina then told me her 'boyfriend' was married and had two children. She went on to say "We love each other. We have been in love for one year." Trying to establish what kind of affair this was, I inquired, I hoped tactfully, if they "stayed together" to which Zarina retorted "Of course not!" as if it was ridiculous of me even to suggest such a thing. Zarina told me how her mother was very angry with her for having fallen in love with a married man when there were so many single men around. Her boyfriend, a policeman, was ready to divorce his wife and marry Zarina. However, she was warned by her mother that if a man divorces once for another woman, you can never be sure that he won't do it again. Admittedly, this seemed like a fair point. I asked half jokingly why he didn't take her on as a second wife, but she replied quite seriously that neither of them wanted that situation.

We waited on the icy street until her boyfriend arrived. All of us, little brother and sister included, piled into his car. I was surprised to see he was chubby, and that his thirty-five years were amply depicted by the many wrinkles around his eyes. To be honest I wouldn't have expected the attractive Zarina to have fallen for such a man.

He took us on a tour of Naryn – which essentially means driving down Lenina Street. He didn't speak any English but gave a running commentary the whole way. Zarina translated. It turned out that the night before he had been called to Kochkor (the next significant settlement, a two hour drive to the north) to assist in the apprehension of an armed robber. The target of the robbery had been one of the continual caravan of lorries coming in on the high road from China. He said it was a common occurrence. Clearly, banditry on the Silk Road had not been resigned to history just yet.

Zarina then went on to tell her own story, and the advantages of having a boyfriend in the police force. Once she was driving her father's car when the police tried to apprehend her. She didn't have a licence, but her father sometimes permitted her to drive the car. With the very low level of traffic in this region of Kyrgyzstan, I did not view this as particularly irresponsible. Once, when the police stopped her she panicked and ran away into the countryside. Needless to say, they chased her down, caught her, and were very angry. However, Zarina phoned her boyfriend who talked to the policemen and they suddenly became very accommodating, letting her go on her way.

She pointed out, giggling, that because of her boyfriend she could also drink and drive without worrying about being caught either.

We drove on along Lenina and the town started to fade out. With no lights, only those from the car, the night was formidably dark. I could just make out looming mountains above, and an expansive black valley bowl below us. The road was rough and gritty. That was until we suddenly reached an absolutely perfect stretch of brand new tarmac that came out of nowhere and lasted for about a mile. It was the best piece of road I've seen anywhere in Kyrgyzstan. Zarina explained it was funded by the Aga Khan as part of the new university he was building in Naryn.

We enjoyed the short soft ride before returning to gravel. We slowly climbed and at the brow of the hill we parked up. To the west I could see a vast dark valley spread below us. Pinpricks of light in a sea of black represented distant Dostyk, the next settlement to the west.

We climbed a small rise through the snow and looked east out over Naryn. The moon was full and I could see for many miles across a rugged landscape where signs of man were few and far between. We posed for many photos. The incredible cold became almost bearable. It seemed to make the air purer and even the smallest noise more resonant. Crisp snow crunched deliciously with every step, and our voices echoed off the shadowy rocks rising above us. Still, after taking every photo I was eager to plunge my hands back deep into my pockets. By the time we returned to the car only ten minutes later, my toes were numb.

Driving back to Naryn, Zarina's boyfriend asked me if I liked hunting, and told me how the very hill we just walked up was once roamed by snow leopards. He said one had to go deep into the hills now to find them, but, almost as a consolation, told me that you could still catch very big fish in the river. Kyrgyzstan was once home to tigers and cheetahs too. Now, of the big cats only the snow leopard remains, and sadly, in ever dwindling numbers.

We drove to my Hotel. Zarina insisted I collect my stuff and return to hers. Indeed, after experiencing the carpeted warmth there, I was only too happy to oblige. Her brother and sister helped collect my bags from the third floor and take them to the car. We then returned to their house.

I was hoping for a chance to lie down and digest the two meals I'd recently eaten. However, there would be no such luck as the hospitality continued unabated. Zarina's brother disappeared through a hatch-door in the kitchen floor and started passing up foodstuffs from an underground storage room. Zarina then informed me that we were having *Beshbalmak*. "When?" I asked, hoping she meant in about four hours, or preferably tomorrow. "Now!" she exclaimed excitedly. "Great!" I smiled back, poorly attempting to match her enthusiasm whilst secretly wondering how exactly I was going to eat it. The oral epics of the Kyrgyz do indeed speak of 'heroic eating', and it was clear I was going to have to 'man[*as*]-up' and do my gastronomic duty.

As I briefly retreated to my room Sarah and I passed in the hallway. Our eyes met. She smiled and I noticed how white her teeth were and the sparkle of her eyes. Slowly, she reached up, touching her hair. Then, rather unexpectedly, she pulled it off! All of her hair! I, for want of a more masculine word, screamed. She had been wearing a wig. That's what had been different about her at dinner. She had appeared with this wonderfully long, straight, glossy black hair that framed her face perfectly with its exacting fringe and somehow turned her from a girl into a woman.

Naturally, she was startled by my reaction, but then burst out laughing as she realised I hadn't known she was wearing a wig. As the rest of the family found out, they all started laughing too. Underneath, Sarah's real hair was cut very short, almost like a boy's. I asked why, but she just said something about it being easier to manage and that she would grow it back for summer.

Dinner (number three) was ready almost immediately, and I consciously opened another compartment in my stomach in preparation for the onslaught. The freshly cooked meat and a huge platter of noodles were brought in by Zarina's mother, a matronly looking lady with grey eyes and henna-coloured hair (perhaps an example of Kyrgyz appearance that was more widespread before the Mongols came). She worked in the local psychiatric hospital. Everyone laughed as she related tales of the crazy inmates, and she even invited me to come along and have a look for myself, implying that it was good entertainment. Finding entertainment value in the mentally defective and delusional seemed a little unsavoury. However, then I recalled the auditioning stages of hit UK television programme the X-factor and similar reality TV shows where, entertainment value is derived from ritual humiliation which allows the audience ('civilised' though they may claim to be) to feel good about themselves – something that may otherwise be hard to achieve when living in a micro-celebrity-obsessed consumer hell.

The meal was certainly prepared in my, the guest's, honour. I was then presented with the best cut of the meat, and watched studiously by the family to make sure I was enjoying it – which I made a good show of doing. Indeed, I may have been already full, but the meat was cooked to perfection and went down easily. Meanwhile, after distributing a chunk of meat to everyone, Zarina's father expertly cut away smaller strips of flesh to be mixed in with the noodles.

It was, in all honesty, a feast. When it was over there was round after round of *chai* and sweets. Later, on my way to the outhouse I found Zarina's father sweeping the drive. It was -25°c and he was wearing shorts, t-shirt and slippers.

When he came back in I decided to show him my map of Central Asia. I had often found on my ride that maps seemed to instantly spark an interest in men, and could be an excellent prop for conversation even when language was difficult. I was proved right, because Zarina's father was very interested in the map, and we spent a long time poring over it together. He showed me that he was from Balichi, at the western end of Issyk Kul, and that his family's ancestral *jailoo* (summer pastures) was near the remote Torugart Pass, Chatr-Kul, and the Chinese border. He explained how he had received his diploma from Tashkent and had then gone to work in a town near the border of what is now Turkmenistan. This was of course in the days of the USSR, before Central Asia emerged from the breakup as five separate nation states.

From there he had gone onto work in East Germany for a while. On the map he traced the Chinese border, indicating areas he claimed were Kyrgyz but had been taken by China. He made similar distinctions along the Uzbek border, saying that the Kyrgyz would one day take these back.

I was then passed the family photo albums to browse through. This seems to happen a lot in Central Asia. Reflecting on it later, I guess it's a good way to tell a story without having to explain it tediously bit by bit. It was almost like saying "here are the highlights, have a look." I noticed a lean, fit looking man in running gear. I asked who it was. Zarina told me it was her uncle who had unfortunately since passed away. Incredibly, however, he had run from Naryn to Mecca to complete his pilgrimage or *Hajj*. I was flabbergasted. Not only was it thousands of miles, but it was thousands of miles through some of the harshest terrain on the planet; beginning in a knot of the greatest mountain ranges on earth and descending into searing desert. The logistics of it beggared belief. I had cycled through that desert and still struggled to carry enough water (The Karakum and Qizilkum deserts together constitute the fourth largest desert on earth and can reach temperatures in excess of 50°c). To have run it really was an amazing feat. I looked at his footwear, just a 1970s pair of plimsolls, none of the gel-cushioned luxury of today's trainers.

The *Hajj* is stated in the Koran to be the obligation of all Muslims who are physically able to undertake it. However, the number of Kyrgyz who make the journey remains low, the sheer cost of travel often cited as the main reason against it. For example, between 1991 and 2005 only two people from Sary Mogul, a town with a population of one thousand, had undertaken a pilgrimage.[11]

The rest of the photos mainly showed snaps from family holidays to Issyk kul, and displayed some interesting retro swimwear. There were also the ubiquitous photos from Ala-Too square in Bishkek; family, friends and classmates all huddled and grinning in front of the fountains or statue of *Erkindik*; 'Bishkek 2009' or 'Bishkek 2007' jotted in the corner.

After we had exhausted both the map and the photos, Zarina's father disappeared downstairs to chuck some more *oogal* in the furnace. The TV had remained on constantly in the background, and the format of every programme was becoming eerily familiar. I recognised I was now watching Russia's twenty-four hour news service as the same feature I had seen earlier appeared on a loop. Before that the Russian equivalent of 'Cash in the attic' had been on, and before that the kind of makeover programme that abounds on British daytime TV, only in Russian. I was disheartened to see nothing new or interesting. It was just the same drivel in a different language. As Zarina pointed out, "Russia takes ideas from Western TV, and then Kyrgyz TV takes ideas from Russian TV, and so on, making it all the same." Whatever ideals I would like to harbour about the inherent nobility of Mankind totally disintegrate when I consider our apparently unwavering world-wide devotion to that little box in the corner of the room. Television represents the new oral tradition, but today's *manaschi* are TV executives far away, their emulation of foreign forms requiring none of the skill of their predecessors and apparently purveying little that is representative of the culture to which it transmits.

In this Kyrgyz household, Russian TV seemed to rule the roost. It was not until three days later that I caught my first glimpse of Kyrgyz television. It was distinguishable by the fact it displayed the channel's conspicuous 'yurt' icon in the top right hand corner of the screen. That was where the differentiation appeared to end, because it was showing Shrek II, dubbed into Russian.

That evening I discussed what I had come to Naryn to see. Zarina's family seemed sceptical that I would be able to go anywhere in the dead of winter, as the snow made many places inaccessible. Nearest and easiest seemed to be the strange forest I had heard about near the village of Tash-Bashat, about 25kms east of Naryn. To start with, no one had any idea what I was talking about. The forest I wanted to see was so odd because it had been deliberately planted to grow into a huge swastika. Why? Nobody knew, but seeing as I was so close to such an anomaly I thought I might as well have a look. In the end, by a bizarre process of drawing trees and swastikas, as if participating in a twisted game of *Pictionary*, a glimmer of comprehension dawned on Zarina's mother's face and she exclaimed "Aaah, Deutsche Christ."

"Yes, the Deutsche Christ" I replied, certain that it must be the same thing. I asked where I would be able to get a bus or *mashutka* to Tash-Bashat and how long they thought it would take. However, Zarina told me not to be silly, and that her father would drive me. Again, I was to be humbled by the hospitality of people I'd known just a few hours really. I tried to tell them that it really wasn't necessary, and that I was sure Zarina's father had more important things to do than drive an unexpected visitor around on an impromptu sight-seeing tour. However, he had offered and nothing I could say would change his mind. I just tried to express my gratitude, and reminded myself how lucky I was to have met such good people. I spent the rest of the evening trying to satisfy Zarina's father's insatiable interest in the comparative costs of England and

Kyrgyzstan, and laboriously explaining the difference between miles and kilometres, which seemed to intrigue and confuse him with equal intensity.

6

The Swastika Forest, Old road to China, and Too Much Vodka

The next morning, after a night of 'heroic' indigestion, I was unable to escape a hearty breakfast. Zarina and I waited while her father went off to get petrol – or 'benzine' as it's known in these parts. She told me about how she had worked with an NGO in Bishkek. It had been concerned mainly with human rights, and had received much of its funding from American donors. This helped explain how so many Americanisms had crept into her English despite the fact she had never been to the States. After working for that NGO she had decided to set up her own, aimed at helping children in Naryn. She explained how many poor families still had eight or nine children, if not more. Some of the parents were drunks or just neglectful, forcing the children out into the streets to beg. Her NGO aimed at breaking this cycle, and also to provide the children with clothes and food to prevent them from begging. Unfortunately, Zarina became the victim of her own success. People began to say that she wasn't using all the money that was donated for the cause she claimed, and was lining her own pockets instead. Faced with such accusations, which completely undermined the good work she was doing, she closed the NGO down.

When her father returned he was wearing a suit and looked very smart as we set off in the spotlessly clean Merc down Lenina Street. The sky was a piercing blue, and the severe cold seemed to lend everything a freshness - like the sterilising power of a naked flame on an old knife.

The scene was still, except for the stumbling progress of a haggard drunk bumbling along the icy street. Zarina's father laughed, flicking the side of his neck, a generic gesture in these parts for getting *very* drunk. That it has its own hand gesture understood by all, gives some indication of the blight alcoholism is on Kyrgyz society - and pretty much any other society to inherit Russia's passion for vodka fuelled self-destruction. Zarina's father pointed to the drunk and said "утреннее начало!" 'He says "morning start"' chuckled Zarina.

We drove east out of the town, entering a starkly beautiful white plain which was contrasted by the sandy orange belt of the river bank. The river was low, and clogged with huge chunks of ice that rotated in slow ricochets downstream. Initially the valley was flanked with corrugated grey hills. These gradually morphed into majestic white mountains. The road was caked hard with ice. The Merc slithered along it. Sleepy Slavic cottages with rickety wooden fences watched silently as we passed. We picked up an old lady, one of the few pedestrians pottering along at the edge of the road. She was wrapped in wool and chatted away relentlessly to no-one in particular from the back seat. We passed horsemen who gazed down indifferently and mud brick ruins that might have been ten, or ten thousand, years old.

Trees glimmered like tangled copper wire in the morning sun, and silver crescents shimmered from the tops of snow-covered tombs. People collected at the manual metal water pumps, eyes narrowed against the double glare of sun and snow. Red faced, and plump-looking from all their layers, they carried their haul away by horse, sledge or wheelbarrow. Wasted water formed an icy rink encircling the pumps. Boys dragged bristling branches for firewood; the plumes of their icy breath preceding them.

Having dropped the old lady off at her destination, we stopped at a turn in the road. We got out, and Zarina's father scouted for the optimal viewing position. We stomped through the snow. Two young lads scrambled past, cajoling a donkey which pulled a sledge. The land looked like a fluffy white blanket. Some cottages were visible in the distance, but other than that the scene was empty until the mountains. Zarina's father pointed up to the peaks, announcing "Deutsche Christ!"

I shielded my eyes from the sun, and followed his hand. The mountains were dappled in black, as great swathes of forest clung to their sides. The woods looked dense and forbidding. My eyes scanned across, and then I saw it, the "Deutsche Christ." How bizarre, I thought. A huge Swastika made of living trees on a mountain side in

Kyrgyzstan. It was a very strange sight, and I wondered why it was there. The shape seemed too exact for it to have been a fluke of nature. I asked Zarina for an explanation, and she referred the question to her father. He said that a German teacher once lived in the area, and that he had been responsible for planting the forest.

There seemed to be a number of theories about how it came to be. Perhaps the most plausible was that it was planted by German prisoners of war who were sent to the area to do forced labour – in this case, plant trees. The story goes that one of the soldiers was a forestry engineer, and that he was able to orchestrate planting the forest without the authorities being aware of its shape until it actually grew – long after the planters had gone. Whether this was the work of a particularly ardent Nazi, or just a final collective act of defiance by men who knew they probably weren't going to see home again, will probably never be known. Either way, I can't imagine that in such circumstances they derived too much satisfaction from their prank.

The fate of German soldiers taken prisoner by the Russians during World War II was bleak to say the least, and the fate of Russian POWs in German hands was even worse, with a staggering 3,000,000 – and that's a conservative estimate – dying in captivity. Having read the tale of Clemens Forell in *As Far As My Feet Will Carry Me,* one might almost consider those German POWs who did forced labour in Kyrgyzstan as fortunate. Forell, a paratrooper, was dropped with his company on a mission behind enemy lines. However, they ran out of food and ammunition, were surrounded by Cossacks and wiped out. Despite being shot in the mouth Forell survived to be sentenced to twenty-five years hard labour in Siberia. There, with thousands of other POWs he was made to live and work in the lead mines. The men were only allowed above ground every few weeks, their teeth falling out as they slowly succumbed to lead poisoning. Aware that they were to be worked to death, Forell managed to escape in 1949, and the book recounts his 8000 mile trek to freedom.

Two years after escaping he was still making arduous westward progress through the wild vastness of Siberia. Towards the end of 1951, when in the region of the Yenisey River - the ancestral homeland of the Kyrgyz – Forell gives an eerie account of abandoned villages he passes. They were not villages of the Kyrgyz, who had migrated to their current domain centuries before. However, Forell's description provides a haunting insight into Stalin's forced migrations; the mechanism by which so many others did end up in Kyrgyzstan:

> *'Forell was glad to get away from the mysteriously deserted village*[s]*... He wondered what the fate of the inhabitants had been. During the war, he had seen how civilians caught in the tide of battle would cling onto their possessions, even beds and heavy pieces of furniture, to the very last moment. Women tottering with heavy chairs on their backs, or coal scuttles and umbrella stands had not been an uncommon sight. Every human instinct seemed to rise up against the thought of abandoning the hard won accumulation of years. It must have been the same with these people in the village*[s]*. Something other than their own freewill must have put them into headlong flight, stripped of almost everything they possessed, and that something could only have been fear – but of what?'*[1]

In one of these Marie Celeste villages '*planes roared down, doing a sweep'* (checking for people), and Forell met an old man hiding, who told him what had happened: *'The inhabitants of the village*[s]*, the entire population, had been forcibly removed elsewhere – where, the old man did not know. He had escaped on the journey and come back... A while ago, he said, the planes had spotted his sheep and tried to bomb them.'*[2]

Amazingly, when Forell reached the town of Abakan on the Yenisey he met another German who was also a former prisoner of war. However, this man had been captured in 1914 during the First World War. Despite years of trying he had been unable to return home. Thus he had set himself up as a baker – his pre-war profession – and resigned himself to life deep in the centre of Soviet Asia. He had only this advice for Forell: 'You haven't a hope of getting home. If I couldn't get away thirty years ago, when things were all upside-down, then you won't now.'[3] It was circumstances such as these that contributed so many Germans POWs to the population of Kyrgyzstan.

Considering the swastika forest again, there are other theories that have nothing to do with POW's. One is that it was planted by Kyrgyz workers under the instruction of a German already living in Kyrgyzstan, and who was sympathetic to the regime of his home country. This could tie in with what Zarina's father had said, as enough ethnic Germans were living in Kyrgyzstan anyway.

However, the swastika forest is perhaps the most marginal and impractical thing left by the Germans. They are recalled for their skill, precision, and quality workmanship. Houses built by Germans are still regarded as the best in Kyrgyz villages. Nazda had proudly told me that her family home in Chayek was a German house. In the Talas region, where many Germans once lived, the Kyrgyz have copied their style of house building. Zarina told me that a bridge nearby was also built by German people. The disproportionate number of German cars on the road in Kyrgyzstan - a country bordering China - must also be a reflection of Kyrgyz faith in things made by Germans.

Others postulate that the forest wasn't planted by Germans at all, POWs or otherwise, but rather that it was officially sanctioned - before the USSR and Germany went to war - as a symbol of friendship and solidarity. Seeing as the age of most trees can be dated to the exact calendar year by their growth rings, I would have thought the truth behind this idea could be quickly resolved.

Perhaps more intriguing than who conceived the forest, is why it has been allowed to remain until the present day. After all, the 'Great Patriotic War' against Fascism was at the core of post-war Soviet ideology, disseminated thoroughly throughout the empire and testified today in the concrete and marble memorials in every town and city across the old Soviet bloc. In Bishkek there is the large stylised granite yurt of 'Victory Square' which covers an entire city block. In the centre stands a sculpture depicting a mother waiting for her son to return from the front. The hearth of the yurt holds an 'eternal' flame.

However, the concrete propaganda of Soviet solidarity masks a somewhat different reality. It has been estimated that of the 1.5 million Central Asians 'requisitioned' by Russia, perhaps as much as half deserted or turned-coat and fought for the Germans. Hitler welcomed this, and did not hesitate in exploiting the animosity many Muslims in the Soviet Union felt for their Russian overlords. The

'Turkestan Legion' was formed in 1942 from Turkic peoples; mostly Red Army POWs who chose to fight with Germany in the hope that the defeat of the Soviet Union would lead to an independent Central Asia. They wore a badge featuring a Mosque and the motto "Allah is with us, Turkistan" which mirrored the German Army's motto "God is with us." There was even an SS unit of Turkic Muslim volunteers. When Germany was defeated these contingents were imprisoned by the Allies and handed back to the Soviets where as 'traitors' to Mother Russia they faced an unenviable fate.

It seems absurd that the symbol of the fascist foe, to which millions of Soviet citizens lost their lives, was left etched in the Soviet landscape itself. However, Fascist ideology had firm foundations in the USSR. Books were printed by the Russian state-run Pravda publishing house right up until the 1980s that even questioned whether the Holocaust actually happened. This official campaign of anti-Semitism only abated during the Gorbachev era. Indeed, there were many disturbing similarities between Nazism and Communism. Both were totalitarian regimes that desired world domination and both aimed to change human nature through science and technology. Whilst the Nazis tried to breed Aryan supermen, Stalin was having humans impregnated with ape sperm in an attempt to create invincible soldiers.

Yet, despite such horrific convergence in outlook and practice, it remains difficult to believe the swastika forest survived for any overt political reason. Likewise, it seems equally unreasonable to assume the forest was simply ignored or forgotten by a regime usually so tenacious in attempts to control the political thought of its subjects. As such, the swastika forest remains more mysterious than ever.

It is unfortunate to reflect on the fact that the ideology represented by the swastika forest now reverberates through the fallen USSR - as neo-Nazism - with greater strength than it ever did when the Soviet Union was intact. The collapse left 25 million Russians in someone else's country and many commentators have noted alarming resemblances between the Weimar Republic and post-Soviet Russia, with mass poverty, high unemployment, falling birth rates and life expectancy, high crime and official corruption. Fortunately, in Kyrgyzstan neo-Nazism does not appear to be an issue. However, as the post-Soviet Kyrgyz reclaim and assert their identity, they do so against a similar backdrop of widespread economic hardship, and within borders where there is long standing inter-ethnic animosity between certain groups - a result of pressures largely created by Russia's colonial experiment in Central Asia. Kyrgyz Nationalism is rising, the most extreme demonstration of this perhaps being the violence between Uzbeks and Kyrgyz in the south of the country in 2010. In a culture where ancestry, blood, and therefore ethnicity, remain such prominent determinants in society, the potential for a fascist-like ideology taking root is, arguably, there.

Getting cold, I took a photo of the curious mountain wood in question, and noticed one of the symbol's arms was dented and deformed. Zarina then told a story that answered my question before I got the chance to ask it. She said how once, an aircraft carrying a 'minister' was flying over the area, and looking out of his window, he was shocked to see the emblem of Nazi Germany staring back at him. So, this 'minister' had ordered it to be chopped down and destroyed. The crippled arm of the swastika forest was apparently indicative of his wishes being carried out. Zarina said "It was just too big; they couldn't cut it all down!" This was certainly an interesting anecdote, but I could not believe that the forest was either too big to be cut down (in the past fifty years Kyrgyzstan has lost half of its forests), or that in a region once riddled with military activities, that the highest authorities were not already well aware of its existence.

We returned to the car and crawled back along the icy track. This time we picked up a school girl and dropped her at a school several miles away. She made the journey by foot twice a day in temperatures well below zero. It perhaps explained why school attendance wasn't always what it should be in rural Kyrgyzstan. A Peace Corps volunteer who had spent two years teaching English somewhere in the Naryn region told me how some kids would just show up once at the beginning of term and once at the end. He complained that even when the parents were told, they were apathetic, saying that if their son was to be a herder what need was there for him to go to school. He would learn his trade in the field, literally. I could see their point. After all, if he is educated, goes to university, and then invariably to the city to seek 'better' things, what becomes of the traditional way of life he has left behind? Education is about socialisation, and about a child learning the skills required for their role in adult life. For most of human history 'education'/socialisation took place within the home and 'on the job.'

The involvement of the state in socialising the young is, like the nation-state, a relatively recent phenomenon. Compulsory school education of the type now found throughout the world originated in Britain during the 19th Century. Contrary to popular belief this 'was motivated not by humanistic longing to open children's minds to the glories of culture, civilisation, and personal growth – but rather for political elites to manage the outlook and behaviour of the working classes through promoting and institutionalising programmes of mass education.'4 This function of schooling remains unchanged. Moreover, such formal education - based on the Western model – which has now been disseminated globally, emphasises literate, essayist 'academic', learning above all else. Despite obvious benefits, it presents a narrow spectrum of what 'knowledge' *is*, and this is often gained at the expense of gradually eroding traditional expertise. Schooling is thus skewed to an economic reality that might not be terribly relevant for many people in many places. In Kyrgyzstan, economic opportunities are limited. For those who continue as traditional pastoralists, and for those who go to Russia where they are generally employed in low status manual jobs, the benefits of a formal education may well seem questionable. Yet it still remains the only legitimate way to transcend these options.

We passed cows and horses shaggy with thick fur to protect them from the elements. Women were wrapped in wool, their faces glowing red in the intense cold. It was a different world, and it was contradictory for its soundtrack to be the endless stream of Western pop emitted from the radio. Zarina said "We will now go and visit a mountain resort, a place where people go in summer to relax." "Sounds good" I replied. I had been to these kinds of places before. They are generally designated scenic spots from the Soviet era, often with sanatoria, and some basic infrastructure to accommodate, feed and water visitors. However, these days that infra-structure tends to be rather dilapidated and overgrown. For me they seem to hark back to the kind of jolly family holiday resorts people used to flock to in the UK half a century ago.

We left the car at an old metal gate and walked into the resort up a snow covered path. It led into the mountains. A river tributary ran adjacent to the track and a thick forest of fir trees climbed both sides of the valley. Long furrows in the snow showed where logs had been dragged down the mountain for use as firewood.

There were a few rusting picnic huts, shaped like medieval tents. Their fading paintwork apparently paying tribute to the décor of a traditional Kyrgyz encampment. We found a donkey tied to a tree, its nose trawling the snow, looking for something edible. Next to it was an empty bottle of vodka. Zarina's father pointed to it and flicked his neck again with a grin. He told me how vodka could be useful in the mountains as it kept one warm and helped against altitude sickness.

I asked Zarina's father how far the path went. He said for many, many miles, and that the forest was so big, one might easily get lost in it and never find a way out. Looking up the expansive valley the woods did indeed seem endless and unbelievably dark. On its periphery the markings of man were already weak; a couple of shoddy picnic tables and an empty stone hut which apparently housed a disco in the summer. A bit further up the path and everything was back on nature's terms.

The wildness was confirmed when Zarina's father started talking about the dangers of wolves. How the winter made them fearless as they could find no food. He said that two weeks before, hungry wolves had come down from the mountains and taken a donkey from a nearby village.

The wolf has a long legacy, real and symbolic, for the nomadic people of Central Asia. For it was the form of a wolf that spirit-guides apparently took when tutoring young shaman, and shamans were believed to have the ability to turn into wolves. The Turks, Mongols, and historic nomadic peoples such as the Wu-sun all traced their origins to a wolf. The warrior elite of nomadic steppe cultures – the comitatus – were often characterised as wolves. Genghis Khan had four; Khubilai, Jelme, Jebe, and Subedi. It is a tradition that dates back to the Saka and prehistoric times. The wolf was likely the ancestral spirit of the ruling Turk clan and the lord's comitatus was known literally as 'bori' – 'wolf.'

I wondered what the risk would be for someone camping up there alone. We looked around at the snow but could only see rabbit tracks, or "carrots" as Zarina called them. I thought she was making a joke, but realised later that she thought the English word for 'rabbit' actually was 'carrot.' Intriguingly, when I stayed with a Uyghur friend in Xinjiang province a few weeks later, he called 'carrots' 'rabbits', apparently illustrating an inextricable linking of the two words in the non-native English speaking mind. I could only hold the global exportation of Bugs Bunny cartoons responsible for this quirky confusion.

We had been walking for about half an hour when Zarina said she wanted to turn back. Looking down, I saw that she was wearing high heels, hardly the best footwear for a mountain hike. Then again her father was only in a suit and shoes. He kept asking me if I could feel the effects of the altitude, and indeed the further we climbed the tighter my temple seemed to get and the more tired I began to feel.

I asked Zarina if she could feel the altitude but she said not really. Instead, she wanted to go back because "I'm worried about turning black." When I asked what she meant she elaborated with "There are four ways that the Kyrgyz turn black. Number one is the wind. Number two is the sun. Number three is the cold, and number four is the snow." She said that 98% of the sun's radiation is reflected back up by the snow. Of course, the Kyrgyz were previously known to the Russians as the *Kara-Kyrgyz* or 'black-Kyrgyz', where as the Kazakhs were named *Kyrgyz* apparently to prevent confusion with the Cossacks.

We started to walk back to the car. Zarina and her father kept telling me to put my hat on, saying "You will go mad if you don't wear your hat in this weather" and then burst out laughing, clearly finding the idea of me 'going mad' hilarious. I noticed they wore no hats, so it seemed it was only the un-acclimatised foreigner who would suffer insanity because of the cold and the altitude.

We carried on back to Naryn. We passed Naryn's Mosque, an ornate building, apparently paid for with Saudi money. During the 1990s sixty new mosques were built in Naryn province alone. That over five hundred were constructed in Osh province in the same period testifies to the more religious nature of southern Kyrgyzstan. Whilst some of these mosques were built with funds from other Islamic countries such as Saudi Arabia, Iran and Turkey, most were built by the Kyrgyz themselves. A traditional system exists for constructing public works, such as mosques, called *ashar*, which uses voluntary donations of money and labour from local people.

It was Friday, the Muslim day of prayer, and a large crowd congregated around the mosque. In winter, mosque attendance always increases due to the seasonal nature of many men's work.

We also passed a yurt that had been set up in someone's front garden. Zarina told me it meant somebody from that house had died.

The yurt was a dirty grey colour, which in reality was the norm for yurts in nomadic times. White, the colour now associated with these felt tents as seen on postcards and displayed in museums, was only the preserve of the extremely wealthy. In fact, the Kyrgyz word for yurt *bozuy* actually means 'grey house', whilst the Turkish word *iurt* means 'clan.'

We stopped at Naryn 'shopping centre' so Zarina could copy some photos. It was pretty much a one-storey scaled down version of Bishkek's Tsum. There was a place to get photos developed and a place to buy stationery and a handful of Russian texts, but other than that it seemed devoted to mobile phones. It was also largely devoid of people, but there were a few, mainly teenagers crowded around the mobile phone displays. Zarina kept on ducking behind me and looking the other way. I asked her what was wrong and she said it was a former boyfriend and that she didn't want him to see her. It was about the third boyfriend - in the traditional Central Asian sense of the word - not including her current boyfriend, we had encountered in the past twenty-four hours. Always, Zarina insisted, they were to be avoided.

Arriving back at the house, old Rex came out wagging his tail, looking up through cataract-clouded eyes, and clearly delighted by his master's return. He was, as always, ignored, with no-one reaching down to stroke or pat him as they passed. I did out of habit from home. Zarina looked at me as if I was doing something really rather strange, almost wrong.

Back at the house the *chai* was brought in by the gallon and I was obliged to nibble constantly at the snacks laid on the table. On TV a Russian soap opera played out. Zarina explained how a character's baby had died, but that she had swapped it with another character's live new-born in the hospital, but obviously that character didn't know this, and everyone was hooked waiting to see how she would find out with all the ensuing drama. I could have been wrong but I was sure my sister had described exactly the same bizarre storyline occurring on a popular soap back home, just before I left.

Next I was treated to what can only be described as the Russian version of 'Family Fortunes' or 'The Generation Game' as contestants answered questions in order to win prizes. A big arrow was spun to see what kind of question they would have to answer. Well, Zarina's father got quite into this and excitedly yelled

"PRESENT! PRESENT!" or "MONEY! MONEY!" depending on which option the contestant was on the brink of winning. There was something quite endearing in his enthusiasm, although it made it odd to reflect that this man came from successive generations of mounted warriors, renowned for their stamina and martial prowess.

Whilst immersed in the evening's entertainment we were constantly eating the fine food Zarina's mother had prepared. Thus, I was very surprised when Zarina turned to me and asked "would you like to go to a restaurant?" Fortunately, I managed to talk her out of it, and she said we would go out with her friends instead.

She phoned her friend Almas and he came to pick us up with another friend called Altay. Altay spoke some English and we were able to converse quite well. We drove back to the shopping centre, which was now closed but served as a good a hangout as anywhere else when it was -25°c and you are car-bound. There was also a Gamburger stall which they all made use of. They asked if I wanted some vodka but I declined, not really being a fan of the stuff. They went to a shop and bought some beer instead; Baltika 5 which is a popular Russian brew throughout Central Asia. It comes in a number of varieties, the actual number following the 'Baltika' part indicating the alcohol content, ranging from Baltika 0 (no alclohol) up to Baltika 9 which can be pretty dangerous.

So I was taken back to my teenage years that evening, sitting around in a parked car on a street corner sipping from tins of beer. They then asked where I had been in Kyrgyzstan and where I planned to go in the future. I said I wanted to visit the far south west of the country, a peninsular of Kyrgyzstan that juts out between Uzbek and Tajik territory - the back leg of the Kyrgyz frog if you will. It serves as a prime example of irrational Soviet state-making and jigsaw borders. This part of Kyrgyzstan even contains isolated pockets of Uzbek territory, known as enclaves, which are completely surrounded by Kyrgyzstan. At the western end of this curiosity of political geography is the Kyrgyz city of Batken. When I said I wanted to go to Batken the car filled with shocked laughter. Altay said "There are many terrorists there" and that if I went "You will die!" Indeed, this part of Kyrgyzstan had earned its reputation due to insurgencies that had taken place there in 1999. The details are shady but the insurgents crossed into Kyrgyzstan from Tajikistan. A Kyrgyz official claimed that these fighters were of many nationalities including Uzbeks, Tajiks, Afghans, Pakistanis, Arabs, Chechens and even Ukrainians. What was clearly a very complicated situation was classed as international terrorism and linked in the Russian and Central Asian press to the conflicts in Chechnya and Dagestan. The military action there was to become known as 'The Battle of Batken.' On top of this, Batken received the additional negative moniker of 'Little Columbia' because of the proliferation of drug smuggling/dealing going on there. All in all it sounded an interesting place to visit and would be my chosen route for reaching Tajikistan later that year.

Closer at hand was Tash Rabat (stone fortress), a caravanserai located in a secluded valley not far from Torugart Pass and the border with China. This isolated, militant-looking building has an elusive history. Little is known about Tash Rabat other than it played some part in the procession of traders and travellers that weaved through this remote region on a branch of what has since become known as the 'Silk Road.' It is one of the very few pre-Soviet/Tsarist structures in Kyrgyzstan, even if it has been subject to renovation by Russian archaeologists.

I wanted to go there. If Kyrgyzstan has an iconic image, then Tash Rabat is probably it. I asked Altay and Zarina if they thought it was possible at this time of year. They didn't know. They said the conditions were very bad in winter. They asked why I came in the winter, "No one comes here in winter" they chorused. They told me there was no public transport going that way, and I knew from my guide book that the road was apparently closed from mid October until May. It was still only January, but if it was possible I was determined to try and find a way.

I asked if I might be able to hitch, but they said very little traffic went that way, especially at this time of year. Maybe, they said, I could hitch to the turn-off, but then, even if the road was not snowed-in, the chance of any vehicle going to Tash Rabat was virtually nil. It was a dead end. No one went there in winter. I would be left high in the mountains in one of the least populated regions of sparsely populated Kyrgyzstan. It would probably be around -30°c, and that was without the wind-chill. They did not think it was a good idea for me to go on my own. I was inclined to agree, although I knew if the worst came to the worst, I had the necessary equipment to survive outside in those conditions. It was just a case of whether I wanted to turn what was a fairly accessible summer day trip into a full blown solo winter expedition that I wasn't really prepared for.

I asked Almas if he would take me. Or at least try and take me, as far as the road and conditions would allow. He said he would try if I paid for the 'benzine.' Altay said he would come too. As we settled on the plan and discussed it further, everyone became excited about what looked to be an adventurous day out. Whether we made it to Tash Rabat or not, visiting that remote region, in the depths of a Kyrgyz winter, would no doubt be an experience in itself.

It was getting late and Almas and Altay assured me that we would have to leave very early if we were going to make it there and back in one day. They said they must also make some preparations for this undertaking. So, Almas dropped us back at Zarina's, saying he would return early in the morning. Zarina, who was less enthusiastic about a mid-winter escapade that seemed destined to fail on snowed-in tracks in the middle of nowhere, said that she would be staying at home. I didn't want to offend my generous host by disappearing with her friends into the back of beyond without her, but she insisted 'If you want to, you must go!'

The next morning I was woken as Zarina's brother and sister came into rifle through the family's collective chest of drawers. It was 7.00am on Saturday morning and they were getting their clothes for school. I wondered what had happened to our early start and dozed on until 9.00am. For breakfast Zarina's mother brought us some delicious cake in the lounge. Zarina phoned the lads, who were 'busy preparing' and didn't arrive till about an hour later. They still considered this an 'early' start.

I had dressed for severe conditions with two pairs of long-johns, multiple thermal under-layers, two fleeces and my down jacket, with more emergency kit stored in a bag. However, Zarina's father came in to inspect my attire and was not impressed at all, handing me some extremely heavy-duty quilted over-trousers and similarly weighty coat. He then stood back, grinned, and nodded in approval at the bulging arctic explorer he had just created. Clearly, he thought this foreigner from temperate climes was now fit to survive out there in Kyrgyza's icy wastes.

Conversely, he didn't bat an eyelid when Zarina - who had now decided she was coming – went to leave wearing knee-high boots, jeans, her normal jacket and - in case of emergencies - a handbag for her phone and make-up.

We went out to the car, Rex wagged his tail excitedly as everyone walked past oblivious to his existence. I gave him a stroke. Altay was quick to tell me "Do not touch. In case they bite." This is probably a sensible attitude where rabies is still common. However, I didn't think Rex seemed particularly rabid.

We drove into town. Naryn seemed even quieter than usual. A woman stood on the pavement, a collection of plastic soft drink bottles refilled with a white liquid sat at her feet. She was selling one, or a variety, of the interesting home-made dairy and malt drinks unique to Kyrgyzstan.

We stopped at a small shop in the high street and Atlay went in, returning with 'supplies.' These consisted of bread, salami and 'salad' (grated carrot) for making sandwiches, and that vital necessity of every Central Asian road trip, a bottle of vodka. Participation in the morning vodka session would be pretty much mandatory. The social contract of vodka consumption in these parts has been referred to as 'terrorist hospitality' – quite simply, you're damned if you do and damned if you don't. The obligation in this particular situation was increased by the widely held belief that vodka has medicinal qualities which allegedly combat the effects of altitude sickness. As it was between three of us I was happy to go along with it. I was very glad of this opportunity to go to Tash Rabat and didn't want to appear ungrateful. Zarina, on the other hand, being a girl, was under no pressure to drink vodka. Instead, Altay handed her two bottles of Baltika 9, the strongest beer on the market, with the alcohol content of wine.

On the edge of town we stopped for benzine. We then left the grey apartment blocks and old Ladas of Soviet civilisation behind. Embarking on a desolate, gravel road we climbed out of Naryn. Snow blew in barrages against the vehicle and only a crumbling mud-brick cemetery bid us farewell from Naryn. It was the first day since I had arrived in Naryn that the sky was low and grey. That great blue bowl and piecing winter sun was replaced with an ominous blanket of cloud that didn't bode well for our journey.

The road was covered in ice, and the air was thick with fog. Speckled brown mountains folded before us like the patterned wings of flexing fowl. Zarina kept receiving phone calls from her boyfriend, the policeman. "He's jealous" she complained, clearly irritated. I can't say I blamed him. His girlfriend was going to be spending the whole day in a car - drinking -with three men, younger and trimmer than he was.

Her phone kept ringing and there ensued a series of troubled sounding conversations until eventually her phone cut out for good. We were out of signal range. As we climbed higher Zarina started to name the Pass and other things of interest. The windows were frozen, and the bare rock of the mountainside passed by in a blur. Zarina talked of how the people in this far flung region of Kyrgyzstan "Are a little bit wild" and how "They might attack, because they think it's their territory."

At the top of the pass I was struck by the all-consuming whiteness that enveloped us. It was blinding. I was glad I had borrowed some of Zarina's sunglasses. Nobody else seemed bothered by it; their eyes instinctively narrowing against the glare their ancestors had known for generations. We pulled over as a Chinese lorry lumbered up the other side of the pass out of the driving snow. Being white as well, it was hardly visible, just the bold black characters on the container stood out. I saw it with a new appreciation after the story told by Zarina's boyfriend. These lorries, chugging over remote mountain passes in extreme weather conditions and facing a real risk of banditry, suddenly made the old Silk Road seem very much alive.

As we sat halted on the pass, Altay said that we must drink some vodka before we went any further. Below us the pass descended to a vast plateau and the grey thread of the road disappeared into a pale murk that was presumably the horizon. Plastic cups were distributed, except for Zarina whose gender granted her exemption. Altay splashed the clear liquid about liberally, announcing calmly "50ml to begin." A few words were said concerning the success of our trip, and then it was down the hatch with the sharp stuff. The dubious 'pleasure' of this pastime was indicated by everyone's acute wince as they disposed of their cup's contents in one, before desperately seeking a slice of salami to chase the taste out of their burning throats.

Of course, upon recovery Altay was ready with a generous top-up. With this dispatched we could finally leave the pass. As the foul taste of the vodka dissipated I began to feel a not entirely disagreeable warmth and pleasantness – something quite out of sync with the wind ravaged snowbound landscape outside.

It seemed our car was utterly alone rattling through the white wilderness. It was a sombre setting, so I was especially surprised when Altay started to clap and sing a song. Singing is something deeply rooted in Kyrgyz tradition. Altay asked me to sing a song, "a traditional English song." I'd been asked by Kyrgyz people if I could sing before, and in other places too, where singing is apparently deemed of more cultural relevance than it is at home. For the Kyrgyz, records, myths, history, their very culture was retained and passed down by the medium of song. Thus explaining why singing is a respected and admired skill to have.

Unfortunately, this proved an awkward situation for me as I have absolutely no interest in singing, and considerably less interest in performing in public. But Altay kept insisting I sing, and I wracked my brains trying to think of something I feasibly could. I could only remember the first line of the national anthem, and that was the only traditional British song I could think of. Is 'kum by ya' British? I wasn't sure. For some obscure reason the only other song that came to mind after that was the last verse of Grandmaster Flash and The Furious Five's 1982 hit 'The Message.' I must have listened to it too much when I was thirteen. So, under increasing pressure from everyone else in the car 'to sing', it was with great reluctance that I launched into a rendition of the above mentioned song, with its harrowing tale of hardship and futility, life and death, as a black man in North America's inner city ghettos. Personally I thought it was quite a good performance, but I don't think it was what Zarina, Altay, and Almas were expecting. However, it was a success in one respect, and that being I wasn't asked to 'sing' again.

Instead, Altay started singing 'If you're happy and you know clap your hands' in Japanese. He had learnt it from a Japanese family who had previously lived in Naryn as volunteers. After singing it in Japanese he switched to English and encouraged us all to join in (no one except for me really needed encouragement). So it was, that as our car continued to crawl into an ivory wasteland and developing blizzard, we (including the driver Almas) sang the whole 'If you're happy and you know it clap your hands' complete with required actions. I felt a strong affinity with the band that carried on playing as it went down with the Titanic.

Altay poured the remains of the vodka into our cups. Out of the white desolation rolled a string of Chinese lorries, grumbling past; ponderous beasts following the trail of their herd. Occasionally we passed such a truck abandoned at the road side. Altay said he did not like the Chinese. The reason he gave was "because they are clever." However, I think he meant something more like 'sly' or 'cunning' as he explained his resentment at their encroachment into Kyrgyzstan. Even here, in essentially the middle of nowhere, we start to pass small camps; a large tent and a few containers, a dog chained up outside, half buried in the snow to escape the cold. I had seen similar encampments north of the Bogda Shan in Xinjiang, another wilderness. These were Chinese scout parties. Surveyors, workmen and such like, sent here because it will be the Chinese that turn this gravel track into a proper road. Altay was annoyed that the Kyrgyz allegedly paid the Chinese to build the road - a road that would probably be of far more benefit to the Chinese; their lorries would increase in number, and their goods would gain greater access to the Central Asian markets, increasing the dependence of Kyrgyzstan on China.

Kyrgyz music blared out from the car radio. A lone horseman cantered through the snow. I wondered where on earth he could have come from. On my map, there were no settlements marked between Naryn and At-Bashi. Altay told me that there were other places out there, isolated homesteads the horseman could have come from. Indeed, a steady stream of dwellings and small settlements started to appear, strung along the roadside. We were close to At-Bashi. Soon we crossed the At-Bashi River. A collection of snow covered roofs marked the town. The houses looked forlorn, weighed down by the snow and Mother Nature in general. A little girl in a red coat was running through the snow. She brought a splash of colour to a view of white and grey, and conjured unavoidable connotations of 'Little Red Riding Hood' in that fairytale wilderness.

Then as if choreographed by the Brothers Grimm, a dark horseman, tracked by his large black dog, came into view. The dog attacked the car, jumping up at the windows as we drove past, snarling viciously. The horseman, whose face was covered, did nothing to dissuade his animal, continuing at the same steady pace, wisps of breath escaping ominously from beneath his hood.

Zarina scraped at her iced up window, straining to see if the dog was still chasing us. "They're a little bit wild in these places" she said again, giggling somewhat nervously.

We passed a pony and trap with a sheep tied to the back as we entered At-Bashi (Horse's head). We turned on to the main street. Altay announced we would wait for his friend, who was working in the town. He said his friend would show us the way. We stood around in the snow. Little sign of life emanated from At-Bashi. An old lady collected water from the communal pump. It flowed continuously and had created a small frozen lake around itself. An old man, misshapen like a crooked coat-hanger, leaned heavily on his staff and goaded some cows to cross the dirt track street.

Cowboys came by with dogs at heel. Calves were tied to the tails of their mothers and traipsed in tandem at the cowboy's command. We retreated to the car's interior for warmth. Even five minutes was too long outside in that weather. Altay produced another bottle of vodka from somewhere and started dishing it out with gusto. Its unfortunate flavour was mildly offset by the salami and carrot rolls served as a chaser.

Finally, another car arrived. It was Altay's friend, and apparently all his friends too, as the car was full of men. I was told that we would first drive to Koshoy Korgan, a citadel that dates from the 10th Century. Our car followed theirs in tight formation back into the white void. Altay asked what word we have in English for this nothingness. I thought maybe 'desert' and used the Turkic word 'kum' to explain myself. They disagreed, making the common assumption that deserts must be hot. I then said I would describe the landscape as 'barren.' Even Zarina did not know this word. I dug out my dictionary and looked it up in Russian. They received the Russian word with shock and then laughter. Clearly, 'barren' in Russian could not be used as a descriptive analogy for something empty. So my comparing the view out of the window to a woman unable to have children, did, to say the least, seem rather unusual to them. Altay told me that for them, the view was more akin to 'field.'

We came to what looked like a forgotten church. In front of it was a long line of crumbling mud-brick walls, like so many brown and broken teeth set in the smooth white jawbone of the countryside. A motley crew of Kyrgyz emerged from the other car. They were all men between thirty and fifty, weathered and tough-looking. They escorted us over to what I thought was a church. It turned out to be the museum for the site. An old man, who they brought with them, was the curator and had the keys. Clearly the place was not staffed permanently at that time of year - hardly surprising considering we had passed no more than two cars since leaving Naryn. He unlocked the doors and let us in. There was no charge, which was humbling. They had come out there only because I wanted to see it.

The old man led us around the small museum. It was surprisingly new and well done. Clearly, it had received some investment, no doubt in the hope of attracting tourist dollars. I was suitably impressed and pushed some Som into the donation box to appease the fates.

The old man spoke of a 'Kalmyk place.' The Kalmyks or Oirats, were the western Mongols who violently resisted the Chinese for 400 years. A long migration now sees the descendents of these Buddhist Mongols living on the shores of the Caspian Sea in the autonomous region of Kalmykia of the Russian Federation. The Kyrgyz from Kizilsu, China, fought a decade long war against the Kalmyks towards the end of the 19th Century. The valley on the approach to Song Kul, named Kalmakashu after the Kalmyks, is also testament to their combative relationship with the Kyrgyz.

However, Koshoy Korgon has been dated to the 10th Century, long before the Kalmyks were in the area, and at a time when the first waves of Kyrgyz were only just arriving in what is now Kyrgyzstan. Thus, the fort is assumed to have been built by the Karakhanids, who ruled from Belasagun (near Tokmok) and Mavarannahr (Ozgon) in Kyrgyzstan, and Kashgar in China. This fits chronologically and geographically with the location of Koshoy Korgon, but does little to elucidate what went on within its walls and around them for the intervening thousand years between the Karakhanid dissolution and my arrival. The sheer scale of the walls denote Koshoy Korgan's importance, yet its remote location and utterly opaque history shroud it in tantalising mystery that can only be guessed at by the modern visitor.

The curator showed evidence of developed settled life; sewers and running water. It is told locally that the Kyrgyz hero Manas built the fort, burying his friend Koshoy there.

Koshoy was one of Manas's comitatus, his body-guard of 'forty friends.' In the epic, Manas's comitatus are always referred to as 'heroes' rather than servants or retainers, and each is given an epithet like 'Kaman, Jaipur, two youths who never lost a horse's track by night; Tas Baimat who brews tea in the cauldron'; and Jamgyrchi 'the mighty wrestler.' [5] Koshoy was known as Koshoy 'who opened the gates of paradise' because he is credited with introducing Islam to Manas's tribe the Sary-Nogai.

The Manas epic was composed at a time of religious transition. The Uyghur and Sary-Nogai had converted to Islam whilst the Kalmycks and Kara-Nogai were still heathen. However, 'religious differences and religious controversy play little part in the poems, and religious bitterness may be said to be absent.'[6]

The comitatus, the lord and his band of chosen warriors, was an inherent part of 'heroic' cultures across the breadth of Eurasia, from Hittites to Huns, from early medieval Germanic peoples to the Koguryo, the early dynastic Japanese. It was a feature of martial societies, of a heroic age, and of an individualism more pronounced than exists in modernity - despite popular rhetoric to the contrary. The heroic ideal of the comitatus was recounted in epic poems as geographically disparate as the Central Asian *Manas* and the Germanic *Beowulf.*

Since the time of the Scythians the comitatus pledged allegiance to their lord with an oath of blood brotherhood. To carry out this rite men mixed their blood together in the same cup and drank it. In many cultures blood was attributed magical qualities, and in the remote past it was believed this bond would allow 'blood brothers' to communicate without actually having to be in each other's physical presence. Indeed, according to this magical tradition Christ's Last Supper and the drinking of wine (his blood) was about creating just such a connection with the disciples. Strange as this may seem to modern thinking, vestiges of such ideas remain today. Take for example the widely held Japanese belief of *haragei* or 'belly talk' (literally 'the art of the stomach'), which refers to the notion that Japanese people can communicate without actually speaking, merely by the virtue of being Japanese, i.e. because of their shared Japanese blood.

Whilst there is no obvious evidence for such esoteric beliefs amongst the nomads, we find a tradition of drinking blood lasting millennia. Despite always being an act of potent symbolism, it is not unanimously related to the oath of the comitatus or blood brotherhood. In the 5th Century B.C. Herodotus mentions oaths made by pouring wine into a bowl, mixing it with blood, and drinking it. He also writes of 'skulls covered with leather and lined with gold used as drinking cups.'[7] Hundreds of years later on the Chinese border, the nomads sanctioned a treaty by mixing blood and gold together in the skull of an enemy and drinking it. Over a millennia after that Genghis Khan was recorded drinking from the skull of an enemy he had encased in silver. In the *Manas* epic we hear how Manas's bereaved wife Kanykai strikes the death blow to her enemy and drinks his blood.

A huge painting on the museum wall told the story of great horse warriors and eagle hunters. History blurred with romantic myth as Manas is depicted doing battle on horseback inside a Yurt, whilst a lion lies majestically at his feet.

After a tour of arrow heads, bits of old pottery, and the dissected yurt that must appear in every Kyrgyz museum, we went outside to the walls. The perimeter was huge and the walls still high. We walked through where the gate once stood and scrambled up the mud-brick walls, in which weeds have now taken hold, and snow covered thickly. The space within the walls was very large and must once have held a sizable population. The men walked a little way into this expanse and crouched down. Where there were once presumably streets and houses there was now nothing, just a tough grass that can withstand the barren conditions, and which bends like sturdy wire against a harsh howling wind coming down from the Tian Shan. The men knelt in a circle in the snow and I was called to join them. They cupped their hands and looked down on them intensely, as if reading palms. The eldest man recited a long prayer. His words were caught and carried off by the wind, just like all the words in all the languages that had been uttered there for the past thousand years. Only the wind's voice endured. When the old man had finished everyone brought their hands over their faces in the standard Islamic gesture of *Omin*. We stood and trudged away through the snow. The mighty perimeter was empty again. The curator locked the gate and turned away, leaving the walls to stand guard over nothing once more. It had been empty for so long, no one even remembered what once filled it. So now they filled it with myths and legends and a sacred meaning – "It is a holy place here" said Altay, with a rare note of seriousness in his voice.

We returned to the cars "Why didn't you come in summer?" the men asked, telling me "People only come here in summer." I replied "That's why I came in winter." They laughed, but looked a little confused. We left Koshoy Korgon and continued down the icy road. After a few miles we stopped and the other car pulled up behind us. Altay said we should get out. We stood around and conversation fluttered between them in Kyrgyz. I couldn't understand, so just studied the men; their fur hats, gold teeth and faces burnt red by the cold. Hard lines extend from their eyes caused by a lifetime of squinting against the sun and snow. Even the young men show wrinkles, the extreme continental climate – alternating from very hot to very cold - apparently affecting humans the same way it does rocks, drying and cracking their outer surface with each successive season.

Soon the purpose of the conversation was clear. Plastic cups are handed out, and yet another bottle of vodka does the rounds. Dry wafers were distributed as chasers, followed by more vodka. I wondered if we had stopped here just to put a respectable few miles between us and the "holy place" before the vodka came out. It was about -20°c. My hands went numb after holding the cup for only a couple of minutes. Lengthy speeches were made. Altay translated and then said that I must make a speech too. I did, thanking the men for opening the museum and site so I was able to see it. This went down well, and they insisted we drink more vodka, ostensibly to reduce the effects of altitude sickness. After ten minutes we parted. The men were returning to At-Bashi, except for one who would come with us to Tash Rabat and then back to Naryn.

Altay introduced him as his friend, and by the nickname 'Gangster.' He was a short man of twenty-eight, but weathered to the age of forty. He spoke no English, but vodka seemed to bridge the language barrier. Approaching Tash Rabat, we joined a plateau between two sets of peaks. Some horses were grazing, but on what I don't know. The absence of green and a sprinkling of beasts took me back to the mountains of Nepal. The road was lost in snow and skirted the mountain's rocky base. Ahead of us the snow was fresh and unmarked. Only one set of horse tracks lined the road. It appeared we were the first vehicle to pass that way in some time. Across the rolling foothills loose snow blew in waves the way water ripples. It was a surreal sight, and in a vista occupied only by the elements. Behind the foothills rose impregnable white peaks until they blended seamlessly with the white clouds. What I thought must be cloud formations turned out to be mountains, and sometimes a mountain would slowly dissolve and be revealed as a cloud.

The track bent round one last rise and Tash Rabat appeared. It lies half submerged in the mountainside, not due to the ravages of time, but from design. What protrudes from the earth may well have been a caravanserai, but it has the appearance of a fortified position – a blockhouse, or bunker, coldly functional in the military fashion. Its hard lines and black stone walls only emphasised this effect when set against the soft white snow. Tash Rabat ('Stone fortress') is another mystery; its location on the trade route to Kashgar being the clearest clue to its purpose – a safe-house and hotel for those traversing this rugged road. I imagined it should have been a welcome sight for those journeying up here in this desolate land, 3500m above sea level. Yet, it is not inviting, only impenetrable and resilient in its aesthetic. 'Rabat' is actually an Arabic term for 'fort', and it seemed fitting. However, it is also a word that came to mean 'caravansary.'

Tash Rabat's stone walls, gatehouse and corner turrets, are without crenulations, arrow slits or windows. Its solid simple structure only makes it look more archaic and mysterious. I read somewhere it was the only construction in Central Asia made of stone. It is an anomaly. The ubiquitous beige of mud-brick is nowhere to be seen, nor the decorative illumination of turquoise tiles. The arched entrance gives only the vaguest hint of Islam, and even that is my inference. The beehive protrusion on the roof is somehow too primitive to call a dome.

Hewn from the mountain rock into which it sinks, there is something primordial about Tash Rabat. Its simplicity defies easy categorisation, or affiliation with an era, style or religion. It has no courtyards, something virtually unknown to the region. It seeks no seclusion behind a perimeter wall, yet conversely, is all the more secretive and obscure for this absence. The dank, dark stone interior bespeaks a remote and ancient Europe far more than the dusty, desiccated assumptions of a Silk Road sanctuary. Tash Rabat's appearance seems to avert hospitality, retreating back into the very mountain on which it is built, as if saying 'stay away' rather than 'come in and rest, weary traveller.' It has the stony, windswept isolation of ruins on the Hebrides. No one knows how old it is.

Some believe it was in fact a monastery, a Nestorian Christian church dating back a thousand years. It's certainly possible. The inside of Tash Rabat is set out in the shape of a cross and Christianity is evidenced in Central Asia long before this date. 7th Century records of the Nestorian church in the metropolitan of Marv tell of a Turkic king who used the sign of the cross to avert a thunderstorm, and Turkic prisoners of war sent to Constantinople (Istanbul) a century before had crosses tattooed on their foreheads. However, whilst perhaps indicative of conversion to Christianity, the tattoos also served as talismans against the plague. Similarly, the king's banishing of the thunderstorm recalls a strong Turco-Mongol shamanic tradition of weather magic, showing how Christianity was appropriated in the context of pre-existing nomadic beliefs.

Yet we know that in the 8th Century the official religion of the Uyghur, - just east of the Tian Shan and Tash Rabat - was Manichean Christianity, and that Turkic shamanism was banned there. One appeal of this religion for the Uyghur was apparently that the Chinese didn't like it. However, it only remained the official religion for 77 years because in 840 the Uyghur were overrun by the Kyrgyz. The Chinese then had their revenge, closing Manichaean temples and executing Manichaean priests.

From the 10th Century it was the Karakhanids, the first Turkic dynasty to officially espouse Islam, which ruled over the region in which Tash Rabat is found. It is from this time that we hear of the conversion of 200,000 tents and of Islam's increased importance in this part of Central Asia. However, 'official' religion only remained so if it was endorsed by the dominant power. When the non-Muslim Mongolian Kara-Khitai displaced the Karakhanids, Islam here was put on the defensive. Something illustrated by the Nestorian Christian metropoly which is known to have existed in 12th Century Kashgar, its power extending into what is now Kyrgyzstan and southern Kazakhstan.

Tash Rabat has also been identified as a Buddhist temple. It is possible that it was all these incarnations. Buddhism, Christianity and Islam all held sway through the region at various times. As one specialist has noted, that Islam 'would emerge dominant once again at the end of the Mongol period... was far from being a given.'[8]

Religion in the region was undoubtedly linked to trade, and its spread connected with adoption by merchant communities. As a link in the Silk Road chain for at least 1000 years, Tash Rabat would have sheltered merchants of many faiths and existed within the dominion of many political masters.

Altay pointed past the caravanserai at a snow filled break in the impenetrable looking mountains. "That's the old road to China" he said. It looked a bleak and desolate prospect now, not even the hint of a road, just a snow-filled maw in mountain jaws. I walked up the rolling white folds of the mountain behind Tash Rabat and looked down on it from above. The corner turrets and low wall ringing the roof were revealed, despite their formidable appearance at ground level, to be poor defensive positions. There was nowhere, if it was a fort, from which defenders could effectively fight. Instead they would have been extremely vulnerable to an enemy coming from the high ground I was standing on. Whilst some local legends talk of Tash Rabat in military terms, as a fortress or such like, the architecture didn't seem to support it, other than as a place to hide in. However, the Soviet restoration could perhaps be held accountable for this. On the roof the central dome has a series of openings, but these served only to let in light and to allow smoke to escape.

We went inside and those openings made it surprisingly light. However, there was still that cave-like dankness, the smell of damp rock and soil deep in the earth. Some say it was in fact built over a cave, one that extends for miles, with an exit somewhere across the Chinese border. The structure is divided into various rooms and cells, including one opposite the entrance allegedly used by the Khan himself. Wide, raised ledges on either side of the entrance were apparently where the soldiers garrisoned there slept. However, no-one really knows, which serves to make Tash Rabat all the more intriguing. The atmosphere, smell, and cacophony of the men and beasts once crowded in there is hard to evoke. Instead, the silence and small cells seem to lend themselves much more to the theory of Tash Rabat's spiritual origins – a place of pious contemplation, rather than trade or war.

At the end of a corridor on the right hand side of the building, the earth opened up into a deep cavity. This was the beginning of a tunnel that apparently leads to a look-out point. Strangely, however, there is no evidence that anyone has explored it for generations. Standing over it, I momentarily considered the glory of going in myself, finding hidden treasure or who knows what. However, motivation subsided as I began to consider the possibility of being buried alive if the tunnel collapsed, wondering what kind of rescue services the Kyrgyz would be able to deploy and how long they would take at that time of year.

We explored every cranny of Tash Rabat, but it did not take long. Soon everyone was feeling the cold, and the stone walls I came to see remained annoyingly silent about the world they once presided over. We returned to the car and began the slow drive back, this time able to use our own tracks to guide us. Almas used the shades I borrowed from Zarina, his eyes finally failing after driving into the blinding glare for hours on end. I put on a fourth pair of socks, Zarina touched up her make-up, and it became apparent how 'Gangster' earned his disreputable namesake. He initiated the buying and consumption of three more bottles of vodka. We had eaten nothing but a couple of salami and carrot rolls all day. My memories ceased to form a coherent narrative from this point on. We passed men on horses and scattered houses. We stopped at empty shops, but always they had vodka. 'Gangster' was constantly laughing and filling our plastic cups with more of the stuff. Night fell. The car filled with cigarette smoke, and the radio blared. At some point Altay asked "Do you want a girl?" saying "we can find a nice girl back in Naryn."

Perhaps I pondered on our intrepid cultural excursion, its transition to a vodka binge in a blizzard, and the prospect of it culminating in a brothel. I can't remember. I recall looking for Zarina to gauge her reaction to this conversation, but I couldn't see her. Almas was in the passenger seat instead. Then I noticed she was driving, laughing wildly, and clenching the steering wheel along with a bottle of 'Baltika 9.' The car lights just illuminated a barrage of snowflakes rushing towards us out of the impenetrable black night.

7

The Long Road to Osh

I was back in Bishkek. This was more out of necessity than choice. My plan had been to push on from Naryn in a south westerly direction across the mountainous spine of Kyrgyzstan, and then descend into the Fergana Valley. Everything I had read about that road said it was hard going and closed from September till May. However, I had read the same thing about Tash Rabat.

Again, transport looked difficult to arrange, but Almas and Altay were willing to take me at least as far as the gold mining town of Kazarman. Unfortunately, they made some phone calls and this time the road really was impassable, a situation that wasn't likely to change for several months.

There were only two other ways of getting to the south of the country. Like I said before, Kyrgyzstan is a nation of few roads. I had cycled both routes, and knew them well. One was pretty backcountry and would be slow and difficult. Having travelled the area already this seemed unnecessary. Thus, I chose to swing back though Bishkek where I could pick up a visa extension. I didn't really need it, but thought it wise in case my proposed route out of the country proved unexpectedly time consuming. It turned out to be a good decision.

I returned to the same cold abode with sporadically functioning electricity. However, after my excursion to the mountains, the cold in Bishkek didn't seem quite so cold. Determined not to get lost in another bureaucratic labyrinth I left early one morning for the office identified in my guidebook as the place to obtain a visa extension. Naturally, I couldn't find it. I was looking for one building but in the location shown on the map there were three very similar houses of officialdom. All the signs were in Russian and slowly digesting the Cyrillic nothing stood out as an obvious place to get a visa extension.

I looked for clues on the notice board outside, but was presented with mug-shots of Kyrgyzstan's MOST WANTED instead. Adopting a process of elimination I tried the first building; the sullen guard waving me on to the next one. That one was even emptier, except for a cleaner who quickly began mopping in the opposite direction of this strange arrival. There were many desks behind glass windows, and I could see a couple of suited functionaries doing what looked like nothing. Presumably they could see me too, so I loitered in the futile expectation that someone would look up and say something like "Excuse me sir, can I help you?" – Or the Russian equivalent.

Of course, I was getting my cultural etiquette mixed up. In the cold corridors of post-Soviet administration, it seemed standard procedure to ignore the stranger in your midst. I approached one of the young bureaucrats and blurted out "Izvinitye Pazhalzsta, viza zdyies?" (Excuse me please, visa here?) accompanied by a mime of an imaginary stamp hitting an imaginary passport. He was pleasingly responsive, glancing up for a second to say "Nyet. KieB." Before looking away again to continue with his sandwich. This meant the place was on Kiev Street, and not here. Thus, the great Central Asian visa chase began anew.

Walking to Kiev Street, I began to wish I had asked for something a little bit more specific, as I faced a façade of similarly non-descript government buildings. I soon managed to decipher 'REGISTRATION' on an unreasonably small sign above one doorway. I didn't need to register – still an archaic bureaucratic requirement in most Central Asian states – but it seemed as good a place to start as any. Inside, at the end of a bare hallway, was a large glass screen. The bottom half of the screen was entirely blacked-out. At about waist height there was a letter-box sized gap in the glass. This was where the inquirer was supposed to inquire, bent over like an unworthy serf before his feudal overlord, and speaking through a hole in a blacked-out window to no-one in particular. Behind the screen, above the blacked-out partition were three uniformed Kyrgyz, only their heads and shoulders visible. I managed to catch the eye of one, who looked at me with indifference and indicated for me to assume *the* position. So, I crouched down to state my question through the hole in the glass. It's quite amazing how well thought out this simple mechanism is psychologically. It instantly forces the member of the public inquiring, to adopt the body language of somebody grovelling. It demeans them, and makes them look ridiculous and pathetic. Meanwhile, the authority figures behind the blacked-out screen are placed in a position of total power, they don't even have to be seen if they don't want to be. Instead they are faceless, omnipotent arbiters of State power. It seemed *proskynesis*[*] was still adhered to in this part of the Orient. However, I knew this screen, like much of Kyrgyzstan's state apparatus was an inheritance from the Soviets that the Kyrgyz simply hadn't got around to changing; assuming anyone had even considered that this method of state interaction with the masses might be inappropriate for a democratic nation and 'open society.'

Placing the same request again through the letter box, I got a reply, in robotic English "Next door." Standing to full height again, I went next door. Unfortunately, next door offered nothing more hopeful than a sign for 'KACCA' (change) and a dingy interior that also hadn't been decorated since circa 1970. From another customer friendly glass hatch a Kyrgyz man in camouflage gazed out nonchalantly. I ignored him and walked up the five storey staircase trying to identify any hopeful looking doorway or sign. Instead I enjoyed a dingy stairwell with a threadbare carpet, and absolutely no indication of where the appropriate office might be. All the doors were shut. I tried some and they were locked. On the third floor I found a door that was half open. I stuck my head in and saw a young Kyrgyz woman was writing. I asked her "Viza zdyies, da?" She replied in Russian that it was on the first floor. I wondered if that meant the 'first floor' or the ground floor, but didn't really have the ability to ask without looking like an imbecile. I checked the first floor – as in the second floor – and every door was locked. I went to the ground floor where there was the "KACCA" window, although the camouflaged man had gone.

I paced up and down. I left the building and re-entered, trying to look at everything with fresh eyes. I did this twice. There was a passage about three metres long immediately on the left of the doorway. The wall was wood panelled, and set amongst the panelling was a similarly panelled door. There was no sign, no writing, whatsoever. I had seen it when I first came in, but instantly dismissed

---

[*] *Proskynesis* was the ancient Persian custom of prostrating oneself before a person of higher social rank. It means 'Kissing towards.'

it as a utility cupboard or something. However, having now reached a level of quiet desperation I thought I would give the cupboard a go. Expecting to find a sink, a vacuum cleaner, and a mop, I was instead greeted by a white-tiled TARDIS, complete with a waiting area, comfortable seating and a row of glass windows, where one might assume diligent public servants waited to assist me.

I was the only person in the room other than two female civil 'servants' at their respective desks. I was quite obviously there, and they were quite obviously ignoring me. I walked over to one and announced myself unnecessarily loudly. She looked up in surprise. I told her what I wanted and she asked for my passport. I handed it over and she flicked through it, not pausing to look at anything in detail. Then she handed it back and said in Russian "Not possible.""Why not?" I asked, but she replied with a torrent of Russian I could not hope to translate. Having reached something of a linguistic wall, I asked if she spoke English. "Nyet!" came the predictable reply as she pointed to her colleague. Approaching that window, I coughed another voluminous "Zdrastvootya" which roused the younger woman to look up and receive me with a withering stare. I asked her in Russian if she spoke English. "Nyet" she replied, stoney-faced. At this I couldn't help laughing, and said that this was strange because her colleague had just informed me she did.

Rolling her eyes in disgust - no doubt at the prospect she was going to have to do something - she asked in flawless English "So, what do you want?" I told her I wanted a visa extension. She demanded my passport, thumbed through it in a surly manner, and instructed me to "Copy this and this" indicating the photo page and my present Kyrgyz visa. So, I spent the next twenty-five minutes tracking down a photocopier in icy Bishkek and rushing back before the office closed for lunch, or for the day, or forever.

Fortunately, I returned through the unmarked cupboard door to find the secret office still 'open' for business. It was however a little galling to see the woman who had told me to go and get photocopies, now happily copying away on a photocopier behind her desk.

I walked over to her desk window and presented my papers. Instead of stepping forward to take them from me, she remained where she was – not at her desk, but about a metre and a half behind the window – and just opened her hand expectantly. Clearly even extending her arm was too much of an effort. This forced me to virtually climb half way through the window to place them in her waiting hand.

I made sure to do this with a big smile on my face, continually expressing my thanks for the wonderful service they were providing. They seemed thoroughly bemused by this, but I've found it to be a better coping mechanism for their unhelpfulness than the natural reaction of sinking to their level – never a beneficial tactic, as these people hold all the cards and they know it.

I was then given a piece of paper and told to "write something." I did't understand what. As a team effort they came up with the explanation "I want to go to Kyrgyzstan, this, this, this." Aah, I realised they wanted me to write my itinerary, or at least what my purpose was for extending my visa in Kyrgyzstan. That was easy enough, for it was simply the truth. I needed more time in the south of the country to make my way to China. There was apparently a bus, but it was only weekly. If I arrived in Osh only a couple of days after it left, then my visa would expire before I could catch the next one.

This done, I was instructed to go to the "KACCA" and pay 1065 Com (about $25) and return with the receipt. I liked this system, because the money isn't given directly to the person dealing with your request, which helps prevent corruption. Returning with the receipt I was told to come back and collect my passport at 5.00pm, which struck me as surprisingly efficient.

This presented me with an opportunity to get some lunch. I went to a fast food kiosk where the friendly guy working there greeted me with a smile and a handshake. I asked for "Dva samsa" to which he replied they were out. I scanned down to the next item on the menu display. "Gamburger?" nope, out again. "Xotdog?" they had none of those either. The guy then suggested "Manti?" Okay, I said, by then just happy that there was something edible available. Manti are dumplings, usually steamed, and containing much the same range of fillings as samsa. In name and substance they're very similar to Korean mandu and Nepali momo. He indicated for me to take a seat inside in the attached cafe.

It appeared I was the only customer. Three young waitresses slouched around engrossed in their mobile phones. They greeted me with surprised looks as the guy from the kiosk relayed my order. Still apparently somewhat startled by their expected role they rumbled lethargically into action. I sat down ordered a Coke and waited for my *manti* to appear. I waited and waited and waited. After half an hour I was getting a little impatient. The waitresses buzzed around on pointless errands in an attempt to look competent. They arranged napkins in neat diamond shapes, which would be destroyed as soon as one was taken from the holder - an aesthetic touch that seemed a little overblown for the surroundings. Eventually one of the waitresses fluttered over to my table and said that unfortunately they didn't actually have any Manti.

Why they couldn't have told me this half an hour before I had no idea, and knew it was fruitless to ask. The waitress continued "Would you like *borsche*?" I asked how long would it take. She said "thirty minutes." I let out a long sigh, and said "Thanks, but no thanks" and left.

I walked away finding this phenomena of apparently staggering ineptness in the service sector absolutely infuriating, but also quite interesting. One obvious reason for it was that no-one got paid enough to care, which could explain the surliness among staff one often encountered. It was almost a reverse of the 'natural' order, with the capitalist psychology of sales inverted. Instead it was I the customer who had to try and get them to sell me things or do me a service. Sometimes it could feel quite conspiratorial.

Geoffrey Moorhouse was in Soviet Kyrgyzstan twenty years ago. His attempts to dine in a restaurant were eerily similar to my own experience: '*Incredulous face[s] looked round the kitchen door to behold the phenomenon of two men obviously expecting to be fed... it was fifteen minutes before one of the waitresses approached, and then only to announce that she would go and find out what food, if any, might be available.*' He commented how '*The abysmal service... had not changed a scrap since I first visited the Soviet Union twenty years before.*'[1]

My own visit was some forty years after his first and for nearly half of that time Kyrgyzstan had been an independent nation. Whatever fears I had about the encroachments of globalisation, it seemed sourness in the 'service' sector was comfortably entrenched, for the time being at least. It also confirmed that this was indeed a Soviet legacy and not some horrible alter-ego to the incredible hospitality I had otherwise experienced in Kyrgyzstan. In a rant induced by the appalling service in that hotel restaurant in the Kyrgyz SSR, it was the Soviet system that Moorhouse was directing his anger at when he wrote: *'How on earth did you people ever get a man on the moon when you can't even organise a doss-house down here? What's the matter with this country?'* [2] That 'country' is now many countries, but some of the less appetising aspects of their former incarnation linger on resiliently.

Returning to the visa office at five, I wondered what other hoops I might be required to jump through. However, despite its Kafkaesque beginnings, the process was at an end by 5.30pm. I had my visa back and another month to get from Bishkek to China.

I went to Osh Bazaar the next day, from where shared taxis leave for the south of Kyrgyzstan. I walked through the slush of ice and mud where the taxis waited; mostly German cars two decades old. The touts were apathetic, maybe because it was so early, and I was left to make my own acquaintances. I chose a vehicle where people were crowded, hoping this was indicative of an immediate departure. The driver, a pot-bellied Kyrgyz man in his fifties wearing a cardigan and woolly hat, made a half-hearted attempt to hustle but we quickly settled on a reasonable price.

Annoyingly, as soon as I put my bag in the boot, the small crowd dispersed, apparently not being fellow passengers at all. I prepared for a long wait whilst the car filled up, but was pleasantly surprised when a middle-aged Kyrgyz man got in. We left with two seats still empty.

The new passenger had a bulbous, drinker's nose, and vein riddled (but far from stupid) eyes. His black hair was receding thinly from his forehead. He was probably in his mid-forties and, somewhat surprisingly, dressed in a purple shell-suit. The smell of vodka preceded him. Not bad going since the sun had only been up for thirty minutes. Initially, he said nothing to me. Instead he concentrated on making a succession of garbled phone calls. We left Osh Bazaar and spent some time driving in circles through the muddy back lanes of Bishkek. We eventually stopped at a nondescript asbestos gate, from which a girl of about eighteen appeared. She seemed to be a relative of the driver and sat in the back, where she stared out of the window or into her phone for the next fourteen hours.

The drunk in the front however now turned his attention to me. After the briefest of formalities, he got to what was for him the crux of the issue, "English man, do you drink?" It seemed wise to say "No" as I assumed he was looking for a drinking partner. He looked crestfallen, but rather than pursue the matter, which was what I had expected, he just shrugged his shoulders in acceptance – although seemingly not quite understanding the mindset of a man who didn't want to get drunk in the back of a car at 9.30 in the morning.

Instead he turned to other matters "So Englishman, why are you going to Osh?" he asked, more in the tone of an interrogator than a friendly inquiry; "There is only burnt buildings and not stable government! You want to see burnt buildings?" he continued. "No" I replied, although what had happened in Osh was connected to why I was going there. However, it was also true that "I want to catch a bus to Kashgar in China." He looked at me suspiciously; "You are humanitarian agency?... There are many America, English, Turkey people in Osh. Many foreigners for humanitarian agencies there. You are too?" I assured him I wasn't. His eyes narrowed "You are CIA, KGB?" I laughed at this ridiculous suggestion. The drunk held my gaze for a long time, clearly trying to figure something out. However it seemed to elude him, so he sighed and turned back in his seat.

We headed west out of Bishkek. However, the driver soon left the main road and zigzagged cross-country on minor lanes, connecting tiny villages of which my map made no reference. In his holey, beige cardigan and brown tea-cosy hat, he didn't look like the boy-racer type. However, he thrashed that Eighties gold-coloured Audi as if in fear of his life. In reality, he was just trying to avoid the fine-demanding police on the main road, whilst not losing time threading through this obscure one.

The landscape we passed through was uninspiring, just a flat, frost covered agricultural plain. However, moving beyond its horizontal monotony was the contrasting grandeur of the dramatic peaks that carved the country in two. The drunk commented "You will see a big difference in Osh. It is very different from here." Indeed, a difference that went far beyond the landscape, and which infused every aspect of life in the south.

We rocketed through inconsequential hamlets, hibernating in the shadows of the hills behind; a blur of rickety asbestos, communal water pumps, locals hunched against the cold, and connotations of noble nomads glimpsed in the passing horsemen. We emerged back on the main road at Sosnovka. This small town sits immediately before the Ala-Too Mountains, which rise up like a wall at the south of the Chuy Valley. It's a scenically glorious 55km climb to cross them at the Tor Ashuu Pass of 3586m. I had done it on the bike twice and was looking forward to seeing it again without the extra effort.

Before we entered the gorge we stopped at a "Magazine." The vodka-laced passenger having gradually become more coherent, jovial, and one might guess more sober. He turned to me again as he got out of the car and reiterated "Do you drink Englishman?" to which I replied "No, I'm fine thanks." He paused momentarily before saying "Englishman, come with me."

He went to the boot to fiddle with his leather satchel complete with inbuilt calculator, and procured a crisp 1000 Som note from its interior. Inside the shop he offered me vodka again. Again I declined. Shrugging, he then purchased a third of a litre bottle of vodka for himself. He also bought some cigarettes and a pickled gherkin. He then asked the gold-teethed babushka at the counter for a glass which she dutifully provided. They chatted casually, full of smiles, in the friendly manner one imagines rural folk at village shops throughout the world to interact. The key difference here seemed to be that my fellow car sharer opened and demolished a third of a litre bottle of vodka in two glasses, and only because the size of the glass didn't permit him to finish it in one. Each glass went straight down in one go. The drinker visibly shuddered as it emptied, and only steadied himself by taking a bite on the pickled gherkin. Meanwhile the hen-like shopkeeper, waited ambivalently for him to finish before they carried on their conversation as if it was nothing out of the ordinary. I tried to imagine a similar scene taking place in rural Britain; Mrs Smith of Bramblestow Village store, sorting through the apples whilst cheerily chatting away with a new customer as he nonchalantly gulped down a third of a litre of hard liquor before 10.30am. It was rather too surreal to seriously contemplate. Yet in Central Asia, they like their vodka, and they don't seem shy with portions. Neither is this bingeing a habit restricted to down-and-outs, but permeates every level of society. The man I was with now, fresh from profitable ventures in the Middle East, was certainly no beggar. In his book *The New Great Game* Lutz Kleveman tells us how 'US Ambassador Steve Mann… acquired notoriety in Central Asian diplomatic circles when the eccentric Turkmen dictator Saparmurat Niyazov, discontented with US foreign policy, once forced Mann at a state banquet to drink a jug full of vodka in one go.'[3] The use of the word 'forced' gives some idea of the pressure that can be brought to bear in these situations. 'Forcing' an Ambassador of the most powerful nation on earth is quite a feat, so I was quite pleased my abstinence had been accepted so lightly. He even bought me a soft drink.

At that point a little red haired Russian boy came in to buy some biscuits. The smiling shopkeeper dutifully weighed them out whilst my hard drinking companion pinched the lads cheeks and teased him about his red hair like a kindly uncle. It was all so 'Little House on the Steppe' and community spirited, the staggering volume of alcohol just consumed seemed inconsequential.

With a cheery goodbye or "Dosveedanya" it was back to the car and through the checkpoint that allowed us into the gorge. Here the drinking man bought some apples from an old lady hawking them at the toll gate. It was his last sentient act.

Looking out of the back window I could see the *Chaikhana* I stayed at in 2009. It was a memory of great hospitality, but again it was tarnished with the ill effects of vodka on this society. I had tried to camp in a field some kilometres back but had been disturbed by an aggressive drunk. With my chosen spot compromised, I cycled on; wary that I had to find somewhere to rest my head before entering the gorge. Fortunately, I met Marat, a Kyrgyz man who said I was welcome to stay with him. We had dinner at his elderly neighbours, an Uzbek, and apparently a WWII veteran.[*] I remember Marat's eagerness to ply me with vodka, but his elderly neighbour came to my aid stating that as a *'sportsman'* I could be excused (this sometimes worked). In this case it meant I got away with only two small glasses. Marat told me with a mixture of admiration and resentment - (for denying him drinking partners) - that "Old Ozgen is not alcoholic!" Something testified by the fact he was still alive.[†]

I recalled being struck by how Marat's obvious drunkenness whilst having a civilised meal with an elderly couple in their garden was apparently a totally acceptable cultural norm. Yet Marat was a kind, intelligent man who took a keen interest in the history book I was carrying, and was eager to discuss politics, complaining about the ignorance of other locals who "No educated very much, and not

---

[*] I say 'apparently', because he did not appear to be old enough. Of course he could have served, even on the front line, as a child.
[†] Kyrgyz menfolk on average only make it to 63, whilst their women survive for a decade longer.

know about George Bush and Toby Bear!" Probably a good thing I thought. The next morning he arrived to treat me to breakfast with a fresh bottle of vodka in his hand. He said as his job consisted of looking after cows and sheep why couldn't he be drunk. It seemed a valid argument. Rampant alcoholism in post-Soviet Central Asia is often blamed on poverty, the favoured excuse for most social ills. However, whilst Marat was evidently not rich, he had a *Chaikhana* that basically ran itself, animals, a wife, and children who were now fully grown and had moved away. Moreover, he lived in a scenically very beautiful place. No doubt many advocates of the 'simple life' would have gladly swapped places with him. Obviously, I can't claim to know the man's problems or what compelled him to drink so much, but on the face of it, I would say he was simply bored and felt he had nothing better to do.

Vodka arrived with the Russians and has certainly had a negative effect on Kyrgyz society. The traditional drink of the Kyrgyz is fermented mare's milk known as *koumiss*. We know this had long been the drink of choice for Eurasian nomads. From the *Iliad* we hear of 'milkers of mares', and from eastern sources we hear of Chinese brides of nomad kings lamenting that they had only 'mare's milk to drink.'[4] A pint of *koumiss* is said to contain all the vitamins that are required to stay healthy. Being fermented, *Koumiss* is very mildly alcoholic. The first inhabitants of Central Asia, the ancient Iranians, drank a stimulant called *soma* to reach an ecstatic frenzy before going into combat. To the ancient Iranians, humans were created to struggle for truth against *drug* (the Lie) and evil. The principal ingredient of *soma* was ephedra which has been found among the Iranian mummies of East Turkestan, now Xinjiang. These people believed everyday life to be an illusion, and that imbibing *soma* allowed one to experience the 'reality' beyond it. Interestingly, clues in ancient Chinese imply that *magi* from this pan-Central Asian Iranian culture were also powerful individuals at the Chinese court 'responsible for divination, astrology, prayer, and healing with medicines.'[5] Turco-Mongol shamans also used stimulants like intoxicating drinks and tobacco. Alcohol was used by the Kyrgyz before the Russians arrived and not just in association with spiritual practice. We hear of Manas and his comitatus sitting in his wife Kanykai's tent, and how the attendant maidens 'brought strong brandy. The forty friends took their seats; and when the "forty friends" were seated, strong brandy was set before them.[6] Nor were the heroes of Manas beyond having one too many. We hear how the strong and powerful Joloi was 'generally only aroused from a drunken sleep by his wife Ak Saikal or his horse Ach Budan' and how Ak Saikal fought at his side displaying 'great activity and strength in battle.'[7] Yet, it seems only with the arrival of the Russians and the institution of vodka has alcohol become such a destructive force amongst the Kyrgyz people. The alcoholism that bedevilled the Soviet Union has been linked to the 'inertia, passivity and frustration' of daily life and a response to the constant pressure from above and 'a feeling of helplessness in the face of authority.'[8] These features of existence were not just realities of Soviet Russia, but also of Tsarist Russia and before. Russian rule brought these elements to Central Asia, and even though it has now retracted, the cultural legacy, and for many the hopelessness too, remains.

After about ten minutes of excited and increasingly incoherent jabber, my Kyrgyz companion of 2011 fell into his own drunken slumber. The car fell silent and we climbed steadily, the road twisting between the gorge walls of purple rock. This road, generously labelled the M41, is never wider than a single lane carriageway. However, it is the only road to effectively connect the north and south of the country. There is of course the route I mentioned earlier, from Naryn, but this is indirect, unsealed, and closed in winter. Moreover, it links up with the M41 at Jalalabat anyway. Similarly, the other road I talked about, and that incidentally is the *only* other road offering partial national transit, merely cuts east to west through the Suusamyr Valley, again meaning that the only way to get further south is the M41. This makes the M41 a veritable lifeline between the two halves of the country. Despite its importance, one can drive its entirety and rarely have another vehicle in view.

It is also a scenically spectacular 700km journey. The road swung in tight turns up numerous switchbacks that pressed against vertical rock walls. There were no verges or lay-bys, only room for the road had been chiselled up the mountain. We slowed to weave through herds of goat being led by horsemen into the pass. This is apparently prohibited, and admittedly a strange thing on a country's premier highway, but I've encountered it every time I've travelled this way. Rising to the top of the pass one looks down on a dramatic rock-cut scene, and a row of epic peaks one now somehow sits above. In 1937, on his adventures, Fitzroy Maclean met three Tajiks who *'Had been sent to Kirgizia to build a road in some horrible mountains. They were far from explicit, but must I think have meant the new road from Frunze* [Bishkek] *to Osh.'* [9] Carving the road through such inhospitable terrain must have indeed been 'horrible.' It also highlights just how divided the nation would be without it, and the somewhat artificial nature of Soviet state-making. The same mountainous topography and tribal political structure hindered the establishment of a centralised state in Iran. Like Central Asia, Iran also served as a buffer between the Russian and British Empires. Eventually, this 'buffer' was reduced to the still unconquerable Afghanistan. What is now Kyrgyzstan was developed by the Russians, later as part of the USSR, and Iran was developed essentially by British Petroleum (BP).

Only the girl and I could appreciate the view. The driver was half concentrating on the road and half concentrating on repelling the strange lunges the unconscious drunk was making in his sleep. He seemed to be trying to embrace the driver, as if thinking himself at home in bed with his wife. Gazing at the brittle edge of the unguarded roadside, and the drop of several hundred feet to the previous loop in the road's long coil, I hoped his troubled dream state would not mean trouble for all of us.

Fortunately he relented into a more stable stupor and we entered the long tunnel that the 3568m Pass culminates in. Inside the tunnel one still climbs at a gentle incline. It is appallingly lit and full of collected fumes. Snow melt runs in waterfalls from cracks in the concrete ceiling. Puddles and potholes riddle the road surface. As a cyclist it had been three kilometres of anxiety and asphyxiation. The guard at the tunnel's entrance had even asked if I had a respirator. What I took as a joke turned out not to be so funny as the level of oxygen inside the tunnel sunk dangerously low. In 2001 this fact cost several lives when a breakdown caused a traffic jam. People kept their engines running and in the confined space ended up suffocating themselves.

As a passenger in a car this time, rather than on a bike, it was certainly easier to breathe, but still a little tense. A convoy of heavy farm equipment rumbled out of the darkness with only the dimmest of headlights announcing their presence.

Emerging on the other side, darkness was suddenly replaced by blinding daylight, intensified by the snow reflecting from every surface. The road was thick with ice, and lorries chugged up the 12% incline so slowly I could almost feel the strain required. Their tyres were wrapped in chains to gain purchase, and they left toxic black clouds hanging in their wake. For one the battle was already lost, as it backslid sideways into a ditch, tipping up into what looked like a position beyond rescue - like a beetle flipped helplessly on its back.

Our own vehicle crawled slowly past on the steep descending switchbacks that unravelled down the mountain. Unlike the confined climb on the northern side, here the world opened up below us in a vast high altitude plateau. From our height it was like seeing the Earth from an aircraft. Totally snowbound the Suusamyr Valley looked like a kingdom of marble, pristine and unmarked; roads and rivers barely distinguishable veins on its broad white back. This great basin of land was encompassed by the distant Suusamyr-Too Mountains. Russian explorer Ivan Mushketov described the sight of the valley as 'An emerald in a silver setting.'[10] However, he clearly came in a more hospitable season. I had seen that great green 'emerald' previously, in the summer months, and it must have looked little different to him, except there is now an asphalt road where there was once just a track. The Kyrgyz still bring their herds to these pastures, and every year their yurts sprout like mushrooms on the felt green valley floor. The Suusamyr Valley, along with the At-Bashi and Naryn Valleys, was one of the few places where, historically, some Kyrgyz lived in exclusively agricultural settlements. This was not really a choice, because only poverty could force Kyrgyz into agriculture. The Kyrgyz who became farmers were disowned by their fellow tribesmen as the age-old antipathy between the settled and the nomadic dictated.

After a cautious, measured descent through thin bands of cloud we reached the expansive ivory plain. A knot of sky blue wagons served as *chaikhanas* on a road otherwise devoid of services. One of only two routes off the plateau splintered away to the east. It was a dirt road leading to a rugged region of Central Kyrgyzstan. Continuing south I was surprised to see some yurts and roadside stalls flanking the white ribbon of road, even in mid-winter and at 2000m+ altitude. I could make out ill matched bottles of murky liquid, looking like a library of potions, amassed for sale. Yet the brewers were not visible, the harsh conditions keeping them confined to their yurts. In the summer the valley is ripe pasture, its broad green breadth awash with life; whole herds of livestock reduced to the appearance of ants swarming at the end of a giant snooker table. On that winter's day, it was odd to note that the only evidence of the annual migration was a few flimsy lean-tos of wood and asbestos; the toilets of the seasonal herders and their families.

In winter, what is always an uncluttered land became almost extinct. Incessantly flat, white and monotonous it continued across the plateau end to end. This continued until we reached the red statue of Manas that signalled the turn off to Otmek Pass (3300m), passage to the isolated Kyrgyz city of Talas, and the Kazakh steppe. The M41 took us over the Ala-Bel Pass (3184m) and down into a different ecosystem, the Chychkan gorge. Again great cliffs began to contract around us, and thick forests somehow held fast on scraggy escarpments. Road and river snaked in symmetry down the jagged corridor of giant rock walls.

In the shamanic tradition, the first faith of this land, those trees, streams, and cliffs were all imbued with a spirit. So too were later manufactured things, tools, guns, or man-made hay meadows.[11] The ancient Indo-Iranians believed even abstract ideas had a spirit. Shamans were intermediaries between their fellow tribesmen and the spirit world. They used the spirits found in nature, the powers and abilities of animals, and of the ancestors. Shamans entered ecstatic trance-like states using song, dance, and the renowned shamanic drum. Indeed, modern science tells us how the human brain will produce hallucinations when tired by repetitious noises such as the shaman's drum or rhythmic repetitive motions such as the shaman's dance. However, it has more difficulty explaining the curative effects of such practices. A traveller struck down by malaria in 1930s Turkestan recounted how a Kyrgyz shaman 'poured water over me again and again, leaped round me to drive the evil spirits out of my body, and beat his magic drum all the while with incomparable perseverance.'[12]

Yet, shamanism has existed on every continent. It is mankind's default religion, the religion of nature. In Ancient Greece, oracles, necromancy, and archaic techniques of ecstasy were survivals of far older shamanic traditions. Socrates admitted to being guided by an inner voice, a *daimon* whose guidance he followed without question, a belief which also represents traces of shamanic practice.

Shamans were associated with metallurgy, for turning earth into metal was also considered a kind of magic. The Yakuts, a Turkic people living in modern Siberia, and who even call themselves 'Saka', have a proverb that 'smiths and shamans are from the same nest.'[13] The Turk and Kyrgyz peoples were renowned as smiths in their homeland of southern Siberia. Like shamans, it was believed smiths had the power to heal and tell the future.

However, 'shaman' is a Russian word. The Turks of Altai, which included the Kyrgyz, used the word *kam*. It is a word that first appears in a Uyghur text from 1069 A.D. A Russian psychiatrist visiting the Altai in the 1990s was told how:

'Things happened here almost a hundred years ago that greatly affected our people's attitude towards strangers. People who were foreign to our land decided to bring their own religion here. One day they called all the kams from near and far for a ritual. They told them they wanted peace between their religions. About thirty kams came bringing only their drums. The strangers took all the kams and put them into a small wooden house. Then they covered the house with kerosene and lit a match. The house with the kams burned for hours. None of the villagers could do anything. When it had burned to the ground, three of the kams got up and walked out of the ashes alive. The strangers were terrified by this. They did not try to stop the three kams but ran from the burned house and watched in shock as the three kams walked away. The three kams went in different directions and continued the 'kamlanie.' But from that time on, the kams have performed their rituals in secret.'[14]

Shamanic practice has always been at odds with the invasive, missionary religions linked to political and military power. The Buriat are a Mongol people who were once neighbours to the Kyrgyz. Indeed, some Buriat had already migrated southwards to Issyk Kul prior to the Kyrgyz, and Chinese records confuse the two peoples. Studies of the Buriat have shown how shamanism survived and prospered in a landscape of forests, mountains, lakes and rivers on the fringes of Mongolia. By contrast, the central plains gave rise to centralised states which tried to impose the religion which was entwined with their power, like the Buddhism of the Manchu state. Religious and political powers perceived a threat to their hereditary or hierarchical power in the power of shamanism which came direct from the Earth.

Kyrgyzstan, with its rugged terrain, seemed such a shamanic landscape. Whilst I had seen no evidence of shamanism, Islam's touch was certainly lighter in Kyrgyzstan than in other Soviet Central Asian states. It has been said before that Islam was essentially an urban religion, that 'Muhammad himself was an urbanite suspicious of nomads' and the 'early Islamic proselytizers were members of the urban bourgeoisie.'[15] So it is perhaps no surprise that Islam took a stronger hold on the settled civilisations of Central Asia, west of Kyrgyzstan. There the population was static, closer to the Islamic heartland, and under the sway of centralised state powers, which despite their rise and fall, were almost exclusively Islamic. On the other hand, it remains a truth that Islam was a religion spread by nomads.

In summer the Chychkan Valley is a beautiful place, with many families coming to picnic under the shade-giving firs next to the churning river. 'Resorts' and eateries have sprung up to serve this scenic spot; people recline on bed-like pieces of furniture (called *topchan* in Russian and *Soru* in Kyrgyz) sipping *chai* as *shashlik* smoke swirls lazily in the sunlight. At the roadside trestle tables are lined with pots; they hold a syrupy substance that glistens like liquid gold. This is *Myod* or honey, for which the valley is renowned. The hives, stacks of wooden boxes painted primary colours, nestle amongst the trees in quaint and quiet industry. In winter the Valley remains beautiful, but in a harsh, foreboding way; the frozen stillness, apparent absence of life, and the impossible angles to which dark woods cling. It is nature in the Gothic style, a cathedral of rock and shadows cast in huge scale.

The driver turned around in his seat and said "Kafe, eat, eat!" We pulled over to a wooden house and went inside. The vodka drinker remained comatose in the passenger seat in spite of the driver's best efforts to rouse him.

Inside was dark, but wallpapered and furnished in that heavy Russian style, much akin to that of Victorian Britain. A pile of firewood filled one corner, and a blackened pot simmered on an open stove. Sanitation came in the form of a free standing basin, where one had to pull a plunger to release a dribble of water from a small metal reservoir. Again it was an archaic contraption that spoke of another age, but without running water they are the best option and remain common throughout Central Asia. A young woman arrived out of the gloom to serve us. She was attractive but there was something distant in her clear eyes that seemed to make her as removed from my experience of the world as the furniture and simple implements around her. This was hardly surprising, as it appeared it was just her and her family out here amongst the snow and the trees. It seemed contradictory that people could live on a country's major highway but still appear to lead an almost pioneer lifestyle. Her cheeks were burnished permanently red by the harsh elements.

She asked us what we wanted. The driver looked at me. I asked in turn for *Shashlik, Manti, Samsa,* and *Plov.* Each time she replied that they didn't have any of those. I asked what they did have. She said *Kordak,* so that's what we ordered. We sat down round a table that leaned to one side. In fact, the whole house seemed slightly wonky, as if it was about to slide down the slope it was set on. After a disturbingly short period of time the hostess returned with three plates of *Kordak. Kordak* is a plate of meat chopped into mouthful sized pieces. Luke warm and unreasonably chewy, our meat floundered in a pool of yellow grease. Still, it wasn't bad, and came with the standard additions of *Nan* and *Chai.* The *chai,* as well as increasing one's metabolic rate is also an effective digestive aid for diets heavy in meat. Once, when complaining about a pain down my side, I was instantly diagnosed with having eaten 'too much oil' and prescribed 'drink tea' as the cure. Among Central Asian cultures east of the Tian Shan, in Tibet, Xinjiang and Mongolia, where meat is also the core of the diet, there is a saying 'can't live without tea, even for a day.'

The girl from our car didn't touch her food, so the driver, who I was starting to assume to be her uncle or grandfather or something, slopped her meal into a ludicrously thin polythene bag, taking special attention to collect every drop of greasy goodness. It was good to see food not being wasted, but it looked a fairly unappetising prospect to return to.

Half a dozen Kyrgyz men then entered, squeezing round the closely packed tables. They were all fur hats, flashes of gold teeth, and drinking glasses of what looked like water, though I imagined probably wasn't. Our driver took the opportunity to introduce me, the foreigner, to them. Mainly they were interested in how much money one could earn working in Britain. However, being displayed as a living embodiment of monetary wealth, I always find a little inaccurate and annoying. Thus, when the first "Skol'ka dollars adin maysat Anglia?" (How much money can you earn in one month in Britian?) came, I lied and told them $700. They didn't seem to believe me, but I insisted it was the truth, which left them visibly disappointed and averted any more tedious questions about money matters.

We paid up and continued down the valley until it broadened out on the approach to the town of Toktogul. Vodka man slept throughout, and the painfully slow speed adopted by the driver indicated he was worried about police and bribes. Toktogul, despite allegedly being a town of 70,000, is an urban non-event, appearing as little more than a collection of crumbling concrete buildings strung along the road. It was once a penal colony, a legacy which apparently still blights the town with a bad reputation today. The name Toktogul is that of the famous 19th Century *Akyn* (poet/songwriter) who was born in the area. Unlike most who live in our times, Toktogul was unmotivated by money, only performing at gatherings of the poor and refusing to sing for the wealthy Kyrgyz nobility. For this he won instant acclaim from the communists who interpreted his actions as pro –socialist, anti-bourgeois class war. It was interesting to learn Toktogul rose to fame through traditional contests where two singers improvised derisory lyrics about each other, with the audience cheering on the most entertaining. Clearly 'rap-battles' and 'freestyle MCs' aren't the modern phenomena one might assume. I would have to remember that the infusion of Hip-hop culture in Kyrgyz youth actually overlays a longstanding cultural heritage.

Today Toktogul seems to be little more than its vast reservoir, which looks almost like an inland sea. The water collected there flows down the Naryn River through a series of hydro-electric power stations, generating a huge amount of electricity, not just for Kyrgyzstan but for her neighbours too. In fact, water and the resulting HEP is Kyrgyzstan's most valuable resource.

The road traced the reservoir's coast, from dowdy moorland reminiscent of Yorkshire, to cafes on sand coloured cliffs like somewhere in the Mediterranean. On its southern side we surmounted a further Pass before dropping down to yet another type of terrain; a land that was red and dry like a newly colonised Mars. The Kara-Suu River weaved through the parched landscape. Kara-Suu translates directly as 'Black water', coincidently the very name of the river that passes through my village in the UK.

The town of Kara-kol (Black Lake) passed in flat, familiar concrete format. Its pleasant summer skin shed for a cold grey winter shell. Beyond it the earth rose and contracted once more in walls of red sandstone. This was the onset of the 67km long gorge of the lower Naryn River. A toll was paid, and we pulled over for "refreshments." As if sensing this, the previously senseless passenger came back to life. Perhaps he had calculated the 300ml of vodka he consumed that morning to be the exact amount needed to sedate him until the next filling station. He was suddenly up and about with a freshness of character that seemed in complete denial of how he had spent the day thus far.

"Englishman, drink?" he challenged boisterously. His spirit clearly buoyed by the certainty that he would soon be ingesting an altogether different type of spirit. I declined again, lingering outside. The driver giggled; his woolly cardigan, tea-cosy hat and ample paunch giving him a Womble-like look. They both lit cigarettes. The re-animated passenger told me how when he was in Saudi Arabia he had smoked 'Rothermans' which, being a British brand, he seemed to believe bonded us in some way. Inside the store – it was too cold to stay outside – the shelves were largely empty, with just some cigarettes, biscuits and soft drinks - except for the middle shelf, which was well stocked with a staggering array of vodka.

The passenger, eager to treat me to something, bought me a boiled egg. He bought himself a third of a litre of vodka. Again, he went through the same routine of one glass, one gulp, down in one. Unfortunately for him, this time there were no gherkins available, or anything else conceivably useful as a chaser. In the end the lady serving gave him a *kurut* yogurt ball. This potently sour Kyrgyz delicacy offered little relief – something testified by his tortured expression as he bit into it.

Clearly, that was his lunch because we promptly returned to the car. The girl had remained there, understandably finding greater amusement in her mobile phone than the antics of the elderly male chauffeur, a drunk, and a mute Americanitz, or whatever exactly it was she took me for. As we pushed into the gorge, vodka man kept up a lively conversation for about three minutes before lapsing into a comatose state once more. He had been trying to explain something about the dam and HEP but passed out before he finished.

However, I learnt the drunk had just returned from a long stint working in the Middle East. Like Zarina he had been a 'guest-worker', imported labour for the Arab states. Whilst paid more money than it was normally possible to earn in Kyrgyzstan, the kind of exploitation related by Zarina was illustrative of a power paradigm that had sucked nomadic Central Asian Turks into the service of the settled Islamic societies of the Middle East for centuries. Previously it was pure slavery, and the nomadic Turks were taken as soldiers. These Turkic 'slaves on horseback' were decisive in spreading Islam though Central Asia to their unconverted brethren. However, it often was not long before the Turkic slave-soldiers rose to power within the Middle Eastern regimes that had enslaved them in the first place; as happened with the Abbasids. Beginning with the Seljuks and culminating with the Ottomans, Turkic peoples even created their own empires within the Middle East.

However, despite this tradition of Central Asian Turkic peoples being imported to the Middle East, it was also the Slavs of Russia who were transported in huge numbers to the Arab world as slaves. Unlike the Turkic nomads, the Russian Slavs were used as domestic slaves, not soldiers. The extent of this practice is testified by the fact that the English word for 'slave' actually derives from the name 'Slav.' Moreover, in Russian the word for 'slave' is *Rab,* and the Russian word for work, *robota,* is derived from it. This has led to the suggestion 'that in Russia there was no such thing as unbounded free work', only slave labour.[16] This is linked to the idea of a nomadic warrior aristocracy which ruled over its settled, farming subjects - a social system evidenced across Eurasia since the time of the Saka. The proliferation of slavery in early Russia – perhaps the most important item in the economy – seems to have been a way of managing the surplus human population in a land not agriculturally productive enough to support them. Slavery persisted when the nomadic Mongols subjugated Russia between the 13th and 15th Centuries. However, domestic slavery in Russia reached its peak in the 17th Century, with an estimated 10 percent of the population enslaved to their fellow Slavs. Many people actually sold themselves into slavery in search of a better life. Despite a later decline, slavery simply merged into serfdom. Slave hunting by Crimean Tartars into Muscovy only stopped in 1738, and the Ottoman Sultan did not order a halt to the white slave trade until the middle of the 19th Century. Of course, this did not stop the Turkmen slavers, and rumours of Christian slaves in the Khanates of Turkestan was a prominent reason given by the Russians for annexing Central Asia.

The absolute power of the Russian autocracy was not dissimilar to the Turkish Sultans or nomad Khans. Moreover, the Russian domination of Central Asia may be viewed as a continuation of a nomadic sociological model whereby a military elite ruled over and extracted labour from subject peoples often ethnically different from themselves. Even today, with the collapse and fragmentation of the Soviet Khanate, the same trends persist; with a symbiotic relationship between a powerful Russia reliant on cheap labour from its former dominions in Central Asia, and those nations' dependence on the remunerations of migrant workers. Thus, Central Asian 'guest-workers' to Russia and the Middle East are part of an ongoing historical continuum. That the situation will, in time, change more to the favour of Central Asians like Zarina and 'the drunk' is as certain as the cyclical nature of historical forces. That a man cannot support his family by working in the country of his people, but rather must sell his labour in distant lands that takes him away from them, is, perhaps, as good a reason to drink as any.

The road clung narrowly to the gorge's rough profile. Below, even in the winter dull, the gorge still carried an oddly exotic turquoise load. The river, held back by the dam, no longer flows as such, but sits in a series of vibrantly coloured green-blue lakes. They extend through the gorge like a dazzling jewelled necklace across the cliffs' red and craggy throat. In between pillars of sheer rock tumbled near vertical slopes of scree. At the base of one such rock-fall there was even a house, trapped between tens of kilometres of narrow gorge either side with only one access road - the M41 - in or out. The road swung round, up and down as the rock dictated. A series of tunnels finally freed us from the gorge's confining corridor, bringing us face to face with the huge modern dam. This mass of forged metal and industrial yellow fixings, stood in stark robotic contrast to the un-hewn landscape which it bridged and tamed.

Beyond the dam, the road unravelled through a broadening vista. Slag heaps were piled like rusting pyramids as we approached Tash Komur, an old mining town. The coal mining industry has totally collapsed in Kyrgyzstan since independence. However, from the road, one looks across a canyon to see the town perched prettily - sometimes precariously - along the opposite cliff. The dirty white houses line their dramatic roost like eggs high up on offshore rookeries. With the turquoise water flowing gently by far below it cut quite a striking scene. Less idyllic were the waterfalls of waste and litter that spilled down the rock; effluent from the cliff top houses. The town's improbable position made it look like some ancient citadel. Only a defunct looking railway and other abandoned relics of aged industry replanted it firmly in the modern era.

The river and road soon drifted apart and we entered the flat of the fertile Fergana Valley. Here the Steppe, Desert, and Mountain terrain so archetypal of Central Asia relent to rich and avidly contested agricultural land. The geographical singularity of this valley is slashed by political lines that carve it between three nations; Kyrgyzstan, Uzbekistan, and Tajikistan. The masterminds behind this division are long since dead and their doctrines disregarded. Yet their legacy is far from resolved, and remains a catalyst for problems both present and future.

When I last passed this way it was *abus* (water-melon) season and the fields were full as the population mobilised to collect its bountiful crop, stuffing trucks and car trunks to bursting with these green football-sized fruits. Today, all was quiet. The wall-less shacks at the end of the fields, where people slept in the summer, were empty. The places I had camped, and was shown wonderful hospitality, were also deserted.

Night was closing in, with a darkness unmediated by street lights or the sparse habitation. Conversely, as everything else faded, the drunk began to slowly surface and revive. He babbled into his phone and I noticed with dismay that when we reached the junction, instead of going straight over on the road to Osh, we turned left towards Jalalabat, Kyrgyzstan's third largest city. Admittedly, I'd never been there before. However, at 10.00pm after more than thirteen hours in the car, and with said company, I was not particularly in the mood for visiting then.

We passed under the grand arches that marked the entrance to the city; 'Jalal City' named after the 13th Century warrior. However, after his heroic statue, I might have been anywhere. It was pitch black and virtually entirely unlit. In fact, it barely seemed to be a town at all. I protested that I really would prefer to go straight to Osh, but was shouted down with calls for "SUPPER! SUPPER!" After a few minutes cruising into this gloom, a flash black Mercedes swung aggressively in front of us forcing the driver to slam on his brakes, before pulling over in tandem to a lay-by. I wondered what was going on, and was a little surprised when a huge man, dressed as a police officer emerged from the unmarked Merc. Any worry that we might be in trouble was put to rest when the driver and passenger from my car got out and greeted him with handshakes; the drunk as if they were old friends, and the driver in a rather more formal fashion. They got back in their respective vehicles and we trailed the Merc as it pulled away. The driver and drunk chatted away in Kyrgyz, the driver sniggering unpleasantly. I felt a little uneasy about this unplanned detour and asked where exactly we were going. The drunk said in English "My policeman friend is taking us to dinner." Resigned to the fact I wouldn't be getting to Osh till the wee hours I stared out of the window in quiet frustration. There was nothing to see, just the red lights of the Merc in front as they floated through the oil-black streets.

We soon pulled into a non-descript looking compound, the lack of light making it impossible to see anything but the black block silhouettes of the buildings. We had apparently arrived at our destination, the driver and drunk exiting excitedly. I stayed put, planning to use the same technique as the girl – distancing myself from social expectation with a blank stare out of the window. More men appeared from the sliver of light created when a door to one of the buildings opened. There was an enthusiastic bout of handshaking. I noticed the entire compound was ringed with wire fencing topped by barbed wire. The driver, grinning broadly at the situation he found himself in, whatever exactly that was, chided me and the girl to get out of the car. We both, in our different languages, feigned lack of appetite. However, he was taking no excuses and his smile subsided in a hint of irritation and anger.

Reluctantly I got out and followed him over to the open door. Stepping inside I was welcomed into a large, brightly lit room, in which was accumulated a sort of showcase of status and wealth. It was not the kind of place I really expected to exist in Kyrgyzstan, let alone to encounter personally.

Dominating the space was two full size billiard tables. They were huge, perhaps even bigger than snooker tables. On them were scattered the balls that make up the game. On the wall hung a very silent and slick air-conditioning unit; hardly necessary mid-winter, but it was on anyway. The opposite wall had a large plasma screen TV fitted. Next to it stood a mahogany coat rack, whilst from the ceiling swung lavish chandeliers. The room was furnished with faux Louis XIV chairs and a table. However, everyone was sitting at one end on a low slung leather sofa in front of a large glass coffee table.

It was set out with fine china and shining cutlery, a far cry from the eateries I normally dined at in Kyrgyzstan, or anywhere else for that matter. The place looked like it had been set up as a penthouse for playboys, filling it with ostentatious items by which to display their wealth, and toys with which to entertain themselves. Yet none of it really fitted together; fine chandeliers hanging from a plain concrete ceiling, replica Louis XIV furniture next to plasma screen TVs. It was a collection of things stereotypically perceived as luxurious, yet they had clearly been acquired with no sense of conformity to the general décor or a larger theme.

There were about half a dozen men present, one of them being the policeman who had shown us the way. None of the others wore a uniform. Instead they wore chinos, fine quality jumpers, polo shirts, and polished leather shoes. They looked dressed for a day at the golf course, or an Ivy League reunion. Thus it was odd that the man who had been habitually downing vodka since I met him, and who - in his purple shell suit - looked an unlikely member of this fraternity, was the one who held court. He took centre stage and with great gusto appeared to be regaling all present with a very exciting story. It was evident from the way he gestured and the place names used, that he was discussing our journey. I just wondered how his tale became so dramatic when he had been effectively dead to the world eleven out of the last thirteen hours.

I heard 'Angliski' mentioned a few times, upon which everyone looked at me. First I was introduced to a dark skinned Kyrgyz man of approximately fifty. He had sharp Mongolian eyes and closely cropped silver tinted hair. He was not big, but held himself with a military bearing. He regarded me with a polite air of superiority as he shook my hand. All the others present were between forty and fifty. The drunk then told me with much repetition and gesticulation that the man who had just shaken my hand was the police chief of Jalalabat. Not only that, he was apparently also the police chief of Osh, and all in between, right up to Bishkek. That he held such huge jurisdiction sounded unlikely, but the man in question just nodded sagely as his status was delivered at length – not that he appeared to understand the English. The drunk then enthusiastically described me in return, but under the slightly less glorious title of "A tourist from London." However, it was nice that my lowly status received recognition at all, and that my place at the table was accepted without question. I tried to imagine a budget backpacker randomly attending an exclusive 'do' with the police chief of a British city or region, and all his wealthy, dignified associates. Personally, I couldn't see the backpacker being treated as the honoured guest I was.

The driver just sat there in his frayed cardigan and navvy's hat with a smile of delight plastered across his face. It seemed he was very happy to be in the presence of such illustrious company. His presence however, was ignored.

Next I was introduced to another man, with solid features and smartly groomed grey hair. His easy smile made him seem instantly genuine. In his chinos and white cashmere pullover, he would have looked at home at an English country club. It was only at the end of the night when he donned his fur hat and flashed his gold teeth, that this notion could be dismissed. He was introduced as a *biznizman* as were the rest. Many of the men did not look typically Kyrgyz and must certainly have had some Russian heritage.

Sitting amongst these *biznizmen* and the chief of police, it was strange to think I was with the elite. I couldn't help but wonder what they talked about, and how they scratched each other's backs. After all, just outside lay a city full of burnt out buildings, a result of the violent ethnic clashes less than a year before. The lid may have been put back on those tensions and order temporarily restored, but nothing had been resolved. By contrast, in this room - evidently very recently renovated - where the paint was barely dry, and which was cluttered with shiny new things, the chief of police and his friends played leisurely games of billiards.

Incidentally, I was there for about two hours and don't recall seeing hardly a ball potted. I assumed they were just incredibly bad players. However, as I was to find out, Russian Billiards, known as *Piramida* or 'Pyramid' is not Pool. The corner pockets are only 4-5mm wider than the diameter of the balls and the middle pockets have a difference of 14-18mm. This makes potting, still the aim of the game, considerably harder. Something probably not helped by large amounts of vodka.

Indeed, large amounts of vodka was the order of the day. Everyone was obliged to gather around the glass table as food was served and drinks poured – *and when the 'forty friends' were seated, strong brandy was set before them.* One might have expected quails eggs and caviar, but, whilst well presented, the food did not quite live up to the surrounding décor. Out came dishes of sliced tomato and cucumber, the ubiquitous salad of Central Asia, along with grated carrot, pickled gherkins, and bowls of oranges and bananas. Nice, but all strangely pedestrian in a room of extravagance. Circular *nan* was broken up and spread across the table as is customary. Again it was interesting to contrast the Western tableware with this Middle Asian habit of putting bread directly on the table top, not on a plate. I was carefully observed to make sure I ate, and everyone passed me plates and broke bread for me. This is a standard experience when dining as a guest in Central Asia.

The main course was *Shorpo,* boiled mutton on the bone served in a watery broth with carrots and potatoes. The second large portion of meat I would eat that day, it was cooked to perfection and absolutely delicious. However, I was light-heartedly rebuked for discarding a bone that still had a little bit of meat on. I was instructed that the "Kyrgyz way" was to strip the bone so that not a shred of anything edible remained - which I duly did.

The girl also did not escape the attention of her hosts. She was not such a compliant guest and had not touched any of her food. This was not appreciated and the police chief host asked why she was not eating. The driver, and her apparent guardian for this journey, squirmed in embarrassment and tried to compel her to eat whilst simultaneously spluttering some excuses so as not to offend his new friends in high places. Shortly afterward, he produced a couple more very thin polythene 'doggy' bags and began enthusiastically collecting food into them, being sure to scrape in all the gravy and grease he could.

The vodka toasts then began in earnest. Everyone's glass was full to the brim with a 50ml serving. Each man took his turn to ramble on, congratulating his companions, before everyone was obliged to stand and down his glass – except for the girl who, as a girl, was of course exempt. Knowing that I was to arrive in Osh past midnight, and not knowing what to expect in a town so recently troubled, getting drunk was not part of my plan. Fortunately, whilst the speakers droned on with their pre-drink monologue, staring at each other with glassy eyes, I was able to discreetly spill some of my serving under the table. Then, when it came to bottoms-up, I was able to hold the rest of the contents in my mouth and spit it back into the tea I was pretending to use as my chaser. Of course, I was again closely observed to see that I was emptying my glass each time. Vodka drinking is a serious business and participation is mandatory. However, out of the first seven rounds, using such clandestine methods I managed to limit my ingestion to about three.

There was then a short intermission for some reason. The billiards continued and I was given a kind of guided tour, which was a bit strange as everything was pretty much in open view as I described it. The police chief attended by the drunk even showed me the toilet which he was clearly very proud of. Admittedly, it was incredibly clean, but as a squat toilet consisted of little more than a porcelain hole in the middle of an empty room. I wasn't exactly sure what kind of reaction he was expecting. He seemed satisfied when I commented "Very good."

I then stood watching two of the 'biznizmen' play un-pot-able *Piramida*. Everyone was very amicable, and I had to admire their resilience to the huge amount of vodka they had just consumed in under an hour. Likewise, they seemed to respect me for the same quantity of vodka they believed I had just drunk, and was holding with remarkable sobriety.

However, we were shortly instructed to reconvene at the table, presumably for more vodka. Indeed, more rambling toasts ensued. The drunk kindly gave a running translation of what was said. The police chief talked of the 'problems' in Jalalabad and Osh, and how they were now on the mend. He then caught my eye, and to my dismay, insisted it was now my turn to make a toast. I started in bad Russian - filling in the gaps in my vocabulary with English – to thank my hosts for the food and their generosity, and looked round the table to see nods of approval. However, with a flash of inspiration, I stood up, raised my glass firmly in the air and loudly exclaimed "LONDON JALALABAT!!!" as if I had just personally brokered peace and declared eternal friendship between two mighty powers.

This was a master stroke, for they loved it, enthusiastically chorusing "LONDON JALALABAT!!! LONDON JALALABAT!!!" the names ringing through the air with such renown you could have sworn I had single-handedly unified Rome and Carthage.

It was a catchphrase I could then roll out every time I was required to speak, and they never tired of it. After another forty-five minutes of shots and speeches it seemed we were leaving. I got up slowly to conceal the puddle of 'misplaced' vodka that had formed under my part of the table. Everyone filed out, except the two who had been playing billiards. They called me back, grinning mischievously whilst holding a glass and a bottle of vodka. They insisted I have one for the road. The glass was filled to the brim and one of them collected a fork full of salad, holding it ready as a chaser, which he apparently intended to spoon feed me with. Not particularly keen on that idea I necked the vodka and pinched the salad from the fork, stuffing it into my mouth. However, the glass was immediately refilled and I was enjoined to drink again. Fortunately, the revving of the car engine outside made my excuses for me. With a flurry of handshakes and a final "LONDON JALALABAT!!" I rushed outside for the last leg of the journey on the long road to Osh.

The drunk was soon out cold in the passenger seat again. The driver quizzed me on which hotel I wanted to stay at when we arrived in Osh. I gave him a name, but he insisted the place had been burnt down during the troubles. I didn't know if this was the case, but intended to find out for myself before being whisked off to his choice, which was rather more expensive. Annoyingly, the journey had taken considerably longer than it needed to. I expected to arrive at 9.00pm and it now appeared that I would not get there till 1.00am. The vodka fuelled delays aside, there was also the fact that from Jalalabat to Osh, anyone without an Uzbek visa is forced to take a time consuming detour in order to avoid Uzbek territory. It is a fine example of the logistical difficulties created by the Soviet border legacy. Indeed, they were conceived with the very notion that no Central Asian nation would be able to operate independently, and that they could only survive as part of the greater whole - the USSR - a classic case of 'divide and rule' policy. Going this way meant ascending another minor pass and driving through the town of Ozgon, the old Karakhanid capital.

It was as we approached this final pass that the drunk momentarily became compos-mentis again and asked, with a tone of triumph in his voice, "So how are you now Englishman?" Clearly expecting the twelve or so glasses obliged me at 'supper' to have taken their toll. Indeed, they would have, but having actually only drunk about a third of that amount I remained in full control of my faculties. I replied in a spritely tone that I was fine and pleased to be eventually getting close to Osh. I don't think my chirpiness was what he anticipated because he just groaned, mumbled something and slumped back into his stupor.

We arrived in Osh past midnight, under cover of an ominous darkness. The driver tried to wake the drunk but he proved difficult to revive. We had to pull over to shake him back into consciousness, and elicit his address. We dropped him somewhere in the backstreets. He collected his holdalls and stumbled down an alleyway without a word of farewell. It was a pathetic flipside to the charismatic party animal in the police chief's den less than two hours before. However, I could not judge him too harshly. He had always been hospitable despite having consumed an unbelievable amount of vodka. I just wished my language skills had been sufficient to learn more about him. If 'supper' was anything to go by, he was clearly well connected. Yet who was he? Whilst the drinking may have been by default, was it underlined by sorrow or celebration? This man seemed to be not doing badly; he had at least some money from working abroad; he had friends; he had family. Everyone he had interacted with from the shopkeeper and red-haired Russian boy at the beginning of our journey to his chums at 'supper' seemed to like him. He could almost be described as charming in his drunken way. Yet he chose oblivion, and he was far from alone in that choice.

The driver was still trying to get me to stay at this other hotel. However, I gave him directions to the one I wanted to go to and told him to drive there. He conformed reluctantly, looking over to inspect me for the signs of the drunkenness I should surely be exhibiting after the earlier binge. He flicked his neck in the tell-tale gesture, asking if I was drunk. I told him I was fine and that for Englishmen "Vodka nyet problem." This ridiculous statement seemed to impress him because he nodded with something akin to respect. At the hotel I said goodbye to the girl who for the first time that day smiled and actually said something, even if it was only 'goodbye.' I paid the driver, but he followed me into the lobby anyway where he asked for another 200 Som on top of the price we had agreed. I asked why. He tapped his watch, indicating the late hour. I had to laugh at this because he knew full well our delayed arrival had nothing to do with me. He took the point, but had clearly thought it was worth a try. We shook hands and parted. I dragged my bag upstairs, realising at that moment all I wanted to do was sleep.

8

Osh

"You know, Osh is older than Rome" the drunk had told me in one of his less garbled moments. Indeed, around the town the odd piece of graffiti remained from the 'Osh 3000' celebrations. Whether or not Osh is really that old remains debatable, but it is certainly a settlement of great antiquity. The reason for such long established habitation is obvious. The Fergana Valley in which Osh finds itself is the most fertile area in the whole of Central Asia and a fifth of the region's entire population is concentrated there. Considering the Valley's agricultural productivity it is perhaps no surprise that in many Turkic languages 'osh' means food.

The history of Central Asia can be opaque and a celebration like 'Osh 3000' is part of a process of legitimisation as this 'new' nation finds its feet. Whilst the Soviet Union gave the 'Stans' form in the modern political sense of lines on maps, the people of Soviet Central Asia can draw on a cultural and historical heritage that extends far enough back to make the Russian/Soviet empire appear a mere blip. Just as Mongolia, since its emergence from communism, venerates Genghis Khan as a symbol of national identity, so too have the new Central Asian states selected historical figures for their respective nationalities to rally round. The Uzbeks have chosen Tamerlane, who was born close to Samarkand. Mostly remembered for his wide ranging military escapades and staggering cruelty (like building pyramids of human skulls and putting 100,000 prisoners to death in a single day) he is perhaps an unlikely choice for 'father figure' of a modern nation.

The Kyrgyz have chosen a slightly less well known person of past greatness, Manas; nomadic hero of the longest poem ever created, not on paper, but carried in men's heads and transmitted by their words. At 500,000 lines, Manas is longer than the Western heroic epics *The Odyssey* and *The Iliad,* combined. It has been questioned whether or not Manas was actually Kyrgyz, or if he even existed at all. However, the answer is to some extent irrelevant as either way he stands at the core of Kyrgyz identity, and all national identities have a mythical element at their heart.

It is often argued that the 'new' countries of post-Soviet Central Asia are entirely 'artificial' creations, as their borders were indeed delineated on Soviet drawing boards. Yet, this is to lose sight of the fact that the nation-state in general is a relatively new invention anyway. Strange as it may seem, those lines that demarcate every scrap of land on the world map today, and which seem to suggest some immutable geographically determined certainty, are often no more than a hundred years old. Any glance at the largely arbitrary borders imposed on Africa and the Middle East should bring such a debate on 'artificial' nations sharply into focus. Even the 'old world' of Europe is not particularly old when it comes to nation-states as the organisational paradigm. Historian Norman Davies writes how 'we habitually think of the European past as the histories of countries which exist today... but often this actually obstructs our view of the past, and blunts our sensitivity to the ever changing political landscape.'[1] After all, who remembers that the western Mediterranean was once dominated by the Empire of Aragon; that the grand Duchy of Lithuania was once the largest country in Europe; or that Glasgow was founded by the Welsh at a time before either England or Scotland even existed?[2]

Take Germany as an example. A people identified as 'Germanic' have been known for more than two thousand years, but only in 1871 was an entity formed that we might really call Germany. Even then, communities of German speaking people remained scattered throughout Eastern Europe and as far afield as Georgia, Russia, and even Kyrgyzstan. Since then, Germany has had territory spliced off, added on, and for half of the last century was actually divided into two separate states altogether. If Germany seems an unfair example in light of her perhaps unduly dramatic history, we might consider Italy (1861), Romania (1877), or India (1947). Also, the majority of nation-states on Earth today are the fragmentary results from a previous age of empires, and in this respect the five new 'Stans' are no different.

Like many peoples throughout Africa and Asia subject to European imperialism, the peoples of Central Asia were conquered by an invading group [the Russians] who were culturally and ethnically different from them and who were attracted to their lands as a source of raw materials. Emphasis on the 'artificial' nature of the 'Stans' is to underplay the 'artificial' nature of all nation states.

However, the Soviet carve-up of Central Asia ensured the existence of minority pockets not culturally homogenous with the majority populations around which the division of Turkestan into separate Soviet Socialist Republics (SSR's) was based. Minority pockets such as Uzbek Osh, historically and culturally contiguous with the settled civilisations of the Fergana Valley, inside a Republic of the traditionally nomadic Kyrgyz was either intentionally divisive or stunningly incompetent. Such latent tension was then exacerbated by the Soviet programme of manufacturing 'national identities' specific to the foreign organisational paradigm they had imposed on the region.

Still, despite the 'artificial' nature of this process, and despite only becoming an independent sovereign state in 1991, the Kyrgyz as a people can claim to be one of the oldest recorded ethnic groups in Asia, appearing in Chinese chronicles under the Mongolian name *Gegun* in the 2nd Century BC. Based on this, the Kyrgyz announced their 2200th year of statehood in 2002. Admittedly, that the *Gegun* truly equate with today's Kyrgyz remains difficult to prove with any certainty. The Kyrgyz were one of many tribal confederations to emerge from the fountainhead of southern Siberia and the Mongolian plain. The continual migrations of peoples from this region had such a knock-on effect across the Steppe that the Romans believed there must be a 'people hatchery' or 'workshop of peoples' somewhere over their eastern horizon. Yet the correlation of names in historic records with historic peoples remains at times uncertain. Historians still debate whether or not the Huns who so violently erupted on the Roman 'radar' are the same people Chinese records identify as the Hsiung-nu.

The Soviet view was that all nationalities had inhabited their respective lands since time immemorial. They claimed that it was only the name 'Kyrgyz' that migrated from the Yenisey in Siberia. In a way there is some truth to this because the Kyrgyz who migrated from their 'Mother River' in Southern Siberia assimilated people from many other tribal groups along the way; such as the Wu-sun, Saka, Turgesh, Oghuz, Qarluq, Qypchaq, Uyghur, Chigil, Turkified Sogdians, and Qara-qitai. However, it was a 'Kyrgyz' Khanate in the Yenisey Valley of the Sixth Century A.D., and it was the Kyrgyz who destroyed the Uyghur Khanate in 840 A.D. In fact, the Kyrgyz had a powerful nomadic empire of their own during the 9th and 10th Centuries. In the West, the first mention of the Kyrgyz still dates from as early as 596 AD, when an envoy of Byzantine Emperor Justinian II received the gift of a Kyrgyz slave. Of course, all this was still at a time when the Kyrgyz were not in present day Kyrgyzstan. Likewise, little more than a century before this date, the Angles of England were still in what is now Denmark, and the Danes for the most part remained in what is today Sweden. Moreover, this Sixth Century reference to the Kyrgyz predates by more than eight hundred years the birth of a certain Italian called Amerigo Vespucci, from whom America and the Americans would in due course take their name.

It has even been claimed that it was the Kyrgyz who reached America first, and that *they* were the original American Indians. Considering the shared Siberian source of both peoples this makes for interesting musing, but actually only amounts to the already established fact that the Amerindians originally came from Asia. However, perhaps it was such a tale that inspired the community of Kyrgyz escaping war in the Afghan Pamir in the 1980s, to try and migrate to Alaska.

The receptionist gave a resounding "Karashou" at the news I would be staying another night. Clearly they didn't have many foreign guests these days. For me Osh recalled a sleepy provincial town despite its status as the country's second largest city. It was a place I'd only seen in summer, and fleetingly at that. I'd been told by people I had met of underlying ethnic tensions, but as a passing visitor the atmosphere had always been one of tranquillity; leafy parks and a central fountain where people relaxed and drank soft drinks or *piva* (beer) with an almost Mediterranean nonchalance. The streets thrummed with the traditional colourful dress and headscarves of Uzbek women. Jayma Bazaar one of the busiest in Central Asia was always filled with a vibrant ethnic mix, a multi-coloured mass of foodstuffs, and a range of goods from traditional *Shyrdaks* (carpets),

Kalpaks (felt hats), even wooden saddles and ibex horns, to modern Turkish and Chinese textiles.

However, only eight months previously, obscure Osh had appeared briefly on the British news. The reports showed images of a town ablaze, traumatised Uzbeks fleeing for their lives, and incoherent reports of an explosion of ethnic violence. As quickly as the media frenzy started it died away, and the truth about what had happened, other than something very bad which left hundreds dead and countless thousands as refugees, remained elusive.

I didn't have to go far to see signs of the violence. Leaving my hotel, I noticed the open air restaurant opposite, where I had enjoyed many a tasty *shashlik,* was now boarded up with charred evidence of serious fire damage. I remembered the waitress with gold teeth and the cook expertly separating the strings of dough for the *laghman,* pulling them across his chest like an edible accordion and slapping them rhythmically off the table in a cloud of flour. I wondered where they both were now.

The grey sky and slush on the ground did little for Osh's general aesthetic mid-winter, but the real change was in the stark, ugly burnt out shells of so many buildings. Broken glass and twisted metal gave ample evidence of the destruction and showed no indication of any attempt at repair or clearance. It was as if it had happened eight days ago, not eight months.

Walking around, Uzbeks, whose womenfolk were easy to identify from their colourful garb*, were conspicuous by their absence. Instead I noticed not a few young Kyrgyz men in traditional *Kalpaks.* There were also many vehicles sporting bumper stickers with the Kyrgyz flag on. Some even had mini flags flying from their bonnets. These were affirmations of Kyrgyz ethnic identity, and clear signs of nationalistic sentiment. Dozens of ethnicities live in Osh, but only the Kyrgyz - with the exception of the occasional Slavic face or South Asian medical student – seemed to be visible on the street that day.

I could see scant evidence of the "Many America, English, Turkey people in Osh... Many foreigners for humanitarian agencies there" that the 'Drunk' had talked about. So I went to the one place I

---

* Uzbek men, like men worldwide have adopted the rather drab uniform of the West.

thought I might find them, or any other foreigners in town, a foreign-owned Café with an English vegetarian menu clearly aimed at expats and tourists. It seemed to have escaped destruction despite its obvious foreign affiliations.

It was a good guess, two women wearing large jackets emblazoned with UNHCR left just as I arrived. Inside there was a table of three Americans and one European, also aid workers/NGO personnel of some description. They were all middle aged women, loud and large, stocking up on pizza and coke. I sat close by, hoping to eavesdrop on the Osh situation. Unfortunately their chat revolved around the internal politics of their organisation and their own careers. The European kept referring to "My time in the Congo" managing to use it as a point of reference or comparison in nearly every sentence. I learned nothing about Osh, but quite a lot about the Congo. Well, actually nothing about the Congo itself, just the sort of food and perks an NGO worker or whatever they were could enjoy as part of an organisation based there.

That was the only human side of the aid effort I saw during my time in Osh; apart from the occasional shiny white UN 4x4 driving through town, and the steel doors daubed with the nationalities of various donors dotted about the place: "UN DENMARK"; "A GIFT FROM THE PEOPLE OF JAPAN."

As I walked along the street, snow which had collected in the troughs of corrugated roofs fell with loud slaps onto the pavement three storeys below. Still, Osh was much warmer than in Bishkek, and comfortable to stroll around. Overlooking Osh is the large rocky outcrop of *Suleiman-Too* or Solomon's Throne. Barren and jagged, it stands alone, a central landmark around which the town orbits. It is named after the Muslim prophet Suleiman who once prayed there. Before the 16th Century it was known as *Bara-Kuh* or 'Beautiful Mountain.' Indeed, it has a certain raw aesthetic, but I had difficulty finding the angle from which locals say it resembles a reclining pregnant woman. Whether this apparent likeness was what first caused women to come here with the hope of boosting their fertility, or if people only started seeing this shape after such powers were already attributed to the mountain, is hard to say. Either way, today hopeful mother's still journey here for this reason. Other people come on more spiritual quests, as pilgrims. As the site at which Prophet Suleiman prayed (some say he's buried here) and where a young

Babur – future Islamic conqueror of large swathes of Central Asia – spent forty days in meditation on a diet of just bread and water, the mountain has become a very holy place for Muslims. Indeed, it is known as *Kichi-Mecca* 'Little Mecca' and is one of the holiest places in Central Asia. Yet one would be unlikely to guess this was the case climbing the steep staircase that claws its way up the mountain side. Whatever its religious and historical credentials, Sulieman-Too remains pretty understated despite some lacklustre Soviet attempts at development.

From the summit I looked down on a vast mosaic of white tiles; the snow covered roofs of the city extending into the distance. 10kms to the north-west lay the Uzbek border. A couple of hundred kilometres to the south was Tajikistan, and approximately the same distance south-east led to China. Above me, at Osh's highest point, flew the Kyrgyz flag, its red background and golden sun so prominent among the mute greys of winter. A strong, and perhaps necessary claim to Kyrgyz nationhood in a city with a population, at least until the violence, which is 40% Uzbek (a source from 2004 put the population as "predominantly Uzbek"[3]) and that is located in the Fergana Valley, most of which lies inside the territory of Uzbekistan.

Despite the artificial borders of Soviet nation-making, it is also true that more than a thousand years ago Osh was still a town on the Turkic frontier separating the settled Persian world from that of the nomadic Turks. We know from Arab sources that Osh at this time had three gates; the 'Mountain gate', 'River Gate', and 'Mughkada Gate.' The latter was 'The Gate of the Fire-Temple' and a clear reference to the pre-Islamic beliefs of the region, something still echoed in the flaming sun that fluttered on the flag above me. The town also had a large *Rabat,* a fort or guardhouse, on top of the hill now called Sulieman-Too. This *Rabat* was filled with 'Warriors of the Faith' who 'kept watch on the preparations of the inhabitants for a Holy War.'[4] The text of Ibn Hawqal infers that these were Turkic soldiers watching over the Persian populace, although the famous historian of Central Asia, Barthold, dismissed this. Either way, we are presented with a picture of Osh as long being on the fault line of two ethnic/cultural complexes and not necessarily something specifically created by Soviet policy and the later emergence of independent nation states.

The bloody expansion of communism in Central Asia might be paralleled with Islam's arrival in the region or the nomadic hordes that periodically exploded from the 'workshop of peoples' to the east. Nomadic life, Islamic and communist ideals can also all be said to have shared a certain egalitarianism. For the nomads this was the reality of life on the steppe, for Islam it is enshrined in the notion of the *Umma,* and for communism it was the Marxist vision of a proletariat utopia. Yet, it was the nomadic way of life, free from institutionalised dogma or social stratification resulting from land ownership, which came closest to this ideal. However, class and material wealth still existed in nomadic society. For example, the Kyrgyz epic *Manas* concerns only the princes and aristocracy. The lower classes take no part in the fighting and at games we hear that 'the lower classes must stand back, only the princes may take their places.'[5] The Kyrgyz tribes were ruled by elders called *manaps,* and although originally elected, these positions later became hereditary. However, when the Bolsheviks brought their Revolution to Central Asia they found none of the class distinctions or resentment familiar to them from European Russia. This was true even in settled Central Asia. Thus, the first task of the Soviet authorities was to manufacture among the 'have-nots' a previously non-existent hatred for the 'haves.'[6] But somewhat absurdly, before this could be done the Russians had to try and remedy the already present genuine hatred that the peoples of Central Asia had for the Russians, who had stolen their lands. This, the Russians failed to achieve, and the nomads resisted bitterly, preferring to slaughter their animals rather than hand them over. Many fled to China, and they endured great suffering in which many died.

Behind the flag, also on the mountain's promontory of *Suleiman-Too*, is 'Babur's House.' This small shrine is the site of the shelter built by Babur towards the end of the Fifteenth Century; the fourteen year old having just been crowned king of the Fergana Valley. Babur, his name derived from the Persian 'babr' which means 'Tiger', went on to campaign widely in Central Asia and founded the Mogul Empire in Northern India. Curiously, the current 'Dom Babur'(Barbur's House) had only been in existence since Kyrgyz independence, the previous structure having been destroyed by an inexplicable explosion in 1961. It's widely believed that this was a deliberate Soviet ploy as part of their ideological campaign against superstition. Even that 'Dom Babur' was only a reconstruction of the one destroyed by an earthquake in 1853. However, the mysterious and unintelligible chanting of a man knelt in the entrance evoked a timelessness that seemed to transcend the age of the current structure.

Some have argued that the communist regime's efforts to undermine religious practice and 'superstition' reveals an ideological continuity with what came before, rather than the radical departure from the 'old ways' it is often presented as being. Stalin has been called 'the last of the steppe politicians' and Lenin's interpretation of Marxist theory has been described as 'nomadic thinking.' Examples of such 'thinking' being the claims to total power once displayed by the great Khans; the quasi-military organisation and discipline; the emphasis on equality, and the dominating role of the community over the individual. Such an ideology required total devotion to its autocratic power structure. Religion was viewed as a force that could potentially undermine the communist agenda. Even during Tsarist times, religion, in the tradition of Byzantium and Eastern Orthodoxy was subservient to the total power of the state ruler.

However, despite these similarities, religions of the 'Silk Road' were - far from being suppressed - frequently accepted and syncretised with existing nomadic beliefs. The Mongols, for example, had representatives of every religion - Christianity, Islam, Buddhism, Taoism, - pray for them. Religion across Central Asia was linked to practical considerations like trade, something probably illustrated by the fact that the Mongols in the East adopted Buddhism and those in the West, Islam. Likewise, skilled persons, whatever their race or religion, were spared from the Mongol onslaught because they were useful. For the Kazakhs and the Kyrgyz, far away from urban religious centres, it seems faiths introduced to the region were felt lightly. When a Russian ethnographer asked Kazakhs in the early part of the 19th Century 'what religion are you?' the general response was apparently 'we don't know.'[7]

The communist 'plot to kill God' actually has far more in common with other modern political doctrines like Fascism and even Western Secularism than it does with Asiatic nomadism. The world view of the nomads saw man as part of nature, and the shamanic tradition on which all other faiths came to be layered was fundamentally the worship of nature. By contrast, Marxism, like Western liberalism, the aegis of which we now live under, are

Enlightenment ideologies which make the mistake of putting man above nature, with a primacy on technological and economic development at the expense of the natural world.

On Sulieman-Too evidence of the pre-communist, pre-Islamic religion also shared the summit with Babur's House. Nearby, there is a smooth slab of rock which had been brought to a shine by the sliding bodies of those who believe it has curative properties. Perhaps unsurprisingly, on that chilly morning no one appeared to feel the need to heal themselves. I walked down the southern staircase, looking out over the Muslim cemetery that scaled the hillside in a flurry of headstones. A small cave next to the path held a modest pile of money left by someone eager to invoke the fertility of the sacred mountain. This was an echo of the shamanic tradition invoking the powers of nature. The Mongol Buriat also used such grottos and caves as shrines to female fertility. They called them *umai* or *eke umai* (womb, mother's womb). However, just as the Islamic shrine of Babur was perceived as a threat by the communists, the Buriat shamanic shrines to fertility spirits in the natural world were seen as a threat to the Manchu Buddhist State in Mongolia. However, rather than blow them up in communist fashion, the Buddhist lamas attempted to suppress the power of the female spirits with the unusual tactic of putting carved wooden penises pointing into the cave entrance.

I continued my tour of Osh through the melting slush, through an empty park and past the dry fountain that had been a place of such colourful congregation two summers before. Fairground rides lay empty and forlorn. Stone busts of important figures stared indifferently. The Yak 40 was still there, in that great Soviet tradition of using large vehicles (usually military) to decorate towns and to subtly highlight the regime's mechanical might. Those days were long gone, but the Yak remained, having taken on a very different symbolism from what was originally intended; now a rusting antique of obsolete aviation technology, relic of a faded superpower. Crossing the rubbish strewn Ak-Buura (White Camel) River which bisects Osh, I found the grimmest sight to be the bazaar. Instead of the vibrant bustle I remembered, it was a shadow of its former self. What people and goods there were could not alleviate the oppression of the bazaar's chilling new backdrop; rows of burnt out buildings, charred walls, and twisted metal.

I returned to the hotel saddened that Osh has lost its spark. I wondered how much was just winter gloom contrasting with the summer nostalgia in my mind. But of course, something had also fundamentally changed under the shadow of 2010's violent upheaval. In the lounge sat three floor ladies or *dezhurnaya*. They didn't return my smile and eyed me warily. *Dezhurnaya* are there to maintain their respective floor, hand out keys and clean rooms. Every time I left the hotel they demanded 'Klooch' (key) assuming I was leaving for good – which seemed strange as I carried no baggage. Other than that, I mostly observed them sitting around drinking tea, clucking in conversation, and having the TV on permanently at a volume that must have permeated every room in the hotel.

I had stayed in the hotel for several nights in the summer of 2009. It had taken me five relatively tough days to cycle from Bishkek. On the final day, as a storm erupted on the outskirts of the city, I had the good fortune to be accosted by three other cyclists; a New Zealander; an American; and an Irishman (it's not a joke). By bizarre coincidence they had also been teaching English in South Korea, and were then, like me, also cycling across Eurasia. The final destination in their case being Ireland, something they aimed to do in just six months. Whereas I had spent the previous nine months leisurely cycling through the Philippines, Borneo, Mainland South East Asia, and China, they had come straight across China, having left Korea a mere three months earlier. However, our directions of travel had now conjoined - there are not too many routes through Central Asia and travellers tend to become bottle-necked. We all aimed to cross into Uzbekistan shortly and agreed we might as well go together. The speedy trio had first to fly back to Bishkek to collect their Uzbek visas and then fly back to Osh again – a carefully calculated time vs. money equation that meant they could still cover distance whilst negotiating the dreaded Central Asian visa chase. I was impressed by their efficiency.

They were eager that I stayed and looked after their things for the three days they would be absent. I assured them this would be my pleasure, time I envisioned being well spent sleeping and eating. The day of my arrival in Osh I had cycled 194km, so felt due a rest. I also had some chores to attend to, and to develop and send some photos to a Kyrgyz family that had put me up along the way when I was unable to find a place to camp. It was whilst I was at the post office, trying to send some of these photos, and struggling to make myself understood, that I met Janyl. With her fluent English and Russian she willingly acted as translator to make sure the letter went where I wanted. When I asked her how long it would take to arrive (this was to a village less than 300kms away) I was staggered when she replied "Maybe two weeks." Evidently the Kyrgyz postal system was not the fastest. However, in fairness, everything I've ever sent from Kyrgyzstan to the UK and vice-versa has always arrived.

At that time Janyl was twenty four years old, two years younger than me. She is an ethnic Kazakh but has lived her whole life in Kyrgyzstan, for the most part in a small town not far from Jalalabat. She is an ecologist by profession and worked, as she still does, in a science institute. I remember as we people-watched in the park, her telling me that the Uzbeks and Kyrgyz "They hate each other!" It was a comment I hadn't paid much attention to at the time, but the authenticity of which was to be grimly demonstrated less than a year later.

When my cycling friends returned from Bishkek I said goodbye to Janyl, not expecting to see or hear from her again. In the following five months I cycled over 9000kms and passed through another eleven countries. Kyrgyzstan became a distant memory. Thus, in the rather depressing dark of a British December, and the midst of a poor re-adjustment to a settled life that had never suited me anyway, it was a pleasant surprise to receive an email from Janyl.

We had kept up a casual correspondence over the next half year until the summer of 2010 when Osh hit the headlines. For four days and nights Janyl was trapped in a flat with her Uzbek friend, whilst outside Osh descended into anarchy. I emailed Janyl for her number and received a reply filled with anguish – of gunshots, screams, and bodies in the street. Even several days after the worst of it she wrote how: "We can't go outside, because it's a little bit dangerous yet. Kyrgyz people are so aggressive. They unsparing no children, neither women. We are very frightened." To venture outside would have been potentially lethal, particularly for her Uzbek friend.

All I could really do was phone each evening and check that they were okay. It was incredibly frustrating to see something horrible unfolding on the news in a far off land, realise you actually know someone in the middle of it, and that you are powerless to help them.

Speaking to her on the phone, the contrast in our situations was absurd. I was sat on the stairs in my safe, comfortable house after work, the TV chattering inanely in the background, whilst Janyl was trapped in fear of her life, with no food, and could only rely on the news and phone calls from friends for updates on the chaos taking place around outside. All I could do was offer platitudes of reassurance. Only when the worst of the violence seemed to have subsided could Janyl risk going out to get some supplies. "Now we have some bread and some jam and some tea" she reported cheerfully after the successful first sortie.

We spoke and wrote to each other often after that as things in Osh returned to something resembling normal. However, most of her Uzbek friends left the city, and she became increasingly worried about her father who was very sick. He had been for an operation but the doctor's diagnosis had been that it was too late. Her parents were pensioners and still lived in the village where she grew up. Her sisters now lived in Kazakhstan. She had told me about a man in her village who made potions that healed the sick. He had apparently healed himself from a fatal disease in such a home-made manner. She said her father was now taking this potion and beginning to feel better. She said she hoped it would work. She had asked "Do you have people who make such potions in England?" I struggled to give an answer; how to sensitively explain the wonder of free healthcare for all, or the standard Western view of men in mountain villages who made 'potions', or perhaps the closest comparable thing being the exhaustive range of alternative therapies in the UK. In the end I could only reply "No, we don't."

As the months passed, her father's condition didn't improve in spite of the 'potions.' Janyl began talking about a 'healer' from Talas, a Kyrgyz city close to Kazakhstan, famed for his ability to heal the sick. Her father had taken a turn for the worse, and the situation was critical. The last I had heard from her before I arrived in Kyrgyzstan, this healer had come to Osh and Janyl was taking him to her father.

My chance encounter with Janyl and our subsequent correspondence had opened my eyes to a different world; life experiences that seemed to have one foot in an all pervasive global system of mobile phones, English language, and western clothing, and the other foot still firmly planted in a traditional culture, which was itself tangled in the snare of the old Soviet set-up. It intrigued me greatly. There is plenty written about the Silk Road in general, but very little about Kyrgyzstan in particular, and almost nothing about how people live there today.

When I phoned Janyl from Bishkek and asked how she was, her voice broke for a moment as she confided "My father, he is dead." I had intended a surprise visit, but having heard this terrible news, the last thing I wanted to do was intrude. However, when Janyl learned I was back in Kyrgyzstan, she insisted I came to Osh and that we should meet.

We met at the place where we had said goodbye after my brief three day break from cycling in the summer of 2009. Petite with brown hair, light skin and large brown eyes, she did not look particularly Kyrgyz or Kazakh. She told me how people often mistook her for Tartar. I had always assumed Tartar people looked more Mongolian, equating them with the Asiatic warrior horde that printed the name so negatively on the West's collective consciousness. The very name Tartar stems from the Greek word for Hell *Tartarus,* giving some idea of the impression they left on my European ancestors. However, today that 'Tartar horde' is disseminated across Eurasia, from China to the Crimea, some of which have been left looking rather more Russian than Asian.

When Janyl was young in her home village she told me how the boys at school had taunted her as "The little Russian girl" and thrown stones at her. This had left her with a lasting dislike of little boys, which she commented on whenever we passed some.

We walked to a café and ate samsa; cutting away the hard pastry base with which they had been stuck to the oven walls. This turned the samsa's into a kind of ready-made pastry bowl, filled with piping hot meat, onion and potato.

Considering we had previously actually only spent about two afternoons in each other's company, we fell into conversation as if we had been friends for years and our last meeting was just the day before. We had spoken regularly by phone since 'the war' (as Janyl called it) and a firm friendship had developed. Whilst our relationship had always been in that context, I would be lying if I said I wasn't attracted to Janyl. However, the fact that we were generally thousands of miles apart had left no room for entertaining anything else.

Janyl told me how she had brought the healer from Talas to see her father. He had prescribed some medicine and assured her father and family that he would surely live. Of course, they were all delighted by this news, her father's condition improved, and everything seemed like it would be okay. Then one morning, after Janyl had returned to Osh, her mother phoned and asked her to come home again, where upon she gave her the dreadful news that her father was gone. "Maybe the medicine was too strong" she lamented. "Maybe" I agreed, wondering what kind of medicine the healer used and what his success rate with such concoctions was. Were those successes merely a matter of the placebo effect or was there something more to it. Kyrgyzstan is famed for its medical herbs and they are sold all over the former Soviet Union. Incredibly, the small country is home to nearly one percent of all the species on earth, yet it constitutes just 0.13% of the world's land mass. Such statistics seem hard to equate with the bare hills and rugged mountains one sees, yet clearly they represent some kind of Alpine Amazon in terms of biodiversity. In a land where till this day large tracts of the mountains remain unexplored and peaks unclimbed, it was hard not to ponder what secrets this secluded state might hold. However, I felt such inquiries must wait until another time.

Janyl invited me to come and stay with her and her mother in their village. Initially, I was reluctant to accept the offer. This was in part because I was uncomfortable about imposing myself after their recent loss, but also because I was guilty about having people much less well off, economically speaking, than myself, housing and feeding me at their expense. It would be nice to be able to accept these offers and follow up by saying, 'and next week you can come to my village and stay with my family.' Yet, unless airfares drop considerably this seems unlikely. Admittedly, with Janyl things were slightly different. Unlike most of the people who had invited me to stay in their homes in Central Asia, she was more than a mere acquaintance providing a place for a weary traveller/cyclist to lay his head.

Still, when I asked Janyl if she really thought it was okay for me to come and stay at her mother's house she just brushed the question aside, assuring me it was fine and that a guest would be a welcome distraction for her mother. Seeing that she was sure about this I gratefully accepted the offer.

However, before I went anywhere I needed to know I would be able to get to China. I had caught a sleeper-bus from Kashgar to Osh in 2007 on my attempt to travel overland from India to the UK. Most of the Kyrgyz section of the journey had been at night. The discomfort of the washer-board road surface was pleasingly alleviated by a stash of valium that had travelled with me overland from Nepal, through India, Pakistan and Xinjiang province. My only notable recollection being when the bus was stopped to allow a platoon of young Kyrgyz soldiers on board. This was for no reason more ominous than to hitch a lift, although highlighting the wants of the Kyrgyz army's logistics corp.

Everything I had read in guides and on the internet suggested that this bus and its return service was still operating. However, Janyl and I both agreed we should make sure I could get a ticket. We caught a *mashutka* to the edge of town to the long distance bus station. I had my money to pay the *mashutka* driver as I got on board, but Janyl told me how in Osh you paid at the end of the journey rather than at the beginning in Bishkek; one of the more trivial differences between north and south. She explained how she had made the same mistake in Bishkek, getting on a *mashutka* and taking a seat without paying, only to be shouted at by the driver "Hey girl, you must pay!"

The *mashutka* rattled through the suburbs of Osh. I noticed the extent of the destruction as we passed more and more burnt out buildings. At one stop four women got on the *mashutka*. They wore the brightly patterned attire and headscarves of Uzbek women, but their faces were different. They were darker and dirtier; their hands stained almost to the point of blackness by an unknown labour, or perhaps they had just never been washed. One of the women could not have been more than four feet tall. She spoke in a squeak and clasped a live chicken in each hand.

"Where are they from?" I whispered. "Maybe Uzbekistan" was Janyl's hushed reply, grinning at these unusual characters, before she followed with the somewhat contradictory observation "But they don't speak Uzbek."

I had become familiar with people who looked like this since I first visited Central Asia. Usually I saw them begging with babe in arms. I had never seen a man in association with them. The thing I found fascinating was that no one I asked seemed to know who they were or where they came from. Whenever I asked locals they pleaded ignorance or suggested "they are Uzbek" or "they are Armenian", and even "they are Indian." It seemed no-one was very clear who they were and that no-one wanted to take responsibility for them; explaining them away with virtually every nationality between India and Azerbaijan. Someone in Bishkek told me "They can work, they just choose not to. I don't know why." The same person also said that they lived in nice houses elsewhere in the city [Bishkek], and that in fact "they are rich." I equated them with gypsy folk and assumed them to be stragglers on the long migration of Romany people from India to Europe. This certainly would help explain their dark complexion and unconventional lifestyle on the fringe of society. However, it became sort of a quest to source some information about their origins. Eventually, in a long out of print book I had to have sent from Canada of all places, I found what I was looking for. These gypsies, although so obscure to the people they live amongst, call themselves *Mughat* which is Arabic plural from Tajik *mug* meaning 'fire worshipper' clearly showing pre-Islamic Zoroastrian roots. This name is also often qualified with a place name indicating the gypsies' location, like *Mughat Samarkand* meaning 'gypsies of Samarkand.' This presumably meant I was encountering *Mughat Bishkek* and *Mughat Osh*. The Uzbeks call these people *Luli* and the Russian's call them *Sredneaziatskije tsygany* (Central Asian gypsy).

Their early history is unknown but they claim they were already in Central Asia by the time of Tamerlane (14th Century). It is indeed thought that they originally came from India, although they have lost the ethnonym *Rom* of the Romany, as well as their own language. Now they generally speak Tajik or Uzbek, intermingled with their own lingo (*lavsi mughat*) which is incomprehensible to outsiders. That explained why Janyl could not understand them. This 'jargon' has been described as being like the medieval beggars' cant, although it reminded me more of the gypsies who live on the fringes of my town in the UK; a society within a society, with different rules and a different language closed to outsiders. The mutual distrust yet interdependence of nomad and settled person in historical Central Asia is still strangely alive in the mix of animosity and reliance of gypsies or 'travellers' on *gorgies* (people who live in houses) in modern Britain. *Gorgies* use the travellers for informal, cheap labour, like cutting down trees and paving driveways, yet at that same time fear them because of stereotypes of violence and dishonesty. Due to this proximity and interaction some of their words became common parlance among local youth even if we did not know what they meant. One such word was *mughady,* and now I wonder if I was actually hearing the linguistic echo of *Mughat* that had travelled with these people from India. Indeed, their origins were just as mysterious to the British who labelled them 'gypsies' because it was thought they came from Egypt.

The *Mughat* of Central Asia are now settled. Their chief occupations remain fortune-telling, begging, tinkering, singing and dancing. However, there is one group of Central Asian gypsies, the *Mazang,* who keep apart from the others, do not intermarry with them, and even follow a specific trade, that of woodworking.

The *mashutka* dropped Janyl and I off in what is best described as an urban wasteland. There was just an expanse of tarmac littered with random lumps of concrete, and succumbing to a subterranean attack of weeds. However, I could identify the large grey shell of a building as the bus station from where I caught the bus to Kashgar four years previously. There was no ticket vendor, kiosks, timetables of buses. It was simply a collection point and just as I remembered it, except for the unfortunate addition that it was singed black with smoke damage and had evidently been ablaze. There was no-one about except for a small group of people huddled in a corner guarding large bags of potatoes. The women nattered and the men smoked.

Whilst my level of Russian was sufficient for the task, it was far simpler to let Janyl ask them about the bus to China. Looking at the state of the building I could already guess at the outcome. After a brief conversation she turned to me and said "The bus to China doesn't run anymore. It hasn't since the war." The people advised us to try the "Peking Hotel" so we started the long walk back to the town centre.

The houses were all one storey, with dirty-white or pastel plaster walls, topped by tin roofs. Occasionally I noticed a house with finely carved eves, a taste of traditional craftsmanship, in an otherwise rather drab looking sprawl. Of course, it is the inside of Central Asian houses where the efforts are lavished, the exterior usually a bland façade. I noticed the few people in the streets were Uzbek. In confirmation of my thought Janyl informed me "This is an Uzbek area." Intrigued by the implications of this I asked "Would Kyrgyz people be scared to come here?" But Janyl replied with an all too obvious point "Why would they come here?" she said it in a tone that suggested mine was a stupid question. Not having lived in a society with such acute segregation, this hadn't occurred to me. She added "Maybe at night they would be scared to come here."

I considered that if there was no bus direct to China, I could hitch from the closest possible settlement on the Kyrgyz side of the border. We decided to call at the 'local bus (i.e. *mashutaka*) station' in town. Crossing back across the Ak-Buura, the bridge was lined with DVD sellers, displaying the latest movies from Russia, Hollywood, and, oddly enough, Korea. A beggar with her face covered sung a mournful melody as we passed, one hand held out, the other clutching a crumpled one Som note. For a woman to cover her head and face entirely is extremely rare in post-Soviet Central Asia. Not even her eyes were visible, just a fine grill of fabric permitted sight. It reminded me of what I had seen a minority of Uyghur women wearing in Kashgar, again, as beggars. It seemed to be far more linked with the desire not to be seen whilst begging rather than with any inherently religious or cultural obligations. By contrast, when I was in the Pashtun tribal areas on the Pakistan/Afghan border, such head gear had been ubiquitous for females and was an absolute social requirement when out of doors.

Behind her a disorderly mass of mainly German cars constituted the taxi-rank; drivers shouted their destinations to passersby: "JALALABAT! JALALABAT!" "BISHKEK! BISHKEK!" The central bus station was a faded building, bustling with people. A row of battered *mashutkas* waited under wooden signs swinging along the length of the tin roof. Each sign was for a destination. I scanned along them, searching for somewhere as far in the south east as I could find, hopefully Sary-Tash. However, I could see nothing. *Babushkas* barged past me overloaded with bags. Hollow-cheeked men touted the destinations of their rusty rides. A man grabbed me, speaking a torrent of Russian; the only word of which I could take in was "Jalalabat." I told him "Nyet" anyway, and he disappeared. Janyl was laughing and told me "He thought you were the driver for Jalalabat, they can't find him." There were no buses to Sary-Tash. A woman told us of a destination vaguely in that direction, but then said it was not possible to get another *mashutka* from there. So it appeared public transport was out of the question.

We went on to Hotel Peking as recommended, but they could only give us taxi numbers. A quick phone call revealed they wanted

$160 to the border. Fine if I could find another three people to split the cost with, but that seemed unlikely. More importantly, I discovered that it was Chinese New Year and that the border was closed for another week. It's something I should have thought about, but would still never have expected it to mean the Chinese closed their borders.

I had one more lead to try. At the back of a muddy car park we found taxis heading southeast. A gypsy woman accosted us, waving a saucepan of a burning herb called *isriq*, sending smoke swirling round us. She wanted money for this service intended to ensure good health and protection against the 'evil eye.' However, we blanked her and she hissed at us for our lack of charity. Despite this it seemed my luck was in because drivers were going to Sary-Tash. This is the town where Kyrgyzstan's main road forks, with one branch heading south to Tajikistan and the legendary Pamir Highway, whilst the other branch goes east to China. How I would get from there to the border remained to be seen but at about $12 a seat, I would cross that bridge when I got to it. Hitching on a lorry seemed like it would be the best option.

Janyl asked me how much I paid to get from Bishkek. I told her 1000 Som (about $25) which she said was good, clearly impressed that a foreigner had got the standard price. She told me last time she made the trip there had been a bomb in Bishkek. I was surprised, having heard nothing of it. I asked who was responsible "I don't know" she replied, apparently finding the question a little irrelevant.

Mission accomplished with regard to my onward travel we went to find something to eat.

We talked about many things, but it was not long before the subject of marriage came up. Seeing as I wasn't married already, at the ripe old age of twenty-eight, it was to any Central Asian a matter I should be attending to with some urgency. I told Janyl I didn't know as it wasn't something I was planning for just yet. I liked to move around. "Maybe when you are forty?" She asked. "Maybe" I replied. "Maybe when you are fifty?" she went on, incredulous. I laughed and told her I'd like to fit it in before then. However, at twenty-six, Janyl, according to the preferences of Central Asian cultural norms, was quite old to be unmarried. Traditionally, a woman beyond the age of twenty who was still not married would become known as a *kara daly* (black back), and it was thereafter increasingly difficult for her to find a husband. However, this was from a context where marriages were once arranged when the groom to be was still a teenager, and the girl prepubescent.

Today things are different, particularly in towns and cities. Arranged marriages are less and less common, and the age at which people get married has been steadily creeping upwards. Janyl was in no danger of becoming a *Kara daly* just yet. Youthful, attractive and with many admirers, she could take her pick. She told me of some marriage proposals that had come her way but she had declined. She told me how two women from her home village came to visit her mother one day. They were the mother and another female relative of a boy Janyl knew. They brought Janyl's mother some cloth, as is their tradition and said something akin to "My son, he likes your daughter very much. Will she be his wife?"

Janyl, a little contrary to tradition, refused point blank, not even taking time to think it over, telling them to their faces that she did not even like the boy in question. Unsurprisingly, this made the women very angry and they left. On another occasion, a male friend introduced Janyl to one of his friends "A man who was thirty and still not married!" I raised my eyebrows in mock horror at what was clearly considered a little beyond the pale. However, he blew his chances with Janyl when he assumed the indecent level of familiarity of putting his arm around her when they had only just met. She mentioned more match-makings and proposals, but all of which she had chosen to rebuff. Her current admirer she referred to as 'Russian boy.' I asked if she would marry him. "Maybe" she said, smiling mischievously, and with the qualifying statement "only God knows who I will marry."

There is an image in the West, based largely on ignorance, of women across the Muslim world living as virtual prisoners, eternal victims of their male oppressors. Of course, Kyrgyzstan is not a microcosm of the Muslim world in general, which is multi-faceted and subject to great diversity across different cultures. Islam in Kyrgyzstan is built on the pre-existing culture and belief systems of the Kyrgyz. Also, as mentioned above, Islam was severely repressed under the Soviet yoke. However, Kyrgyzstan remains a society heavily influenced by traditions pre-dating Soviet social engineering, and where the dominant faith is Islam.

However, contrary to popular Western stereotypes this is far from synonymous with an absence of female assertion or 'power.' In fact, Janyl seemed to have as much 'power' as any of us do, man or woman, when it comes to shaping our own destiny. Petite but fiery, she takes no nonsense from anyone. She was living her life as she wanted to as far as her circumstances would allow. Her only limitations were related to the economic realities of life in Kyrgyzstan, not because she was the victim of a rampant gender inequality.

Janyl was working as an ecologist and studying for the equivalent of a Master's Degree. She had chosen to study ecology despite the wishes of her family that she choose English, which they considered to have more potential. Again, when it came to marriage, she was not under any pressure from her family to marry a particular individual or only another Kazakh. She admitted that this was sometimes the case in Kyrgyzstan and Kazakhstan, but said that her parents had always respected her choice in matters of the heart. She was then sharing a flat in Osh with a Kyrgyz girl and had previously lived with an Uzbek friend, whilst her family remained in their village. Thus her life was one of independence, not of restriction, and certainly not one subordinate to men. If anything, listening to the many tales of suitors she had spurned, it seemed that the men in her life were all subordinate to her.

Kyrgyzstan may be a 'patrilineal society' and one that is often described as 'male dominated' - whatever that means - yet what I've witnessed has often been indicative of anything but female subservience. It seems to be the girls who study hard, who master the foreign languages, and who create the opportunities for themselves. If one looks at the oral literature of the Kyrgyz we learn that in the past 'apart from the professional shaman the intellectual life of the steppe is largely feminine.'[8] Indeed, there were female shamans too, *shamanka,* a Russian term used to denote a 'seeress', but also other female skilled 'professionals' among the Turkic nomads.

Soviet influence and its ideological stress on sexual equality had a huge influence on the role of women in Kyrgyzstan. However, women in nomadic society had enjoyed physical freedom and high status long before the Russians arrived, certainly more so than their agrarian settled counterparts. In nomadic times Kyrgyz women were able to divorce their husbands, and upon his death could remain single or marry outside the family, rather than being forced to marry his brother as occurred in some societies.

A Chinese historian who visited Fergana in the First Millennium A.D. commented on the high regard in which women were held and the complementary nature of relations between the sexes. From ancient times we hear of the Scythian Queen Tomyris who defeated the Persians in a battle judged by contemporaries to have been 'more violent than any other fought.' The Greek myth of Amazon warriors seems to be evidenced by the burials of Central Asian women with weapons, and in the 8th Century A.D. we hear of women archers among the Uyghur. In the Kyrgyz epic *Manas* the women are often as heroic and militant as the men. In the poem *Joloi* (Joloi was a member of Manas's comitatus) it is his wife Ak Saikal who repeatedly saves him from his enemies, and in the early episodes is the heroine more than Joloi is the hero.

However, this martial capacity exhibited historically by Kyrgyz women and their forebears should not be likened to the Western project of so-called 'sexual equality' which seeks to make the genders interchangeable in modernism's ultimate hubris which is the denial of sex-difference. The *Manas* epic presents an ideal of Kyrgyz femininity as kind, gentle, hospitable, courteous, capable and wise. They are portrayed as *shamankas,* skilled as cooks and doctors, and women of great honour and culture. In all societies gender roles have been related to a division of labour in accordance with the mode of production. Due to their reproductive capabilities women have generally worked in what has been labelled as the 'domestic sphere', something the modern West in its confused war against nature seems to resent as inferior to its opposed imaginary construct of the 'public sphere.'

However, in Manas the high-born women function in both 'spheres', which are complementary aspects of a single social system. In fact, it was the women in nomadic societies, working from the 'domestic sphere' that produced all the value added products of the nomad herds, like dairy products, textiles and carpets. This vital economic function was undoubtedly conducive to a high status for women of the steppe.

The coming of communism, through brutal policies of collectivisation, crushed this traditional nomadic way of life. The imposed economic system - aimed at extracting the natural resources of Central Asia essentially for the benefit of Russia - meant new gender roles within a new division of labour. Mass education was made universal in Central Asia and thus literacy rates rose from perhaps a couple of percent to being comparable with 'developed' nations of the West. The benefits of this are self evident as they are necessary tools for individual advancement in the economic model which created them. Men and women of a previously nomadic culture could now become scientists, journalists, doctors, and many of the other economic roles which characterise modern society.

However, these education, literacy and judicial reforms were imposed as a package aimed at serving the ends of the colonising power. Through these modern reforms the Soviets wanted to destroy the existing social system which was based on loyalties to the family, clan and tribe. Instead a westernised way of family life was encouraged. The purpose of this was to erode all aspects of traditional culture which stood in the way of the 'Great Russian Dream'; the ethnic fusion of all peoples in the USSR into *Homo Sovieticus*. Such social engineering, with less coercive methods, had already been practised by other colonial powers elsewhere in the world.* In the case of Soviet Central Asia the aim was to direct the labour of Central Asians, male and female, to the Russian project of universal communism. Ironically, and somewhat tragically, the violent imposition of communism's egalitarian ideal created a new class system and social hierarchy far less egalitarian than the nomadic way of life it sought to 'improve.'

The indigenous culture of Central Asia which the Soviets worked so hard to undermine survived in a large part thanks to an oral culture transmitted by women to their children. According to one scholar, this 'formed the backbone of Central Asian religious life throughout the Soviet Period.'[9]

Today, with regards to 'gender equality', the president of Kyrgyzstan at the time of writing was a woman, and opportunities for women in the economy are legally equal to those of men. No doubt

---

*For example, the British colonial administration in Egypt aimed at the Europeanization of the class structure and the Europeanization of the family in order to more efficiently exploit Egyptian labour and maximize production. Starrett, *Putting Islam to Work,* 32-56.

men still hold the majority of high level public positions, but this is just as true for the United States or Denmark.

However, for most men in Kyrgyzstan, often disenfranchised from their pastoralist past, and deprived of employment in the now diminished heavy industry of Soviet times, opportunities are far from favourable. Bride-knapping, alcoholism, even the ethnic violence in Osh, can be attributed to this economic uncertainty and its dislocating effect on the traditional pattern of life. These are not the defects of Kyrgyz culture in need of instruction from benevolent foreign agencies, but rather they are the direct result of foreign intervention which destroyed the traditional order and then failed, leaving a vacuum and fertile soil for a whole range of social ills to say nothing of nationalism and Islamic fundamentalism. This is the end result of a 'modernising' process that has destroyed the balance between people and the Earth, and persons with each other.

In Kyrgyzstan the free market arrived in the wreckage of the Soviet centralised economy which deliberately 'developed' Kyrgyzstan in a way that prevented economic self-sufficiency. The Kyrgyz could however find work in their own country. Today, as a direct result of the centralised economy, many are forced to do menial jobs in Russia, or as we have seen, the Middle East, as migrant labour.

Whilst Kyrgyzstan certainly needs to move forward from this economic situation, there is considerable reason to be sceptical of the benefits of the free market in terms of social stability. Modern free markets turn people into atomised wage labourers at the whim of market forces. The result of this has been social fragmentation and the dissolution of the family; processes most advanced in the 'developed' West.

Unfortunately, even 'development' projects sponsored by foreign powers, no matter how ostensibly altruistic, are always about creating social and economic change in accordance with foreign interests. In a continuation of Soviet policy the 'New Great Game' players use 'development' as a tactic to exploit Central Asia's vast natural resources. The IMF and World Bank are particularly notable for using 'aid', and thus debt, to turn 'less-developed' countries into

America's client states.* Such development is about making the world in America's image to serve America's needs, and those 'needs' are the unsustainable consumption of the world's resources to maintain a culture of over-indulgence for a very small proportion of the world's population (Chinese or other foreign development projects in the region are no less self-interested). The idea that this model can be spread in a way that elevates everyone to the same standard of living (level of consumption) 'enjoyed' by the West is a fiction and would require the resources of another dozen Earths.

---

* American Professor Chalmers Johnson writes that 'Soviet citizens never understood Marxism-Leninism as an ideology until after it collapsed, just as Americans like to think (or pretend) that their economics is a branch of science, not a fighting doctrine to defend and advance their interests against those of others.' Johnson, *Blowback,* 180.

9

A trip to The Valleys

We left the restaurant at 7.30pm. Already the streets were empty. "It's been like this since the war" said Janyl. Clearly no-one wanted to be out after dark. It was eerie. Speaking to people had revealed great animosity and blame between the Uzbeks and the Kyrgyz. I didn't know what to think. How could I? I could only judge things from what I was told, and that all depended on who I spoke too. There were many circulating rumours on who had been responsible and why things had unfolded as they had.

One thing however was certain, and that was that the fuse to this powder keg of ethnic tension had been lit a long time ago. Osh lies in a region with the highest population density in Central Asia, and its resources are in great contention. How these resources are distributed, and inequalities of wealth between various ethnic groups, has been a source of considerable resentment, cementing ethnic divisions and acting as a catalyst for the terrible violence that erupted in Osh in 2010 and in Ozgon a decade previously.

When I had first passed through Osh a young Kyrgyz man told me "Uzbeks are bad people. They look like they are good [presumably a reference to the greater proportion of Uzbek women wearing headscarves as a more visible symbol of Islamic identity] but underneath they are bad." Yet, at the same time I had met Kyrgyz people who lived with Uzbeks and shared none of this bias. Similarly, the same young man thought "the Germans are a cruel people." I asked how many Germans he had met, and he said none. I chuckled at this, and so did he, clearly appreciating the problem it shone on his original comment. Considering the large number of Kyrgyz I had met who spoke German, who went to Germany to work or on scholarships, such a negative stereotype seemed very outdated. Yet in a way, his views were hardly surprising. As I've already mentioned, memorials to the 'Great Patriotic War' are everywhere. It was one of the building blocks of Soviet solidarity and has clearly left a deep imprint. He had told me how in his village when the boys played war they still pretended to fight the Germans. Indeed, just as I had in Britain, and where even today the tabloid press occasionally - tongue in cheek - attempt to rally some patriotic fervour related to our 'finest hour' battling the 'Bosch.' I had that conversation four years previously and wondered if today the Kyrgyz boys in their villages pretended to fight the Uzbeks.

In the internet cafes of Osh, playing first person 'shoot 'em ups', the young lads certainly weren't fighting either. The computer games that absorb the current generation worldwide certainly seem to have moved on from WWII. Now the player fights across a global theatre against the foot-soldiers of global terrorism, with the 'hero' - by default of the manufacturer's affiliations - being Western, and the enemy to be blasted, although not explicitly identified as such, generally set in locations where in the real world the population is Muslim. In Osh this generic narrative had added relevance as the Fergana Valley was home to the terrorist organisation the IMU (Islamic movement of Uzbekistan) and the Islamist group Hizb-ut-Tahrir. Yet, with no apparent conflict of identity, these games are just as popular among the youth of Muslim Central Asia as they are in British suburbia.

Twenty years after independence I wondered how the school syllabus had changed, and if the 'Great Patriotic War' retained the prominence it was no doubt given during Soviet times. I wondered to what degree a growing nationalism would cast local people against their former Russian colonisers. A traveller to Kyrgyzstan just after independence had described how Russians were already finding themselves sidelined from state employment opportunities, like the police, and that there were plans to replace the Russian way of naming people with a Kyrgyz tribal system.[1] Certainly there weren't many Russians left in Osh.

Janyl's school day stories of being bullied as the "Little Russian Girl" (when she's not even Russian) revealed that ethnocentrism, at the root of nationalism, is nothing new here. It was just repressed under the cloaking ideology of a multi-national/multi-ethnic communism where everyone was equal, just with the Russians being a little more equal than everyone else.

Janyl told me how immediately in the wake of the 'war' she had hailed a taxi in the centre of town. After she got in, three Kyrgyz women came over and shouted at her to get out. When she asked 'Why?' one of them threatened her with a bottle (I believe it was plastic) and said "Because you are Uzbek!" I'm not an expert on Central Asian physiology, but Janyl's facial features, pale skin and Western style dress alone was a good indication that she probably wasn't Uzbek. She retorted that she wasn't Uzbek at all, and that she was Kazakh, but it had little effect on her assailers. She was in their eyes after all, still not Kyrgyz. Fortunately, the driver, who was also Kyrgyz was not swayed by ethnic solidarity at the expense of what was fair, and defended Janyl as having been in the taxi before them. It was a minor example of how ethnic tensions, heightened by the 'war', had really galvanised communities along ethnic lines in a 'them and us' mindset.

From Kyrgyz students at Osh University I heard of atrocities against Kyrgyz people committed by Uzbeks, of Uzbek plans for an armed takeover, and of their genuine fear of going into 'Uzbek areas' of the town. These views were held in a context where Kyrgyz and Uzbeks shared the same classrooms, where there were Kyrgyz and Uzbek teachers, where some people were of mixed parentage, and where everyone used the same shops and services. Whenever I witnessed one of the students who had voiced such an opinion interacting with an Uzbek, I would often ask afterwards 'but that Uzbek is okay?' to which I would always get a response that 'yes, some Uzbeks are okay.' The fear was of the Uzbeks elsewhere, in the 'Uzbek areas' 'plotting,' they were the ones responsible. From another Kyrgyz student I even heard it was a Uyghur, to which he was related, who masterminded the 'accident' (as the violence was sometimes euphemistically referred to). Similarly, it was the commonly held opinion that the Kyrgyz who took part in the violence were not from Osh, but outsiders from 'wild places', the mountainous Alay region to the south. When two huge Kyrgyz men, hearing me speak English, asked about work as 'guards' in England, I was advised by the students in attendance 'not to speak to such men.' They too were from the mountains, the 'wild places.' I was reminded of Zarina's comment about the people beyond Naryn as 'a little bit wild' and how 'they might attack, because they think it's their territory.' Clearly an urban-rural divide, like the old nomadic-settled dichotomy remains pervasive regardless of ethnicity. The truth behind any of what I was told is beyond my knowledge or perception. Yet it was evidently what people believe, and it revealed an animosity to a labelled 'other' somewhere else, rarely the Uzbeks or Kyrgyz encountered in daily life.

Janyl, with her ethnically ambiguous appearance, seemed to be somewhat of a chameleon, constantly identified as the 'other'; Tartar, Russian, Uzbek, but never actually Kazakh. In a telephone call she even told me that another taxi driver had been angry with her for speaking Russian. This was because he believed her to be Kyrgyz, and didn't think the Kyrgyz should be speaking Russian anymore. Again, this has been a trend since Independence, but one that has accelerated massively since the 'war.' What these anecdotes highlighted for me was the absurdity and danger of nationalism in such a polyglot, multi-ethnic region.

The fact that Janyl found herself constantly identified with an ethnicity she didn't belong too, made only too clear the ambiguous reality behind nationalist ideology, and the tragedy it could result in. In many ways it seemed to resemble Rwanda, Yugoslavia or Northern Ireland, where apparently quite superficial 'ethnic' differences led to such devastating results. In conflicts like this, where opposing groups live in such close proximity, the spiralling arbitrariness of retaliation is vicious and disturbing. Janyl told me that some days after the 'war' she witnessed a car stop in the street and three young men drag another man off the street kicking and screaming in protest into the back of their car before speeding off. Janyl could only look on in horror and shout for the attackers to leave him be. As I mentioned before, Janyl was not afraid of confrontation, especially if her strong sense of justice had been offended.

The issue of Nationalism is perhaps illustrated most acutely in the Osh region, but it is on the rise throughout Central Asia. Janyl told me how angry she was with her Kazakh brother (cousin) when he expressed disgust at seeing a mixed Kazakh and Russian couple. Yet in all likelihood the Russian in question was probably a Kazakh citizen anyway. However, that she was ethnically Russian meant she was not ethnically Kazakh, giving rise to a whole range of awkward contradictions about what it means to be Kazakh. After all, if she was

Kazakh, did she speak Kazakh? Most ethnically Russian Kazakh citizens do not. However, seeing as it was the Russians who pegged out the borders, Russian Kazakhs no doubt feel a default right to the land they have lived on for generations; just as European Americans and Antipodeans claim the right to the countries and borders they created after displacing the indigenous population. In Kazakhstan the population was not displaced (although collectivised and moved about, it remained in what is still now Kazakhstan).

The Kazakh people have a claim to their land that pre-dates the Russian intervention. Despite being nomads, the Kazakhs, like all nomads, ranged within a set territory. Their movements were not random, and were associated with identification with a certain territory. However, it is only through Russian colonisation that we arrive at the situation where there is now an independent sovereign state of Kazakhstan. Whether a Kazakh state (as opposed to a collection of ethnically homogenous tribes) would have emerged otherwise is unknowable and much debated. Yet, the Kazakh khanate of the 15th Century seems indicative of just such a 'state' based on a Kazakh ethnic identity. Similarly, the 18th Century lamentation 'O my nation' is expressive of a national consciousness well before the Soviet 'nation making' exercise of the 20th century. The Kazakh word for 'nation' *yel,* and emotive attachment to it, is the core of the poem; 'Dirt and dust storm down from the blue heavens, more wicked than the winter of January, [with] its cold days. O my nation, O my nation!'[2]

In a broad historical context, arguments that Russia 'created' or 'invented' Kazakhstan and Kyrgyzstan, must be measured against the influence nomads and nomadic culture had in creating Russia. The formative Russian state was dominated by a warrior elite which subordinated a sedentary underclass of agrarian peasantry; a sociological model common between settled and nomadic peoples of Eurasia. It has been suggested that the warrior elite of Kievan Russia were nomadic. The ruling class of their predecessors in the region, the Khazar Khanate, certainly were. Even the agricultural peasants of these times were partially nomadic, and had to move every few years due to the unproductive nature of the land and their primitive farming technology. In Russia, the economic value of land was not even recognised until the Eighteenth Century. Instead, the nomadic idea dominated, that it was people who were really the valuable property.[3]

In the tradition of a nomadic universalism, all under heaven belonged to the supreme leader, be it the khan or the Tsar. The Mongol conquest of Russia was extremely influential on the political and economic development of the country. Many Russian words relating to administration and finance like *den'gi* (money) or *tamozhyna* (custom house) are actually of Mongolian origin. The Mongol domination of ethnic Russians, like the Russian domination of ethnic Kazaks, merely imposed new organisational forms on an existing ethnic 'nation', with a minimum of cultural mixing between rulers and ruled.

With regard to the Russians left stranded as citizens in the relics of their former empire, it is difficult to make comparisons with other colonial empires. Unlike the former British colonies in South Asia, the Russian Empire was an overland expansion quite in accordance with the tradition of nomadic empires that had swept across the Eurasian steppe for the previous two millennia. Also, acquiring territory in Central Asia meant no significant differences in climate or vegetation from what Russians were used too. In contrast to the British in India or the French in Indo-China, Russian settlers in Central Asia often lived in conditions materially similar to the natives. Moreover, Tartars of the Volga region had been part of Russia since the 16th Century, and the fact that the Mongols had ruled Russia for 250 years, limited the potential for feelings of biological or social superiority that existed between rulers and ruled in other colonial empires.

However, Kazakhstan and Kyrgyzstan - like India, Algeria, or so many others - were only realised as unified nation-states in the modern sense by the process of foreign imperialism. It was British imperialism that unified the sub-continent as a single political entity,[*] and secondly, it brought Indians into contact with the nationalist ideas they would eventually use to win independence. Indeed, 'there was no way to teach a man to read the Bible… which did not also enable him to read the radical press.'[4] Likewise, Pakistan and Bangladesh (formerly West and East Pakistan) would not exist if it were not for the resulting Indian, namely Hindu, nationalist movement. That

---

[*] Of course, at various points in history the Sub-continent has been in part, and on occasion, nearly wholly unified under the aegis of various kingdoms and empires other than the British.

Indian independence was understood and planned for meant that the Britons administering the colonies did not simply wake up one morning to find they were part of a new nation state; the majority of the population with whom they had little in the way of ethnic, cultural, or linguistic affinity (although English remains a lingua-franca in South Asia, in a way comparable to Russian in Central Asia). In other Western colonial possessions, such as Algeria, protracted wars of de-colonisation were fought that often left no more than a tiny remnant of the original colonial population.

However, due to the sudden collapse of the USSR many Russians did awake to find themselves suddenly in a country where they were the ethnic minority. Moreover, there were millions of them, not like the relatively small expat populations that administered and settled in the European colonies. Thus, those Russians who remain in Kazakhstan as Kazakh citizens (or any of the other 'new' nations) face a dilemma of identity, as do the states – named after their dominant ethnic group – that accommodate them. After all, what does it mean to be a Kazakh, a Kyrgyz, Tajik, Turkmen, or Uzbek citizen? And is that the same as being an ethnic Russian citizen of Kazakhstan, an ethnic Kazakh citizen of Kyrgyzstan (like Janyl), or an ethnic Uzbek citizen of Kyrgyzstan. Moreover, this does not even begin to account for the ethnic groups living across Central Asia that either have no state of their own, or have been dislocated from their ethnic homeland for so long that they are not in a position to return even if they wanted to. Take for example, the Korean, Dungan, Uyghur, Tartar, and Karakalpak minorities.

The next day as we had lunch Janyl repeatedly filled my cup only half full. I on the other hand would always fill both our cups to the brim. When I asked her why she only filled the cups half full she told me it was the 'Kazakh way'; by filling them nearer to the brim I was apparently pouring tea in the Russian fashion. So, I thought, a Kazakh who's spent her whole life in Kyrgyzstan is still a Kazakh.

Janyl belongs to Kazakhstan's 'Little Horde', one of the three 'hordes' into which the Kazakhs arranged themselves. Within the 'Little Horde' she belongs to the Ongyt Clan. These clans are each made up from a number of lineages; Janyl's being called the Ongyt Mailibai. Tradition prevents her from marrying anyone from this sub-lineage as they would share the same male ancestor, a situation loosely analogous with our concept of incest, although clearly the degree of blood relation is far less acute.

However, Janyl can still marry someone from the Ongyt clan as long as they do not belong to that particular sub-lineage. Hence, questions of lineage are among the first that any Kazakh or Kyrgyz will ask each other when they first meet. "Maili" means 'butter' and "bai" means 'rich', a definite testament to her people's old pastoralist ways. Janyl has taken the name of her father's tribe. Her mother is also of the Ongyt clan, but of the sub-lineage Ongyt-Kayaka. She also calls her cousins her brothers and sisters.

It had snowed the night before, and we cut a path along fluffy white pavements. We walked up to the Lenin Statue, still proudly pointing the way, even if he had snow on his shoulders and a pigeon on his head. Nearby a raucous Kyrgyz wedding celebration was taking place. The bride wore a white dress in the Western style, and the men similarly so in their dark suits, clutching bottles of beer. After their photo shoot close to the Lenin Statue, the wedding party drove down the wide avenue in a convoy of cars, luxury 4x4s, and even a Hummer (hired for the occasion).

We walked around the town. We went to a small art gallery, a boutique of local work that would be at home in any Western city. Similarly, there was a clothes shop that looked like it belonged in a European shopping centre, all white tiles and mirrors, with tight t-shirts by the rack load. Apparently it was a Turkish owned business. Whilst these signs of development were refreshing oases in the sea of communism's concrete uniformity, I could not help but resent their familiar façade.

Fortunately, as we passed the shop a gypsy – quite the anti-thesis of global uniformity – brought me crashing back to Central Asian reality with a healthy dose of herb smoke from her saucepan. In hindsight I wish I had given her some money in recognition of her unusual profession that seemed an echo from more enchanted times. However misplaced my romantic view of the past might be, I was pleased to have it indulged by a story that showed such superstitious thinking is far from forgotten in Central Asia. Janyl told me about a respected old gypsy woman who lived in her home village. People went to this gypsy to have their fortunes told or to have problems solved by methods other than those you or I would be likely to consider. This gypsy had told Janyl that she had a double.

Admittedly, the idea of a double, as in a body and a soul is quite common in human belief. The ancient Egyptians even thought a person was made up of five living elements; the body, a spirit called the *ka*, a *Ba* which lived in the tomb when the body died, the name, and the shadow. However, Janyl was talking about an exact physical replica of herself walking around somewhere else. According to the gypsy Janyl's double lived in Europe and - I particularly liked the accuracy of this – had a degree in environmental management. That a gypsy woman living in the hills of Kyrgyzstan knew about degrees in environmental management seemed very much to lend credence to her abilities in my opinion. Janyl's double was also apparently a little bit taller than she was. Janyl then asked me if I believed this. After thinking it over for about half a second I had to say "No." Janyl insisted that the gypsy in question was a very old and wise lady, but I couldn't be persuaded to change my mind. I had suspected Janyl was just having fun seeing what fantastical yarn she could spin a gullible foreigner. However, it's a yarn she's sticking to.

At the weekend I went to meet Janyl in her hometown in the hills north east of Jalalabat. I received a hearty 'goodbye' from the hotel receptionists and assured them they would see me again. On the way to the bus station I even managed to procure some notebooks with lined pages rather than squares. The stall owner who didn't have enough money in small denominations gave me a roll of sticky-tape as change. I wondered if I could use it to buy my fare on the *mashutka*. Even my Som was sometimes studied with reservation. This was because the Kyrgyz mint had recently printed a new issue of bank notes, presumably to erase any reference to the former government that might be found on the old money. However, at this time the new notes had yet to really filter down to southern Kyrgyzstan and so were regarded in every exchange with the greatest curiosity. However, their crispness and colour was always appreciated, the older Kyrgyz money often being of the appearance that it had been in circulation for several centuries. I was frequently to find that the wad of one Som notes which tended to collect at the bottom of my pocket, upon removal, had turned into an amorphous brown blob beyond separation into its single components. In the traditional nomadic economy money was of little use, and more a source of danger to its possessor than anything else. For nomads, their wealth was in their herds. Russian Roubles and Indian Annas were used as ornaments and jewellery by the nomadic peoples, notably the Kyrgyz, Turkmen and Mongols. Conversely, it was unworked metals and lumps of turquoise that were used as currency in Eastern Central Asia. Russia also had a poorly developed money economy for much of its history, with money being used mainly by the state to pay foreign specialist and soldiers. In Kievan Russia a barter economy persisted with currency largely constituted of squirrel and martin furs, and pieces of cloth. In the same period, living at the other end of Eurasia, Kyrgyz wealth came from supplying furs, musk and lumber to the Silk Road trade.

In order to reach Janyl's hometown I first had to catch a *mashutka* to Jalalabat. On the outskirts of Osh there were roadblocks manned by armed police, a clear sign of the troubled times. However, more alarming to me was the new development of red tiled, yellow brick houses, laid out in the archetypal style of Western suburbia. I had seen the same thing happening across the world. Cycling across Eurasia, from huts and houses, farms and villages, I was greeted almost unanimously by friendly, curious people. Yet, with these new developments, from China to Eastern Turkey, there was always a change in the attitudes of the people who lived there. As a wall went up around their houses, a wall went up in their minds. Suburbia is the architecture of anomie. By the time I got to Western Europe friendliness from strangers was an alien concept. They just peered at me with suspicion; protective of all the accumulated junk they had given their lives to collecting. Indeed, in the most bourgeois countries like Austria, outside the cities I almost stopped seeing people altogether. Yet all the houses and lawns were immaculate; little show homes for atomised lives based on artificial appearance rather than real interaction. It makes your blood run cold. Moreover, it's a way of living that's completely unsustainable. In Britain we have already run out of space, and the houses they build keep getting more expensive and of poorer quality. Whatever its material advantages for the few, it's an ideal that will cost us the Earth, literally. The houses were unfinished and empty. I wondered how long in the current economic and political climate it would take for them to be complete and occupied. And who would live there? The classic geographical model of people flocking to the cities, and then, as they become more affluent moving back out to plush suburban pads, still seemed hard to envisage in Kyrgyzstan.

Janyl met me at the bus station in Jalalabat. She was surprisingly punctual. 'Time' as a concept is not really adhered to with any great precision in Central Asia. Indeed, I've found this to varying degrees across much of the world, where time is a loose framework rather than a rigid rule.

Apart from my midnight tour on the journey from Bishkek, this was the first time I'd actually seen Jalalabat. I was shocked by the number of burnt out buildings. I had no idea there had been such extensive disturbances outside of Osh. Janyl pointed out what she called the "Uzbek University" which was now just a burnt out shell with its windows smashed in. She called it the "Uzbek University" apparently only because its director had been Uzbek. Allegedly he had made some remarks about Osh and Jalalabat being part of Uzbekistan. As you might expect these remarks did not go down too well, and according to Janyl, were the reason the university suffered such a fate.

However, I had to wonder how instrumental these words, if even spoken, were. How much of this destruction was really politically or ethnically motivated, and how much of it just represented an unleashing of frustrations caused by many factors. Core issues aside, how much of it was just fuelled by the boredom of disillusioned young men, who are always the key demographic in such events. In Northern Ireland, riots were often started by local youth more as a form of entertainment rather than as a political statement. When I returned from my travels there was outrage over the spontaneous and widespread riots that broke out in the UK, with apparently no higher ideal driving them other than an anarchic desire to destroy and plunder. Obviously the death toll in the Kyrgyz events reveals their far more serious nature, but the mechanics of the mob mentality that sustained them was probably largely the same. I wondered how many of the participants in the violence really needed a reason, and how many were just looking for an excuse – the 'other' being a convenient scapegoat for all life's woes.

With the exception of the burnt out buildings I'm afraid Jalalabat left very little else imprinted on my memory. We went to a café for tea and watched as men came in and bought sealed plastic cups of vodka that could be drunk in one and then disposed of - A convenient alternative to lugging around a whole bottle, and a clever, no doubt very profitable, marketing ploy. However, the reality of people casually popping into a café for their mid-morning hit, before going back to do whatever it was they did, was a little disturbing. Whatever the town is like in summer, in winter it is a lacklustre place and there seemed no reason to hang around. However, I decided to visit the local springs and sanatorium. 4kms from the centre, they were the only ostensible attraction Jalalabat was reported to offer. Thus, I thought I might as well try to see them whilst I was there.

The way to the springs and sanatorium was a road that twisted up round the hills out of the city. Young men jogged past up the steep incline. It was a display of recreational exercise unusual to Central Asia. We passed one lad doing step-ups very fast on some concrete stairs. Janyl, having apparently never seen such an activity before, asked why someone would do such a thing. 'To get fit' I said, as his mate timed him on a stopwatch whilst smoking a cigarette.

As we climbed the meandering hill I looked across to the mountains rising in the north. They stood in sombre magnificence, pressed down upon by a heavy grey sky. We made it to Sary Bulak, the first spring of twenty eight apparently. These springs of health giving water are popular phenomena throughout Central Asia, and to judge from the now crumbling health resorts built round them, were enthusiastically endorsed by the Soviets. Unfortunately, winter was not the time to visit. Icy steps led to a broken tap and basin filled with empty bottles. Apparently the spring no longer worked, the 'resort' shut up and deserted. Walking a little further up the hill, a small trickle of water ran down the wooded slope. Janyl scurried to meet it, in search of the spring. Sure enough, a pipe running along the ground poured its contents onto the bare earth, creating a muddy cascade. There was a lady amongst the trees collecting firewood. With her colourful traditional dress and bundle of sticks she was a fairy tale caricature. The fairy tales we are all familiar with are of course handed down to us from a time when people in Europe still dressed 'traditionally' and collected firewood. The connection was complemented by the huge white dog that accompanied the Kyrgyz woman. Without collar or leash, and sporting a well scarred, battle worn snout, it was a fitting wolf. With ears and tail removed - as is the custom throughout Central Asia – it looked a potentially dangerous beast and I was a little surprised when she said it was still just a puppy.

As for the spring, she told us someone had stolen the rest of the pipes, and that was why water no longer reached the basin we had just visited.

Undeterred, Janyl cupped her hands under the remaining pipe and drank from it. I followed suit, but to me the 'health giving' water just tasted like metal. Perhaps, I hoped, this was testament to some healthy iron deposits further upstream. We continued up the path, past the statue of some Kyrgyz hero, a chain-mailed, helmeted warrior from the Kyrgyz nomadic past. A flat-bed lorry came hurtling down the hill. It was full of young men hanging off it and shouting wildly, like a scene from *Mad Max*. We instinctively moved off the road, wary of this excited and ominous looking mob as they sped towards us. Incongruously, it was "Auf wiedersehen!!" They yelled as they passed. Presumably my backpack had led them to mistake us for German tourists.

We reached the top of the hill and the sanatorium. There was little to see but a group of youths who asked us for cigarettes. The effect of winter had drained the colour from everything, and what would have been a wonderful view and scenic spot in the summer instead became rather dull. Back in the town we went to the bazaar so I could buy some fruit for Janyl's mother. I had told her I wanted to arrive with a gift, and Janyl had suggested fruit. Walking through Jalalabat, the black fur hats, rusty Ladas, and concrete extravaganza were all symbols of Soviet times impressed on the landscape, as had been the crumbling sanatorium. However, there was a parallel world amongst it that spoke of a more colourful, ancient 'orient.' It shimmered in the sequins of bold turquoise and blood red headscarves. It was the woman hunched in an Indian shawl, with Mongolian eyes that shone green like a cats; it was the man with half his face consumed by an abscess – blighted by something that in the West was long ago banished to a distant past. It was the woman with the jewelled red earrings, and a dot tattooed in the middle of her forehead. It was the corpulent stall owner sat atop a pyramid of fruit, cross-legged in her robes and turban-like headscarf, like a Buddha or Eastern potentate holding court. It was the girl with a jade headscarf, who Janyl disliked for wearing "too much eye make-up", but to me the dark rings of kohl round silver eyes on caramel skin made her look like an Egyptian princess. It was the relentless brown gypsy boy, dressed in rags patting Janyl's arm for alms. It was the elfish *kalpaks* and noble flowing facial hair of the old Kyrgyz men – the *white beards*. And yet with the rare exception of these hats and beards, the men were the dowdier of the sexes. In an inverse of nature, there were no lions' manes or peacock feathers here. The colourful plumage was for females only, the men having absorbed the wardrobe of *Homo Sovieticus* if nothing else. However, from their dark hats and coats peered strong faces. There was no pretence in their attire as their boots stomped through the muddy slush. Instead there was an egalitarianism of appearance, and something quasi militaristic in the drab regimentation of their dress. It spoke not only of Soviet social ethos, but also of the equality and militarism inherent to the pre-Soviet nomadic culture. For it was men with the same faces as these who had stormed out of the east with Genghis and Attila, and who formed and fought for myriad tribal domains throughout the steppe and hills of these inner-Asian lands.

There was no public transport to Janyl's hometown. Instead taxis waited outside the bazaar until full. Once ours was full we left Jalalabad and ascended the snow laden hills to the north east. The small road wound across the rising relief. Flocks of dark woollen sheep splattered the white folds of land. Looking down into the valley where Kok-Janggak nestles I was overwhelmingly reminded of Wales, where I had lived for three years. It was an impression that was strengthened when I learnt of the town's coal mining heritage. As in South Wales, that industry is nomore in Kok-Janggak, and the community it sustained has suffered accordingly as a result.

However, unlike the ethnic homogeneity of the Welsh valleys where heavy industry also once flourished, Kok-Janggak is home to many nationalities. Whilst the ethnic divide rocked Jalalabad and Osh, in the village of kok-Janggak where many nationalities live alongside each other, the contagion did not spread. Undoubtedly, this was due to the intimacy of living in such a small community. It is harder to kill or burn out people whose names you know; harder to justify. The 'other' becomes a human being. Psychologists say that the 'other' must be dehumanised if normal people (not psychopaths) are to be compelled to kill.

After those troubled times Janyl came to Kok-Janggak, a peaceful place, to be with her family. However, during the height of the violence she was in Osh. Everyone urged her to leave for her home village, but she refused to leave her Uzbek friend to fend for herself. When the situation stabilised, her friend, like so many Uzbeks left Osh. Still, again like so many of her Uzbek compatriots, she returned. After all it was her home, despite what ethnic nationalists might think to the contrary. Janyl told me how her friend now works in a bank and lives with three Kyrgyz colleagues. I asked what would happen if violence erupted again. Janyl said her friend trusts them. However, Janyl has doubts about their loyalty, should it be required in the face of fresh disorder. She recalled how the Kyrgyz boys in the flat opposite "changed" when the violence started. I asked what she meant, but she could only articulate it as "They just changed. It was not good!"

She then went on to say how relieved she had been that she was not Kyrgyz. This was because she wouldn't have wanted to be in a position where her loyalties were split. Of course, Janyl believed she would have remained loyal to her friend even if she was Kyrgyz, but was glad her neutral Kazakh identity did not put her in a position where she had to choose.

I asked what nationalities lived in Kok-Janggak. She told me Kyrgyz, Uzbek, Tartar, and Russian, but that the Slavic population had decreased significantly since independence. She said there had also once been Kurdish people living in the town, but a Kurdish boy had done 'something' to a Kyrgyz girl, so the whole Kurdish population had been chased out of town – showing that there was a limit to tolerance even in this multi-ethnic community. It also illustrated how the alleged wrong-doings of an individual could by association make that individual's whole ethnicity culpable. Indeed, I had heard stories of inter-ethnic sexual wrongs being blamed as the catalyst for the 'war.'

The taxi dropped us at a snow covered verge that was revealed to be a railway embankment. However, the track was now defunct. The railway had long ceased to take out the *oogal* (coal) that brought in the wealth. Now it was nothing more than an interesting snow covered footpath by which we picked our way to Janyl's house. Someone back in Jalalabat had told the taxi driver he had a foreigner in his car, but he hadn't believed them until I got out and started speaking English to Janyl. Such anonymity was nice, but surprising considering the day before a shop owner in Osh had asked if I was Pakistani.

Janyl's house was fronted by the ubiquitous steel gate, which led to a large garden that held fruit trees, and sheds for animals. The rickety plank huts housed sheep and chickens. In one corner of the garden stood the wooden outhouse and in the centre were two small hutches. These turned out to be the homes of two scraggly looking dogs. Kept on short chains, the dogs acted as living burglar alarms announcing our arrival with a barrage of barking. I was a little shocked to see ecologically minded Janyl keep her dogs in what, by British standards, and in light of the very cold temperature, would be considered cruelty. It seemed a perfect coincidence that the word for dog in Kazakh, Kyrgyz and Uzbek is simply '*it.*'

However, Janyl reminded me that keeping dogs in such a way was normal in Kyrgyzstan. I knew she was right. I thought of poor old Rex in Naryn and recalled how at least he was free to roam the yard. Being fed and cared for, Janyl's dogs probably had it better than most. As in most of the world, they had a function to fulfil (to guard the property), and were not members of the family as we might consider our pets in more prosperous lands. Poverty prevents the pampering of animals as we do in the West. I was recently told that the famed English fondness for animals was a result of the country's rapid industrialisation; people flocked to the cities, but brought animals with them, cherishing them as reminders of the countryside they had left behind.

It is in the tenets of Islam that dogs are unclean, although I don't know how relevant that is for the dogs in Kyrgyzstan, considering the Kyrgyz's often flexible interpretation of this faith. For example, although Janyl was a Muslim, she said her family had no taboo against eating pork, and had always done so. Indeed, for the Muslim men of Central Asia obliged to serve in the Soviet armed forces, if pork was on the menu they ate it. Even today conscripts in the Russian army are blighted by malnutrition.

Close to the house was a huge water tank. I was to learn a great deal about the water situation in Kyrgyzstan from Janyl as it was her ecological specialisation. Despite Kyrgyzstan's vast reserves of fresh water, the country's one great resource, a stable and clean water supply was still a pressing issue for many people. The tank in the back garden was to provide the household with water when the main supply was stopped, as happened regularly.

Janyl's house was a cottage in the Slavic style; whitewashed with the wooden frames picked out in that sky blue so reminiscent of Mediterranean Santorini and yet so at odds with a Kyrgyz winter. The interior was quite bare, just white walls and an uncarpeted floor. In the cloakroom a dresser-like basin stood in one corner, and as there was no running water, it had to be refilled regularly. There were other parts of the cottage which I did not see, but the home centred on a large room divided by a partition into two. It was where the large wood burning stove could provide heat and where meals were prepared. Furniture was sparse, just a low table, and a small cupboard that served as the kitchen work top. The area behind the partition was for sleeping, and blankets were piled up against the back wall on top of a carved wooden chest called a *Juk*, just as they would have been in the traditional yurts. This absence of stuff was to some extent reflective of poverty, but it is also inherent to a cultural tradition that is nomadic and as such unsuited to amassing material things. Among the Kazakhs and Kyrgyz the nomadic way of life was *the* way of life a mere two or three generations ago. Indeed, whilst the Khans maybe gone, the people still move. Janyl's mother had come from Qizilorda in Kazakhstan and would one day return. Since I had known Janyl she had lived in Osh, Kok-Janggak, spent two months in Qizilorda and also some time in Almaty. Indeed, even in her most regular locale, Osh, she had lived in four different places, each with different people, all in a mere two years, and even then she had often returned to Kok-Janggak at the weekends. Neither, if Zarina and Nazda were anything to go by, was this transience particularly unusual. What would be a decidedly stressful way of life for most people in the Western world – where even going to university entails a convoy-like transfer of material possessions just for the duration of mere ten week terms – seemed to be undertaken as a matter of course in Kyrgyzstan with a minimum of either stuff or stress. With a vast Central Asian diaspora migrating seasonally to Russia, Kyrgyzstan is still in many respects a very nomadic society. Moreover, this nomadism is assisted and underpinned by family connections and obligations; a web of kinship ties that contrasts it with the isolation and atomisation of individuals pursuing 'independent' lives in the West.

Janyl's mother was perched on a low stool next to the stove. Janyl had mentioned before-hand that her mother was sixty-five years old, but had been keen to stress that she looked much older because she had had a hard life. She was petite like her daughter, with the same spritely face, but with a web of wrinkles lining her features. She wore a simple blue woollen dress, more like a tunic really, and a blue headscarf from the bottom of which dangled a long grey plait. Her legs were bandaged in thick stockings against the formidable cold. Personally, I did not think she looked much older than her years, but her attire was of quite another century. Indeed, the scene was one of peasant life, seemingly simple and harsh. Yet the smell of wood-smoke, the warmth of the hearth, coupled with the sound of my hosts' mysterious chattering and the wind buffeting against the small, single paned window, again conspired to evoke what was for me a forgotten world. It was an environment that seemed closer to both people and to nature, unimpeded by the space and things people crave and yet that often serve to keep them apart. There was no retreating to separate rooms and seeking isolated amusement in individual choices of television or music. There was no distribution of chairs and tables from which to stare at each other across the void, whilst our eyes grazed the clutter and decoration of personal accumulation which is displayed in people's houses like an embodiment of their life's achievement and very being. There was no such affectation in Janyl's house. Instead there was just one main room where the life of an entire family had been lived, sitting and sleeping on the floor, preparing and eating food, where living together really was living together, and the centre of that collective family life was still the stove, just the latest adaptation of the hearth and ancient nomadic *tunduk* of the yurt. The stove was built out of the whitewashed wall, and hunched over on a stool Janyl's mother fed kindling through its metal hatch door. That she had spent a lifetime in such a pose could be read in the stoop of her shoulders, but her eyes sparkled with the same energy and mischief that I saw in her daughter's.

I was received kindly and told to take a seat on the cushioned floor area around the table. Janyl and her mother nattered in Kazakh, the language of the home. As their guest I was aware I was now due for a stuffing. I watched as a feast was prepared in a radius of about 4ft square with a single knife, pot, and pan. I thought of all the swanky kitchens people spend small fortunes on at home; the designer granite work-surfaces, the range of utensils and crockery, most of which is probably used only very rarely. It seemed quite ridiculous when the same, if not better results can be achieved with so much less. It was even more ironic when I considered the current fad for 'minimalist' décor – a way to stylishly conceal all the expensive hardly used things you have behind a costly veneer which paradoxically displays very little.

The *chai* flowed steadily until the food was prepared. I was given *manti*. I had been expecting *Plov* but of course that is an Uzbek dish, and Janyl's family are Kazakh. Whilst I ate they exchanged gossip, which Janyl graciously translated for me. They were discussing how some relatives had found a husband for her elder sister, who was divorced. It was interesting to me how spouse finding here could be a family affair. Janyl acknowledged this but is quite adamant that she keeps her own counsel when it comes to her marriage prospects. She then told me something rather strange: "But I would not make someone fall in love with me."

Wondering if I had heard her correctly, I replied "And how exactly would you *make* somebody fall in love with you?" She gave me a surprised look, as if it was common knowledge. "There are certain ladies who can… (she used a word I don't know and haven't been able to find since, but seems to equate with 'witch') …make a person fall in love with another person against their will."

"How?" was my obvious follow up question. "I don't know their ways, but they can!" she insisted, clearly convinced of it herself. To illustrate the point she proceeded to tell me about her sister (cousin) who apparently had such a fate befall her. This 'sister' had a boyfriend who she was happy with but another man kept proposing to her. She rejected him, and according to Janyl, really disliked the chap. However, after a short period of time, and mysteriously (so the story goes) she all of a sudden married the man she had rejected. This was apparently accompanied by a similarly drastic change in behaviour. The 'sister' suddenly appeared distant to those that knew her well, and started to undertake heavy domestic work with enthusiasm, something she had always detested before. She also started to wear a headscarf. Intrigued but sceptical I had to wonder were these not all unfortunate, but completely explicable, pitfalls of married life, rather than outright sorcery. According to Janyl, apparently not, and witchcraft was deemed the only reasonable explanation. She said that many other people shared her opinion. Janyl's real sister, unnerved by the events and the change in her cousin, went to a 'witch' who was able to divine that her cousin had indeed been cursed. Janyl's real sister then paid for the curse to be lifted. Among other things the spell was broken by putting nails (as in hammer and nails) inside the afflicted cousin's house. That this worked was apparently demonstrated by the cousin getting divorced shortly afterwards. Freed from the curse, (or just the marriage, depending on your interpretation of the story) Janyl's cousin stopped doing chores and even claims not to remember being married at all. With a final grim twist which Janyl cited almost as proof that the union was forged by forces diabolical, she told how the unborn baby from this cousin's marriage then "died inside her."

I asked Janyl if the 'witch' who performed this counter spell was rich. I was unsurprised when Janyl told me she was poor. I queried why somebody with such power would be poor. Janyl agreed that it was strange, but would only acknowledge that "all such women are poor." Janyl then said that she too had been accused of being a 'witch' by her classmate because she kept appearing in his dreams. I found this pretty funny and laughed, but Janyl continued in complete seriousness "I would not do that. I don't think it's right." It was as if to even entertain the idea that she could possibly be responsible for appearing in someone else's dream would be to cast doubt on her morality. She also told me about the 'evil eye' and that if she came home from school feeling tired, her mother told her it was because someone had used the 'evil eye' against her. I found it all quite fascinating, especially considering Janyl was a scientific professional. It was strangely refreshing. The Soviet campaign against superstition had evidently not been a complete success.

That night I slept next to the table whilst Janyl and her mother slept on the other side of the partition. Janyl's mother, or 'Kazakh mama,' as it had now been decided I should call her, stocked up the stove before retiring. The room remained wonderfully warm and I drifted off to sleep easily. However, I was woken sometime in the wee hours by an unnervingly aggressive thumping at the door. It continued, getting louder and more violent. "What's that?" I called out to Janyl who was just a few yards away. "It's Drinking Uncle!" She replied with some alarm. I recalled that she had mentioned "Drinking Uncle" before. He had stolen Janyl's father's boots and some tools to sell so he could buy vodka. However, I hadn't been expecting to meet him, and had no particular desire to do so, especially not in the middle of the night. The banging continued vigorously and I thought he was going to break the door down. I wondered what reaction I could expect from 'Drinking uncle' when he found a strange foreign man in the house of his deceased brother, alone with the recently departed's widow and unmarried daughter. I imagined his response might be less than favourable, and on the face of it could indeed see why that might be the case.

I got up and dressed quickly so that at least I wouldn't be entering into any possible confrontation in just my underwear. The banging persisted and I wondered what ogre I was about to face. The name 'drinking uncle' was hardly conjuring up anticipation of meeting a benign individual, who was going to come in and start handing out sweets. I glanced around the bare room and noted the position of the knife resting by the stove. Thankfully, my imagination was getting ahead of itself. Janyl went to let him in and diverted him off down the porch before he even saw me. She then just grabbed some blankets and banished him to the icy wooden annex, which didn't even have walls. "He will sleep there?" I asked, astonished, because it was well below freezing. "Yes" she replied sternly "It is cold, but it is okay for *him*!" a note of disgust crept into her voice when she spoke of the man. Personally, I thought "cold" (as in -20°c) was a fantastic understatement, and wondered what manner of man could so easily endure such privations. Going back to bed I hoped that if I did meet him, we got on.

In the morning I awoke to hear the whistle of the kettle on the stove. I opened my bleary eyes and was shocked to come face to face with a wild looking man. His skin was as dark as an African's, and deep lines extended from unreadable Mongolian eyes. Strands of thick black hair shot erratically from under the beige fox-skin hat he wore on his head. It was the whole pelt, and the fox's tail hung down over his shoulder. He looked like one of Attila's boys fresh from a war party on the steppe. That he was related to Janyl, or even of the same species, seemed incredulous.

Our eyes met and we just stared in silence. If he was surprised by my presence, I couldn't see it on his face. All the time I was trying to think of something to say that would break the ice, but in my morning stupor which was compounded by mild panic, I failed utterly. What could I say? "Morning, did you sleep well? Oh that's right, you slept outside whilst I slept next to the stove in your relatives house. Fancy a cup of tea?" However, there was no need to make conversation as he stoked the stove and left before I could muster the Russian to speak.

For breakfast 'Kazakh mama' made a huge omelette, accompanied by bread, jam and biscuits. One spoon moved freely from butter, to jam to tea, with none of the pointless division of labour (and extra washing up) created by excessive cutlery. The table cloth doubled as a plate. I asked Janyl about 'Drinking Uncle.' She explained that he was a carpenter and furniture maker, and not without talent. I said that surely he should have some money then, and not need to take the tools which he stole from them. However, Janyl said she thinks that he probably just works for payment in vodka.

That morning we went for a walk around the town. We followed the broken railway track that ran directly behind Janyl's house. In parts, the embankment underneath had given way, so one was forced to hop from sleeper to sleeper with nothing but air in between. Sometimes snow and ice had collected in the gaps giving the appearance of solid ground, creating a grave danger for the unwary. We continued along this precarious ladder until we came to a path across snow-covered ground. Skeletons of old industry stood in stark silhouette against the blinding glare of sun and snow. Still, I had yet to see hardly anyone in Kyrgyzstan wear sunglasses. A building next to the railway track was stripped to exposed girders and concrete. A rhythmic clanging came from within it. As we got closer and my eyes adjusted to the sun's searing glow, I saw figures of men on the second floor, the wall having given way long ago. They were beating at something with metal bars; the clanging was the sound of metal on metal. "What are they doing?" I asked Janyl. "Stealing" she replied with clear disapproval. They were stripping a building that looked like it had already been gutted many years before. It was a clear sign of their poverty; to be bothered to hunt for pipes sealed in concrete, or the most firmly fixed fittings, any bit of metal that might be worth a few Som. The ratio of effort exerted to profit made must have been pitiful.

It was an odd sound to be ringing through the morning quiet. All around us climbed white hills, dappled with the dark dots of trees and patches of grey/green vegetation. The undulating relief with monochrome colour and no hint of movement was quite beautiful, like the upland country of the UK.

We left black footprints in the snow, for the *oogal* was just below the surface. It seemed that once the streets here really had been paved with gold - that black gold of former times. Mining had sustained the town. It was what Janyl's father had done all his working life. However, the coal was no longer mined. The trains had stopped coming to collect it, and Mother Russia, the driving force behind it all, had recoiled back within her own borders, with most of her sons following shortly in her wake. Now a community was left scavenging through the rubble for the metal innards of the industrial body that had once given it life.

We turned away from the railway, up a small lane. All the roads were small lanes here. It was lined with Slavic cottages. A group of men in dark jackets and fur hats watched silently as we passed. A boy of about ten galloped past on a large sand-coloured steed, riding bareback. He then effortlessly wheeled the creature around and cantered back past us, looking down at us nonchalantly. And why not, I thought. The control that boy had over such a powerful animal was extremely impressive, and a little disconcerting in the hands of one so young. There was no guardian or instructor around to tell him what to do or catch him if he fell; no helmet, saddle, or stirrups. He was free, his own man, yet he was still just a boy. When I was ten I had a bicycle. I can't imagine the sensation being comparable. Horses are in the blood of the Kyrgyz people, and are at the core of their identity. The symbiotic relationship between man and horse gave the nomads their place in the world. Horses were the nomad's most precious possessions. In Central Asian epic poetry, all the horses are individualised and mentioned by name. There are many different words for horses used to denote each class according to its exact age and condition. The description of Manas's horse *Manykar,* at one point in the poem takes up fifty-three lines.

I tried to imagine being that boy; having that ability, freedom and power when I was just a child. But then I imagined growing up to the wretched economic legacy bestowed on Kyrgyzstan by the Soviets, and the country's pains to integrate into the doctrine of the free market. At school that boy will no doubt be told that if he wants to succeed he must learn to use a computer – moving little icons around on a glass screen – and that he should learn English, the language of a people who go pink in the sun, and most of whom don't even know Kyrgyzstan exists. As for the horse-riding skills, he can become a herder, or perhaps get seasonal work taking tourists on horse treks. It all seemed pretty degrading after the glory days of mounted warfare on the open steppe. No wonder so many grew to seek solace in the vodka. One way of life had been imposed on another, then it had collapsed, and now adjustment to yet another system is required with little actual provision for this existing; destruction, 'development', and dissolution - dismembering in little more than a century the nomadic way of life that had lasted virtually unchanged in the region for millennia.

We passed another abandoned building which Janyl told me was the old rope factory. There was a car outside and I asked if people still worked there. "No, they are just stealing" was the weary reply from Janyl. I could try and relate this to a fine nomadic tradition of raiding, the battered *Lada* merely a modern metaphor for a dozen chestnut steeds and lance-bearing warriors of the finest Eurasian heroic mould, seeking plunder in the ruins of the despicable settled estates of the displaced Sarts. But I can't. There was no romantic spin on an economic situation that obliged people to spend their Saturday scavenging in the wreckage of old factories so they could feed their families. It was desperate and sad. Nobody should have to live like that. But was the only alternative really Western consumerism; with everyone just getting fat and seeking spiritual fulfilment buying things they don't need and worshipping talentless celebrities?

Across the street was the town spring which Janyl proudly introduced me to, clearly feeling it was one thing in Kok-Janggak worth seeing. I wished I could have shared her enthusiasm. It was a metal pipe protruding from the bare hillside. The weak flow emptied into a muddy puddle shared with plastic bottles and cigarette packets. Janyl cupped her hands delicately to catch the clear stream and gulped down a couple of mouthfuls. I tried some too and was pleasantly surprised, pleased that it didn't taste like metal.

We climbed up the hillside behind the rope factory. It looked out over a great crumpled white cloth that was the landscape; an intricate cross-stitch of houses and trees threading through the folds and creases of successive valley and ridge. The air was thin and silent accept for the distant clanging of the scavengers. We scrambled down the sodden slag heap summit, to grassy hillocks like British moorland, ambled along the wood and wire fences of white-washed cottages, and across muddy tracks of stone and slush. So much stood empty from more prosperous days. There were too many abandoned buildings and smashed windows. Not enough people left to fill those gaps. The melancholy of the place was exacerbated by a melancholy inherent to the frozen landscape. Barren windswept hills and fog filled lanes, Russian relics that in the shadows turned to Gothic ruins - like a walk through the world of *Jayne Eyre*.

Back at Janyl's I helped with some chores; feeding the goats, and filling up churns of water for use inside the house from the large cistern outside, marching backwards and forwards with pails of water. It was time consuming, laborious work. Having slipped over on the hills whilst trying to make a particularly debonair descent (and failing) I had got covered in mud. I washed my jeans in a bowl, the way people here wash all their clothes. I joked I was a '*pratchka*' (washer woman) and Janyl laughed, complimenting my technique, asking "At home you have a machine to do this work?" "Yes", I replied, a little ashamed. After about five minutes the rustic appeal of washing by hand had worn off, but Janyl insisted I rinse and wash several more times until the water in the bowl remained clear no matter how hard I scrubbed. I'd paid the floor lady at the hotel in Osh a dollar or two to do a large bag of laundry. The whole lot arrived back less than 24 hours later, neatly folded and smelling of roses. After washing one item myself, I could see she had certainly earned her money.

Janyl then went on to casually make some bread as 'Kazakh mama' prepared an extravagant supper from the simplest of ingredients. I was impressed by their proficiency in tasks where I really wouldn't have known where to start. These seemed like real skills, where what you consume is moulded by your own hands, what you wear is washed by them, and what you use is often made or at least maintained and cherished by them. Everything had a value tangible in labour and time that people in the world from which I hailed were largely disconnected from. Yet, these are the skills that the collective 'we' of the West would no doubt interpret as the trappings of poverty. Indeed, 'poverty', or at least an absence of material luxury means that for many such chores are still a requirement of daily life. Time consuming and tedious though they may be, I wondered what mechanism of social evolution had led 'us' to believe that our way was better; where labour saving devices just freed up more time to sit in gridlock and watch TV, where honest life sustaining skills were disregarded in favour of ready-meals and becoming adepts of superficial service sector non-skills whose only value lies in a self-referential system of consumption.

I may not have been overly enthralled with the hand washing, but the simple life has its charms, especially when I was required to do nothing. Leaning back against the wall I yawned contentedly. Janyl glanced up and expressed immediate concern, asking "Are you okay?" I told her "I'm fine", before promptly yawning again. "Stop it!" she said, a little agitated, before continuing "You know you shouldn't yawn so much?" Bemused, I asked "why not?" She told me that to yawn many times (I had yawned twice) is thought of as very bad. Apparently too much yawning means you are weak and that therefore you may have absorbed some bad energy. Luckily, she went on to tell me "There is a cure. Someone else must rub you with a newspaper whilst you both yawn. Afterwards you must burn the newspaper. This will remove the bad energy." Well, that's a relief I thought, and we did just that. Janyl told me how she used to yawn when she came home from school, and she used to go through the same ritual with her mother, fearful that someone had used the evil eye to give her bad energy.

That evening we had the pleasure of being joined for dinner by "Drinking Uncle." He took off the fox he wore for a hat and sat down, revealing a brown crag of a face, and a shock of black hair. He shook my hand with a huge grizzled paw. I noticed on his thumb joint he had a small tattoo in Arabic. He was drinking water from a large glass pasta sauce jar. I had seen Janyl give it to him the previous evening. Now it had bits floating in it, but he seemed unbothered. Fortunately "Drinking Uncle", despite his bad reputation actually struck me as quite amicable, at least at that time of the evening. However, I acquired yet another new identity when he asked me if I was Jewish - quite a contrast from my last mistaken identity as a Pakistani. However, calling me Jewish became one of his favourite jokes, along with one about killing the cat, which had slunk around the edge of the table in search of titbits. "Drinking Uncle" then pulled out a large knife from his jacket pocket and rested it on the table. I asked why he was carrying such an implement around with him. He grinned, saying "I'm a carpenter", as he mimed using it to skin the cat.

He was always smiling at his jokes, but Janyl and 'Kazakh mama' did not respond in kind. Janyl was harsh with him and rebuked all his attempts at friendly chatter. She increasingly revealed herself as a very strong and determined character. She was the boss; "Drinking Uncle" did what he was told and moved on to the more palatable topic of our respective ages and star signs. It was a little disconcerting to discover that we were both the year of the dog. However, the twelve or so years between us could have been twenty, as he looked out from a face so weathered it almost obscured his features. After dinner "Drinking Uncle" didn't linger and presumably returned to the habit that had earned him his nickname, somewhere outside in the bitter cold.

'Kazakh mama' went to bed early and Janyl and I stayed up talking. Inevitably conversation seemed to circle back to Osh and the 'war.' Janyl told me how on that fateful day she received a phone call from a friend telling her "Don't you Know?! The war between the Uzbeks and the Kyrgyz has started! Be careful! Don't go outside!" Then as the hours passed and she and her friend stayed housebound, they heard gunshots and screaming, and began to see smoke rising over the city as Osh burned. She feared for herself, but feared for her Uzbek friend more. She told me that for the first time in her life she felt that she could die for someone – defending her friend. I could do little but nod in admiration, having no such personal experience to relate it too.

Janyl told me that she had heard the 'War' started with a simple fist fight which escalated. Then later "More Kyrgyz came from 'wild places'" as she called them. "Maybe they drink some vodka to make them crazy" she continued. I asked if she thought it had anything to do with the coup in the north; that the violence had somehow been orchestrated by the deposed president perhaps to destabilise the country and see him returned to power. However, she dismissed this, suggesting instead that the Uzbeks knew about it all along. She said that Uzbek workers were mysteriously absent from their work at the hospital as "D-day" approached. She also thought the call to prayer may have been used to signal the start of the violence. She now hated that sound. Using the *muezzin* as a call to battle struck me as an interesting idea, but it all sounded a bit like an urban myth. After all, where was the need in this age of mobile phones and internet? Indeed, if there was such an Uzbek plot it seemed to have backfired as all the figures I've seen indicate that it was the Uzbeks who came off substantially worse.

Janyl then told me of another theory, again rather conspiratorial, that the whole thing was merely a diversion to allow drug smugglers to get their cargo through. The drug trade in Central Asia is big business, as narcotics from Afghanistan make their way north via the other 'Stans' to Russia and on to Europe. Later, Janyl would email me and write that neither the Kyrgyz nor the Uzbeks were responsible, 'but it was someone else and who this is we will never know.'

At midnight we went to bed. Laying out blankets on our respective patches of floor either side of the partition. I got into the habit of sleeping on the floor when I lived in Korea. It agrees with me, and I've been doing it ever since. The ability to just fold up your bed, put it in the corner, and free up the whole room seems far more sensible than clogging it up with a bed.

With the light out, I saw Janyl's silhouette standing in the doorway. "You know, my mother says you are handsome" she told me. "Thank you" I replied, before I could think of anything better to say. I sensed her smile. Her silhouette shrank from the doorway. "Have good dreams" She called out. Then it was silent except for the purring of the cat and the crackle of the stove.

10

To The Border

"Phone me when you are safe in China" said Janyl as I got into a taxi for Sari Tash. The 4x4 roared onto the high street but as I expected, such vigorous progress was to be short lived as we just drove around the corner to wait for another passenger. The driver was a taciturn fellow, permanently obscured by his sunglasses and cigarette smoke. Yet he cut the sort of strong silent type that seemed appropriate for such a journey – no superfluous chatter and certainly no vodka; just a hunter's stare for the road ahead and the occasional flash of gold as he grimaced at something noticed only by him.

In the back were two other Kyrgyz men. They both lived in villages to the west of Sari Tash and were wedged in amongst the horde of boxes and bags being ferried to this remote wing of the country. Every taxi to such areas also acts as a freight vehicle, delivering goods that would certainly not be available there otherwise. We were also eventually joined by a mother and daughter who somehow managed to find space for themselves in between the cargo.

By now it was no surprise to me that of the five adults in the jeep it was only the female who spoke English to a level that made more than elementary communication possible. Like the other passengers she was also returning home to a village beyond Sari Tash. She and her daughter had come to Osh on a shopping spree. This was a two day undertaking. Not because of the huge distances involved, but because the quality of the road (singular) and the lie of the land - which included a 3600m pass – still served to make travel here slow and unpredictable. It seemed an epic venture just to visit humble Osh, but of course everything's relative, and when you live in a small village in a remote region of a 'remote' country, Osh is probably quite the metropolis. However, it still seemed like the equivalent of crossing the Alps to visit your 'local' shops.

The lady wore a headscarf which I remember thinking unusual as I had not met a young Kyrgyz woman wearing one before. Whilst there are plenty of headscarves in Osh, they seem to be the preserve of Uzbeks and older Kyrgyz women. However, her most striking feature was her eyes; a piecing green, which framed by the headscarf instantly evoked that iconic *National Geographic* photograph of the 'Afghan girl.'

Leaving Osh, we began to climb into Christmas card scenery. Broad, snow-white folds of land fell in layers below the sharp peaks of the Alay Shan. Through my window the familiar props of the Kyrgyz countryside presented themselves on set. Horsemen rode alone or in pairs, coaxing their flocks of fat-tailed sheep, which spread like woolly brown blemishes on the ivory hills. Settlements of milky white cottages only distinguished themselves against the snow covered land by their smoking chimneys trailing black across a baby blue sky. Colourfully clad school children ambled in pairs along the roadside like little elves in Lapland. Our vehicle sped past them with disturbing indifference to their presence on the pavement-less, icy track. The driver's lips just parted enough to omit a sliver of gold as he hammered the horn to herald our arrival.

The winter wonderland whizzed passed in a pleasingly repetitious sequence; its glacial cold basked in the reflective warmth of a sun which seemed to strike everywhere, unimpeded by cloud or contour.

Only when we entered a deep stone-filled valley did the sun retreat behind the high peaks. With it gone, the cold increased ten-fold. The wind delivered its chill like a weapon along the dry rocky channel of the desiccated river valley. It seemed a peculiar place to stop for lunch, but seeing as someone had already gone as far to build a café there, the decision was perhaps understandable. The café was standard, as was the menu. I opted for that Russian classic *borsche* – a beetroot soup.

"What's it like in England?"; "How much does a ticket cost there?", and invariably "Could you help me get a job there?" came the predictable questions from my fellow passengers. I don't like to dash people's dreams, but I'm hardly in a position to help fulfil them either. Their view of the West was from pirated DVDs of Hollywood movies, pop-videos, and the Western brand image, whose tentacles have reached even into the remote Alay Shan. If they ever did get there I'm sure they would be in for a big disappointment. However, I often (as many travellers must), find myself appointed by default as ambassador for this dream world that doesn't even exist, except in its self-created media images and the heads of the people it exports them to. What *is* real, is the gross inequalities in wealth that separate us. This is what they know about, and it's what they want a part of in order to better their own lives. Usually, I lamely refer them to the internet, because the answers to most of the questions they ask I've never needed to know. After all, I don't need a visa to visit the UK and don't have the first idea about how one would go about getting one.

However, whilst I can avoid the questions, I can't avoid the irony that the very thing I like to escape from, that brings me to Kyrgyzstan, is the very thing they think they are seeking. They aspire to the West's ideal of a consumer paradise, and the money that would certainly make aspects of their lives much easier. Even my moderate, deliberately toned-down estimates of average wages in the UK can seem fantastic, and explanations of costs of living do little to douse their enthusiasm. They imagine a land of riches, something unavoidably illustrated by the fact that I was meeting them in their country and they were not meeting me in mine. There is little one can do to temper this reaction. For someone with evident abundance to start telling those living without it about the virtues of scarcity would be as absurd as it is wrong. However, whilst perpetual growth and increasing material prosperity may have become a global religion, the destructive effects of this doctrine on the societies where the process is most advanced are well documented. I've worked and spoken with many immigrants to the UK and it has rarely met their expectations. Some are enamoured with the vibrancy of London, and all, regardless of age or background, are attracted by a Dick Whittington dream of wealth, but few find much to envy in the general state of British society.

We are led to believe such dissolution is the price of modernity; a trade off for supposedly greater freedoms and material well-being. Yet, for all of human history and across all cultures, economics was embedded within, and therefore subordinate to, society. Only today, has society, most acutely in the West, become embedded within and subordinate to its economic system. This situation has not evolved 'naturally', but has rather been purposefully created and maintained in the misguided belief of the self-regulating market. However, as I write, the myth of a global utopia based on this assumption is visibly disintegrating. Of course, it is this system that has undoubtedly allowed me to live my life as I have, for better or for worse. Indeed, I would not have been able to really converse with people on my travels if some of them had not felt obliged to learn English, a language mostly learnt because of the economic dominance of the English speaking world. Moreover, I cannot flatter myself to the point of pretending my origin from this world was of total irrelevance when making their acquaintance. Yet, it is the same system that means most people in the world could never do the same even if they chose to. For the Kyrgyz, like all Central Asians, these gripes against the current world order may seem of little relevance as they struggle from the legacy of Soviet communism. The forced incorporation of the Kyrgyz into the USSR was, as one contemporary observer put it 'to suppress the economical and political freedom of the last of all genuinely free peoples on Earth.'[1] Now they are free of that oppression and the gateway to Western-style material abundance seems open. Yet, this is far from a return to their former freedom, and what is their future in 'the vortex of globalisation'[2] as the capitalist system reaches its 'apocalyptic zero-point.'[3] The path to stability and sustainability is uncertain for all of us, and for those at the bottom of the global pecking order things are perhaps most bleak. As people attempt, or are obliged to climb the ladder of this failing system, we must wonder what will be lost along the way, like so much has been already. British explorer Wilfred Thesiger spent the middle of last century travelling in 'remote' places because he knew the ancient ways were dying. Now they are mostly dead, or more accurately speaking, they have been killed. As such I can only share his 'deep seated resentment of Western innovations in other lands, and a distaste for the drab uniformity of the modern world.'[4]

I had come to Kyrgyzstan looking for echoes of an older world, one which I believed I had glimpsed on previous visits; somewhere I felt to be as yet beyond the homogenising influences of globalisation, a culture not yet commoditised and therefore degraded to the whims of mass tourism.

Unlike those journeys this had not been a summertime odyssey of chance encounters and refreshing novelty. With the stunning green expanse of Kirgizia's land under snow I had been restricted to the considerably less appealing urban centres. However, I had still been greeted with unbelievable hospitality and found first-hand experience of traditions and folk beliefs utterly removed from my own life or what I had even heard about previously. I also had the opportunity to visit places and see things that reverberated with a history little known in the West, and which I found so fascinating.

I had hoped to write a book that exuded the magical quality I had encountered before in Kyrgyzstan. However, in the depths of winter, and in the face of such recent social upheavals, I feel I have done quite the opposite. Winter, and time, allowed me to see beyond the scenery and hospitable people to some very unattractive social problems, namely alcoholism and bride-knapping. The romantic charm a tourist can find in the nomadic past had crashed into the brick wall of some grim realities. Yet these are problems largely created by modern impositions, and the only proposed model out of this situation, despite its fluffy image and fashionable buzz words seems unlikely to fulfil the promises its Hollywood propaganda wing presents. 'Progress', communist or capitalist, despite considerable material benefits, has been overwhelmingly a process of destruction. Contrary to popular belief, it is these secular political religions and their god science that have been responsible for far more devastating wars, and indeed peace, than anything that came before. The Kyrgyz, like most people in the world today, live in the aftermath of incursions by 'progressive' militarised ideologies that sought to alter, if not obliterate, the way of life they found because *they* knew better. This is not to deny genuine benefits such as modern health care, which may have been brought to people, but they must be measured against the wider social and environmental costs the imperial/modernising agenda has entailed. Obviously we cannot go back, but looking at the problems the world faces after a couple of centuries of Western-style material 'progress'(and reaping the associated profit) it is perhaps time to challenge this paradigm.

After lunch we left the shaded valley for glowing white hills once more. We passed two cyclists, Westerners, their bikes fully loaded with weighty looking panniers, and faces burnt red by the high-altitude sun. Souvenir *kalpaks* perched on their heads. They climbed up the white ribbon of the road, their progress defined in glorious clarity against the clear blue sky. It was a fine image of man immersed in nature, yet challenging himself against it; no noise or exhaust from a combustion engine, just the steady struggle of ascent; of muscle and will conquering cold and contours.

A chuckle rippled through the jeep, no doubt some mild amusement at these foreigners choosing to cycle into the mountains in the dead of winter for *fun*. However, I did not laugh. Instead I felt a little jealous of their freedom in the fresh mountain air, and a little ashamed that I wasn't out there doing it the 'hard' way too. It was an aspect of 'my' civilization I could be proud of; to embrace the physical and mental challenge, the unknown, and to pursue an endeavour - that whilst the necessity of which is negated by modern technology - the rewards to the individual spirit are immeasurable. It is to take off the security blanket of career and mortgage payments and to engage life as a human being again, not merely as a cog in the impersonal innards of modern society's machine. It is to be a nomad once more.

As the sun was shut behind rocky curtains our vehicle climbed up a series of steep switchbacks in driving snow. The view was a flurry of white, snowflakes whizzing past like stars as if we were travelling at warp speed. But it was the wind and not our rate of progress that gave this effect. Instead the jeep lurched and crunched on the irregular road, rocks popping continually under the tyres as the driver navigated in slow tumultuous zigzags. This was the climb to the pass. It seemed to take an age for us to reach it as we were rocked violently up every foot of the track. It is an odd sensation indeed when merely being a passenger in a vehicle can induce the feeling of physical exertion. Such was the gritty, tumbling nature of our jeep tackling the pass. At the summit we stopped. The night was all consuming and unrelieved by even the most distant light. The shining white of the day had sunk into an ominous black out of which spat a continuous barrage of freezing projectiles. It was not a place you would want to stay long without shelter. I wondered where the cyclists had made their bed for the night. I had many a memory of frantic searching for somewhere sheltered enough to camp on my own cycling odyssey.

At the pass and either side of it there was only unforgiving rock walls and the rutted road to contend with. The driver got out to fiddle with the engine. We all got out as well to stretch our legs, with the exception of the mother and daughter who preferred to stay in the warmth. Even a couple of minutes outside felt too long. With the wind-chill the temperature must have dropped many tens of degrees below freezing. Thankfully the driver quickly amended whatever problem it was he perceived with the engine and we retreated back to the car interior. Descending the other side, the road seemed smoother. Its undulations became hypnotic rather than violent. Everyone was cocooned by the darkness and warmth, and soon consumed with their own thoughts. The haze of sparkling snow drops stuttered strobe-like in the headlights and the jeep bounced with sleep inducing rhythm.

Sari Tash arrived out of the night with no warning. It appeared as a light in a doorway, nothing else. The driver pointed to it saying "Gostinitsa" (hotel). The men in the back escorted me across the stretch of snow and sea black night to reach it. It was almost too cold for pleasantries and I barely had time to shake their hands before being deposited in a large empty room all to myself. Traditional carpets were spread across the floor and up the walls in colourful and intricately patterned insulation. The rugs depicted rutting stags, magnificent mountain valleys, and the eagles of the hunt. To one side was a mattress and thick blanket, evidently my bed for the night. Many more articles of bedding lay rolled up against the back wall, indicating that the room was communal. I just happened to be the only guest there that night.

Heat came from a piece of coiled wire wrapped around a stone pipe. There was no guard and the coil glowed like orange magma. Next to it, in rather an ill chosen position, sat an open tub of water for washing and drinking. The fact that water and electricity do not mix well had clearly not occurred to whoever placed it there. I went outside. The night was like crystal, the air so cold it seemed stretched tight and felt it might snap. There was no light from the settlement, but the moon ignited the mountains as blue beacons, and above them stood Orion, poised to release his bow across the Alay Shan.

For some reason I did not sleep until the grey promise of dawn seeped through the window. Then I found myself following a neat pair of footprints through the snow. They were black from the *oogal* that lay just below the surface. The sky was a particularly gorgeous blue and the snow a pure white. However, a repetitive clanging rang through the air, bestowing me with a strange sense of urgency, and turning my walk into a run. The glare of the sun on the snow made it difficult to see, but up ahead I could make out the silhouette of a figure facing away from me. The clanging became louder and more demanding so I began jumping the sleepers of the railway track two at a time. I had nearly reached the figure when she turned around. It was Janyl. She was smiling warmly and holding out her hand for me to take. She was saying something but the clanging drowned out her words. Her eyes sparkled. They said 'come back.' Yes, I thought, I will stop here. I reached for her hand, but I could not stop. My legs were no longer my own, obeying the beat of the clanging they carried me past her... faster and faster towards the horizon... that horizon I could never quite reach, an invisible force pulling me onwards to the East.

I awoke a couple of hours later, when a man with a face as rugged as tree bark delivered some breakfast. It was a bowl of butter and a flask of tea. Fortunately, I wasn't hungry. The man's wrinkles were deep and many. Skin formed knots and folds around his eyes and along his brow, liked the gnarled bulges of an ancient oak. Yet something told me this man was not that old, maybe around fifty at most. A cigarette hung permanently in his mouth, a smoking branch on the weathered trunk of his face.

I asked him if there were any lorries passing. "Nyet Kamaz" he responded; *Kamaz* being the Russian trucks that still indomitably ply the old empire with freight, normally followed by a fug of toxic black fumes. He told me they had all passed very early that morning. I was annoyed for having overslept. There was no public transport to the border, so I needed to hitch, and lorries were the most frequent traffic. If the lorries had already gone, I was stuck.

Outside the cold carved the landscape in colours beyond their normal spectrum. Somehow the blue was bluer and the white whiter. I scouted the town, which is little more than a crossroads, hoping to spy a vehicle trawling east. It was 90kms to the border, but after fifteen minutes my face was stinging from the biting cold and my eyes sought salvation from the luminosity it was impossible to escape. The road climbed on eastward, milky white and silent. No vehicles passed. I trudged back to Sari Tash puzzling over my dilemma. The tree man, who appeared to have been waiting for me, beckoned. He pulled back the gate on his shed and revealed a shiny black BMW, somewhat at odds with the simple settlement and rugged wilderness around it. Seeing where this gesture was going I asked "Skolka sto'it?" (How much?).

Before he saw fit to answer we exhumed the car, which required pushing out of its icy lair. For some reason he insisted he couldn't take me to the border, only to a place that appeared on none of my maps called Karagandy ('black' something). He told me it's not a settlement, just a place where I should be able to find a truck. Curious, and with no option other than to wait around with nothing to do, I agreed. We bartered a price by writing figures with our fingers on the frosted windows.

The car was twenty years old, but polished like a show car. The front grill was covered with a picture of a pretty lady; a 1940s honey, in the style that once adorned WWII bombers. The tree-man produced a saucepan full of smoking herbs and set it on the engine. Naked flame and engine, electricity and water, I was beginning to notice a pattern emerging. We were enveloped by the herb's pungent smoke. He seemed to be using it to warm up the engine. For good measure he then wafted the smoke around the inside of the car as some kind of blessing.

We left immediately, traditional Kyrgyz music flowing from the tape deck. The first rise gave way to a vast paper-flat plain below the great blue bowl of the sky. The road was like a washboard and our progress painfully slow. However, Karagandy appeared on the horizon disturbingly quickly, and I wondered should I not have haggled a little harder. Had the lucky lady mascot and fortune bringing fumigation really been required for such an undemanding journey.

Karagandy was rather a pitiful place consisting of a hut and three trucks. I was quickly coming round to the idea of Osh the mighty metropolis and why people might undertake a two day journey to get there. In the snow three men laboured over a disembodied wheel. They looked huge, like bears. It was an effect amplified by the half-dozen woollen jumpers they each wore. A brief chat with one of these drivers secured me a place on the next kamaz to Qitai (China). When that would be, however, depended on how long it took to repair their vehicles.

I walked around, trudging through the snow in a panorama of white and blue, as if on the surface of a glacier mint. Three Chinese trucks passed in convoy the other way along the road; as white as the snow around them with huge black characters marked on their sides. I mused on this latest stage in the Silk Road's story; camels had become combustion engines.

One of the Kyrgyz drivers asked 'Carta?' (map), clearly in expectation that it was the kind of thing a foreign fellow such as myself might be carrying. I was not to disappoint, and repair work stopped briefly as the three truckers pondered with grave deliberation over my two dimensional representation of the lands they traversed daily and knew intimately. I was always struck by the reverence with which maps were regarded in these parts, for it was as if they were not seen very often. Indeed, maps had little precedence in Kyrgyzstan's past. The country was very much sealed off in the Soviet era, and across the communist world in general secrecy was the spirit of the times. Maps were probably not made too readily available; and even today the only ones I've come across in Kyrgyzstan itself are those produced by and for the Russian military. After they had taken their cartographic fill the drivers instructed me to go and wait in the hovel that constituted the mighty settlement of Karagandy.

As my eyes adjusted to the gloom I saw five men sat crossed legged on the *soru* in Oriental fashion. It was a sight that made me wonder if things on this ancient trade route had changed that much. They were gathered around the low table too absorbed in their *laghman* and *chai* to notice me. They slurped from their bowls noisily, and ate large lumps of meat on the bone with their hands. I felt I could have been in any caravanserai at any point in history along the old trading trails to and from the East. One looked like a well fed slave master, with narrow darting eyes and a shiny, sweat-soaked brow. Another had a face that might have come straight from the Saka, sculpted by the wind from a life in the saddle. It was a face easy to imagine framed by chain mail, a strong visage not quite from our age.

A stove in the corner gave off a hint of heat. A Kyrgyz girl stamped her feet to try and stay warm. Her cheeks had gone blue with burst blood vessels. Clearly she had spent a lot of time in such cold, her complexion suffering as a result. She travelled with the trucks. I didn't ask her what she did. After the men had finished eating they left, and the girl with them, back to the Kyrgyz interior. A snake's head and some herbs were nailed to either side of the doorway.

Having seen the faces of those running the kitchen, I assumed the hovel of Karagandy was run by a Chinese family. However, I got speaking to the lanky young man who had come out of the kitchen for a cigarette and he told me he was Kyrgyz. His name was Dastan and he had been at Karagandy for four years without leaving. Considering where I was sitting pretty much amounted to what Karagandy had to offer, Dastan's time there seemed almost like a prison sentence.

I asked if he liked it and he said he did. He wanted me to take a photo and send it to him, which I did. He then gave me the shortest address I had ever seen: Karagandy, Kyrgyzstan. I was sure there must have been a mistake but he assured me it was correct. After all, it was the only house between Sari Tash and China.

The hours ticked by slowly. I drank lots of tea and stamped my feet which were failing to stay warm even inside. Bored, I went for a walk outside, my legs sinking up to the knee in snow. There was no *oogal* beneath it though, just snow that seemed to go down forever. I noticed there was a compound filled with containers. Mandarin characters identified it as Chinese. They were there to build the road, but the place seemed deserted. Unlike Dastan, many of the Chinese who found themselves at Karagandy working on the road crews *were* serving a prison sentence.

Returning, I found the truck drivers still tampering with their vehicles. A Chinese worker appeared from the compound and came over to look. He was short, dark, with a heavily lined face. His was the face of rural China, peasant life, and the underclass of heavy industry; not the ageless, pale complexions of the new pampered Han middle class. He was conspicuously ignored by the Kyrgyz drivers. Someone told me the Chinese workers were sent there as punishment for having a second child. No one Chinese wanted to work there. For them it's still the barbarian lands, barren and dangerous.

I helped with the repairs, at least as much as my mechanical ignorance would allow; just providing an extra pair of hands when things needed to be carried and pulled. The Kyrgyz drivers started to change and fiddle with the trucks weighty batteries. I was instructed to hold a copper pipe onto the terminals of two batteries. Being fairly certain that copper conducts electricity, and remembering the electric heater in its potentially lethal position next to the tub of water the night before, I became increasingly unsure about holding that pipe.

However, I didn't want to make a fuss. After all, these chaps were going to take me to the border. I thought I would just 'go with the flow', though hopefully not in the literal sense. I just managed to ask "electricity ZZZZZZZ!!" accompanied by my best impression of being electrocuted. The driver waved his hand in reassurance, "Nyet, Nyet!"

However, as soon as he started the engine a huge jet of sparks shot out of the terminal that was attached to the pipe, and that was attached to my hands. Needless to say I abandoned my post, and jumped about six foot backwards in the snow. The driver whistled and shook his head, I hoped in apology. No problem I thought, I'm still alive.

We then started swapping the batteries, ferrying them on sledges between trucks. What exactly was taking place mechanically I'm not sure, but six hours after arriving at Karagandy, one of the trucks spluttered into life under a cloud of black smoke. I took this as a good sign. The ancient Kamaz looked like it had come into service circa World War II. The second truck was newer and it was the one I was told to ride in. Our two truck convoy left in tandem, the third remained. We set off at the blistering pace of about 15km per hour. I thought that we were just warming up and that we would soon increase to a more satisfying speed. However, we did not.

We chugged along with chain-bound wheels that sought purchase on the frequent ice-clad inclines. Sometimes, our lead lorry stopped and waited for the old Kamaz to catch up.

Tired, I pulled the window curtain shut against the sun, but the driver looked at me as if I had committed a small blasphemy. Clearly he expected me to marvel at the spectacular scenery passing by outside, not sleep. Indeed, it was a hard view not to marvel at.

"Karashu?" the driver asked. "Da, ochen karashu, ochen prekrasna!" I responded. We climbed into ever more breathtaking vistas. Clouds crashed like surf below plunging grey mountains. The polished snow line curved across the horizon like a gargantuan whale's rib. It stretched behind us for hours, as our snail's pace saw us sailing slowly through the snow-scape. Eventually we descended into a sandy brown valley. The landscape changed to one pock-marked with mud-brick hovels, hay piles, dithering livestock, and a rusty wagon. We also passed a strangely artificial looking settlement, an urban suburbia of cake-yellow houses isolated in the wilderness.

The regular rows of houses looked ridiculous against the random ruggedness of the rust coloured rocky peaks around them. It wasn't on my map, and I could only guess at what purpose it served. There was nothing there to support it.

Soon after came the preliminary border post, a crude camouflaged cabin with a couple of young soldiers in attendance. They carried the standard Kalashnikovs but I noticed the magazines were safely stored in their webbing rather than in their weapons. I wondered why this was. I knew that during the battle of Batken twelve years previously Kyrgyz soldiers had been ordered to fire as few rounds as possible because the state could not afford to buy replacements. However, that funds for security forces remained so restrictively tight in light of Kyrgyzstan's ever increasing geopolitical importance seemed unlikely.

They asked me if I was Tajik and were surprised when I told them I was English. My name and passport number were recorded in an ancient looking log book, the computer age having not quite filtered down to this distant outpost. They lifted the barrier and our lorry climbed again, up a narrow, rocky road that rose in steep switchbacks. Stones popped under the tyres and red dust hung over the gravel track.

As the sun waned we reached the border. It was already closed for the day. "Nyet problem" the driver told me, "Gostinitza tam" (Hotel there). Really? I wondered. Looking from the window at a mass of cluttered trucks, a 'hotel' was something I found difficult to imagine. There weren't even any buildings, only lorries waiting to cross to China, a hut labelled 'café' and an old metal military trailer. I was soon to discover that the military trailer was the 'hotel.'

I thanked the driver, who wanted no payment, and went to investigate my bed for the night. Two large shelves at the back of the khaki trailer had been turned into communal beds. Along the side ran space for two single mattresses. Altogether it could house eight men. A coal heater and TV made it that little bit more homely. I was charged 100 Som, or a little over £1 for the privilege.

My only room-mate was a seventeen year old Kyrgyz driver. He plied the roads from Kashgar to Dushanbe, Osh and Bishkek. He asked if I wanted a drink, but I declined, assuming he was offering vodka. However, I was wrong, for he told me that he neither drank alcohol nor smoked.

Apparently eager that I was entertained, he put a DVD on; a modern Russian thriller with frequent flashbacks to WWII that just got confusing. WWII, 'The Great Patriotic War', and (as I was soon to find) the Sino-Japanese war which raged in China at the same time, seemed impossible to escape. Even nearly seventy years after the end of these conflicts, their regurgitated myths continue to abound in the popular media and legitimise the respective ideologies of the West, Russia, and China, all of course from very different perspectives.

When it was about half way through, and I had thoroughly lost interest, three men burst in; they wore blazers and flat caps, looking like old cockney barrow boys. My young room-mate greeted them with the Muslim 'asalamu aley kom' but received just a cursory nod in reply. I offered a chirpy 'Zdrastvootya' and was soundly ignored. They cast their eyes around moodily then left. Admittedly, if they too had just been directed to a 'hotel' I could quite understand their disappointment. "Uyghur" said my Kyrgyz room-mate, turning his nose up dismissively. "You don't like them?" I asked. "Uyghur, Kyrgyz, some problem" he replied, turning a fist in the palm of his hand to emphasis the point. I could extract no more from him on the reason for this apparent animosity, but was quite relieved that we didn't have to accommodate any more bodies in our spartan quarters.

In hindsight, some more bodies might not have been such a bad thing, even if it meant cosying up on the communal bed. That night in the trailer was the coldest I think I've ever experienced. The coal ran out and there was nothing to refuel the heater with. The trailer had no insulation save its metal walls, and as the temperature dropped outside it simply sucked the heat from our tin foil abode. I put on all my clothes, my sleeping bag and the Kyrgyz driver and I split the trailers remaining blankets between us. We each lay under a pile of cloth two feet deep and I was still shivering frantically.

Daylight could not come soon enough. When it did I went outside to stamp my feet and walk in circles, anything to warm up. The hardy Kyrgyz seemed to be sleeping like a baby. The border opened at nine o'clock, and it seemed I was the only one crossing by foot.

The hut labelled 'café' was as well stocked as I had come to expect in Central Asia and was serving fried eggs, and only fried eggs. I bought four of them and was exceedingly grateful for their warming qualities. Outside the engines of the amassed freight lorries roared in unison as if on the starting line of a race. The occupants of their cabs, who had somehow avoided freezing to death during the night, creaked around outside in the grey air, visibly thawing.

I briefly returned to the 'hotel' to grab my stuff and bid fair well to the Kyrgyz lad, before loitering eagerly at the barrier separating me from China. I was ushered through quickly enough, the first person that day. I was directed from pillar to post for seemingly cursory checks on my passport whilst the guards waited to hail a truck to put me on. It is not permitted to cross the five miles of no man's land unless in a vehicle. The first trucks took longer to clear customs than me so I fell into conversation with one of the guards; a very jolly chap. He was an ethnic Russian, and once he found out I was British, turned out to be quite the fount of knowledge on the remaining British dominions. He told me excitedly how Gibraltar held the status of British 'crown colony', a fact I had not been aware of myself. He then went onto talk about the Orangemen of Northern Ireland, even doing an impression of their marching. I wondered how on earth he had amassed this knowledge. Perhaps he had spent a lot of time in front of the Discovery Channel.

He then complained about the altitude of his current post, saying "too much radiation bad!" He chuckled jovially, before holding up a straight index finger then letting it droop illustratively. "Too much radiation bad!" He repeated, chuckling again. This seemed to lead his mind in a direction that prompted an odd question. He asked if Chinese girls, somehow in correlation with their slanted eyes, were horizontal downstairs too. More chuckles followed. It may sound like a ridiculous question, but little over a century ago the belief that Chinese women had horizontal vaginas was commonplace. Until the 1860's Chinese females were displayed in zoos and exhibitions of the West. One poor Chinese lady was exhibited in Hyde Park from 1843 to 1851. However, such anatomical ignorance was far from being all one way, as the Chinese once believed Europeans to be in possession of four testicles.[5]

On that note a truck was stopped to take me across the border. Here the road inexplicably degenerated to its worst state yet. We drove through no-man's land, barren and brown, a vast boulder strewn valley. There was even one last treacherous hairpin climb before the Chinese border post came into view. Then the tarmac began in earnest and a different red flag was fluttering against the clear morning blue. It was not emblazoned with the flaming golden sun of *Tengri's* domain, but instead golden stars that marked the outer limits of the modern Middle Kingdom; a new 'Mandate of Heaven', that of the People's Republic of China. Soldiers in forest green dress uniforms with gold braid and red epaulettes marched out for inspection. A loud speaker blasted out marshal music and Mandarin, but the wind carried it away; away from the Heavenly Mountains, and away from Eurasia's secret garden and the nomad's lament, out to the Taklimakan, old East Turkestan, Tibet, and beyond.

Notes

Preface

[1] Herodotus *The Histories* Book IV 25-7.

[2] 'The lament of His-Chun' in Sitwell, *Outside The Empire: The World The Romans Knew,* 175.

[3] Ammianus Marcellinus, Book 31, in Hildinger, *Warriors of the Steppe,* 58.

[4] Ibid., 57.

[5] Ibid., 13.

[6] Rashid, *The Resurgence of Central Asia,* 9.

[7] Beckwith, *Empires of the Silk Road,*76.

[8] Ibid., 44.

[9] Ch'ien Han Shu, 96A, in Sitwell, *Outside The Empire: The World The Romans Knew,* 179.

[10] The name 'Turkestan' as the country of the Turks was first used in a somewhat derogatory sense by the Persians of the Sasanian dynasty (A.D. 226-637). It never seems to have been used by the actual inhabitants of Central Asia until it was revived by the Russians as a convenient name for the Governate-General which they created in 1867. Wheeler, *The Peoples of Central Asia*, 64-5.

Chapter One

[1] Halliday, *'Orientalism' and Its Critics,* 160.

[2] Gray, *False Dawn,* 38.

[3] The base was shut down in 2005 after American protests against the Andijan massacre.

[4] Kleveman, *The New Great Game,*188.

[5] From the novel *The Russian House* by John Le Carre.

Chapter Two

[1] Roy, *The New Central Asia: The Creation of Nations,* 163

[2] Herodotus, *The Histories,* Book IV 46.

[3] Carter Vaughn Findley, *The Turks in World History,* 19.

[4] Golden, *Central Asia in World History,* 63.

[5] Moorhouse, *Apples in the Snow,* 39.

[6] McCauley, *Afghanistan and Central Asia,* 93.

[7] Lonely Planet, (2010), *Central Asia,* 74.

[8] McCauley, *Afghanistan and Central Asia,* 95.

[9] Knobloch, *Russia & Asia,* 289.

[10] http://www.gaurdian.co.uk/commentsfree/2010/apr/08/kyrgyzstan-vladimir-putin-barrak-obaba.

Chapter Three

[1] Huntington, *The Clash of Civilisations,* 58.

[2] Ibid., 58.

[3] Ferguson, *The War of The World.* 49.

[4] Beckwith, *Empires of The Silk Road,* 13.

[5] Kokaisl & Kokaislova, 96.

[6] Kokaisl & Kokaislova, 187.

Chapter Four

[1] Dunbang, *56 Ethnic Groups in China,* 94.

[2] Baumer, *The Southern Silk Road,* 2.

[3] Ferguson, *The War of The World,* 50.

[4] Dikotter, *The Discourse of Race in Modern China,* 4; E.g. a northern tribe called the Di were assimilated with dogs. Min people of the south shared attributes of reptiles etc.

[5] Ibid, 84.

[6] Ibid, 84.

[7] 'Last mass of the Caballeros' track 10 from the album "There's a poison goin' on…"

[8] Dikotter, *The Discourse of Race in Modern China,* 48.

[9] Dikotter, *The Discourse of Race in Modern China,* 46.

[10] Chadwick, *Oral Epics of Central Asia,* 48.

[11] Kleveman, *The New Great Game,* 91.

[12] www.eurasianet.org/departments/insight/articles/eav032510.shtml

[13] Wheeler, *The Peoples of Soviet Central Asia,* 90.

Chapter Five

[1] Maclean, *Eastern Approaches,* 36.

[2] Lonely Planet (1996), *Central Asia,* 355.

[3] Rashid, *The Resurgence of Central Asia,* 139.

[4] Ibid.

[5] Foltz, *Religions of The Silk Road*, 70.

[6] http://www.chinadaily.com.cn/cndy/2011-06/15/content_12697737.htm

[7] Sinor, 'The establishment and dissolution of the Turk empire', 297. In Sinor, D. *The Cambridge History of Inner Asia.*

[8] Ibid.

[9] Orwell, *Burmese Days*, 139.

[10] Whittell, *Extreme Continental*, 127.

[11] Kokaisl & Kokaislova, 100.

Chapter Six

[1] Bauer, *As Far As My Feet Will Carry Me*, 251.

[2] Ibid, 252.

[3] Ibid, 256.

[4] Starrett, *Putting Islam To Work*, 25.

[5] Chadwick, *Oral Epics of Central Asia*, 80.

[6] Ibid.

[7] Parker, *A Thousand Years of the Tartars*, 42.

[8] Foltz, *Religions of the Silk Road*, 109.

Chapter Seven

[1] Moorehouse, *Apples in the Snow*, 55.

[2] Ibid., 56.

[3] Kleveman, *The New Great Game*, 93.

[4] Sitwell, *Outside The Empire*, 175.

[5] Barber, *The Mummies of Urumchi*, 201.

[6] Chadwick, *Oral Epics of Central Asia*, 37.

[7] Ibid, 38.

[8] Knobloch, *Russia & Asia*, 361.

[9] Maclean, *Eastern Approaches*, 126.

[10] Stewart, *Kyrgyz Republic*, 195.

[11] Humphrey, 'Chiefly and Shamanist Landscapes in Mongolia', 141.

[12] Krist, *Through The Forbidden Land*, 61.

[13] Eliade, *Shamanism*, 470.

[14] Kharitidi, 63.

[15] Abu-Lughod, *The Islamic City*, 156.

[16] Knobloch, *Russia & Asia*, 78.

Chapter Eight

[1] Davies, *Vanished Kingdoms.*
[2] Ibid.
[3] Stewart, *Kyrgyz Republic,* 230.
[4] Barthold, *Turkestan Down to the Mongol Invasion,* 156.
[5] Chadwick, *Oral Epics of Central Asia,* 79.
[6] Wheeler, *Peoples of Soviet Central Asia,* 70-1.
[7] Golden, *Central Asia in World History,* 116.
[8] Chadwick, *Oral Epics of Central Asia,* 236.
[9] Foltz, *Religions of the Silk Road,* 18.

Chapter Nine

[1] Whittell, *Extreme continental,* 138.
[2] Weller, *Rethinking Kazakh & Central Asian Nationhood,* 194-196.
[3] Knobloch, *Russia & Asia.*
[4] Starrett, *Putting Islam to Work,* 58.

Chapter Ten

[1] Krist, *Through the Forbidden Land,* 155.
[2] Zizek, *Living in The End Times,* viii.
[3] Ibid., x.
[4] Thesiger, *The Life of My Choice,* 56.
[5] Dikotter, *The Discourse of Race in Modern China,* 43.

Bibliography

Abazov, *The Palgrave Concise Historical Atlas of Central Asia,* Palgrave Macmillan, 2008.

Abu-Lughod, J. L. 'Do Muslim Women Really Need Saving? Anthropological Reflections on Cultural Relativism and Its Others', *American Anthropologist* 104(3): 783-790. 2002.

Abu-Lughod, J. L. 'The Islamic City – Historic Myth, Islamic Essence, And Contemporary Relevance', *International Journal of Middle East Studies.* 19 (1987), 155-176.

Akiner, S. *Islamic Peoples of The Soviet Union,* Kegan Paul International, 1983.

Anthony, D. W. *The Horse, The Wheel, And Language,* Princeton. 2007.

Barber, E. W. *The Mummies of Urumchi,* Pan, 1999.

Barthold, W. *Turkestan Down to the Mongol Invasion,* GIBB, 2007.

Bauer, J. M. *As Far As My Feet Will Carry Me,* Robinson, 2003.

Baumer, C. *Southern Silk Road: In the Footsteps of Sir Aural Stein and Sven Hedin,* Orchid Press, 2003.

Beckwith, C. *Empires of The Silk Road,* Princeton, 2009.

Bonavia, J. *The Silk Road,* Odyssey, 1999.

Brody, H, *Maps and Dreams,* Faber & Faber, 2002.

Cawthorne, N. *The Iron Cage,* Fourth Estate, 1994.

Carter Vaughn Findley, *The Turks in World History,* Oxford, 2005.

Chadwick, N. K. & Zhirmunsky, V. *Oral Epics of Central Asia,* Cambridge, 1969.

Ching, F. *China: The Truth About its Human Rights Record,* Rider, 2008.

Christa, P. *The Road to Miran,* Flamingo, 1994.

Davis, N. *Vanished Kingdoms – The History of Half Forgotten Europe,* Allen Lane, 2011.

Dikotter, F. *The Discourse of Race in Modern China,* Hurst, 1992.

Dunbang, D. *56 Ethnic Groups in China,* Reader's Digest, 2010.

Eliade, M, *Shamanism: Archaic techniques of ecstasy,* Penguin Arkana, 1989.

Evola, J. *Ride The Tiger: A Survival Manual for the Aristocrats of the Soul,* 2002. Vermont.

Ferguson, N. *War Of The World: History's Age of Hatred,* Penguin, 2007.

Foltz, R. *Religions of the Silk Road,* St. Martin's Press, 1999.

Geiss, P. G. *Pre-Tsarist and Tsarist Central Asia: communal commitment and political order in change,* Routledge, 2003.

Golden, P. B. *Central Asia in World History,* Oxford, 2011.

Gray, J. *False Dawn,* Granta, 2009.

Gray, J. *Black Mass,* Granta, 2008.

Gray, J. *Straw Dogs,* Granta, 2003.

Halliday, F. 'Orientalism' And Its Critics', *BrSMES.* 20 (1993), 145-163.

Hambly, G. *Central Asia,* Weidenfield & Nicolson, 1969.

Herodotus, *The Histories.* Translated by Aubery De Selincourt, Penguin Books, 2003.

Hildinger, E. *Warriors of The Steppe: A Military History of Central Asia, 500 B.C. To 1700 A.D.* Spellmount, 1997.

Hopkirk, P. *The Great Game: On Secret Service in High Asia,* Oxford, 2001.

Hopkirk, P. *Setting The East Ablaze,* Oxford, 1984.

Hosking, G. *Russia And The Russian: From Earliest Times To 2001,* Penguin Books, 2001.

Humphrey, C. 'Chiefly and Shamanist Landscapes in Mongolia', in Hirsch, E. & O' Hanlon, M. (eds) *The Anthropology of Landscape,* Oxford, 1995.

Humphreys, A., King, J., Noble, K. *Central Asia,* Lonely Planet, 1st Ed. 1996.

Huntington, S. P. *The Clash of Civilisations And The Remaking Of The World Order,* Penguin, 1997.

Johnson, C. *Blowback: The Costs And Consequences Of American Empire,* Little, Brown and Company, 2000.

Keddie, N. R. 'Is There A Middle East?', *International Journal of Middle East Studies*, 4 (1973), 255-271.

Keesing, R. *Cultural Anthropology: A Contemporary Perspective*, Harcourt Brace Jonanovich College Publishers, 1975.

Khan, A. *A Historical Atlas of Kyrgyzstan*, Rosen, 2004.

Kharitidi, O. *Entering The Circle: Ancient Secrets of Siberian Wisdom Discovered by a Russian Psychiatrist*, HarperSanFrancisco, 1996.

King, D. *Cultures of the World: Kyrgyzstan*, New York, 2005.

Kleveman, L. *The New Great Game*, Atlantic Books, 2003.

Knobloch, E, *Russia & Asia: Nomadic & Oriental Traditions in Russian History*, Odyssey, 2007.

Krist, G. *Alone Through Forbidden Lands: Journeys in Disguise through Soviet Central Asia*, Reader's Union Limited, 1939.

Kokaisl, P. & Kokaislova, P. *The Kyrgyz – Children of Manas*, Prague, Fellowship of Development Cooperation, 2009.

Lee, M. *The Beast Reawakens*, Little, Brown & Company, 1997.

Maclean, F. *Eastern Approaches*, J.and J. Gray, 1951.

Mayhew, B., Bloom, G., Clammer, P., Kohn, M., Noble, J., *Central Asia*, Lonely Planet, 5th Ed. 2010.

McCauley, M. *Afghanistan And Central Asia: A Modern History*, Longman, 2002.

Moorhouse, G, *Apples in the Snow: A Journey to Samarkand*, Hodder&Stoughton, 1990.

Nicolle, D. *Attila and the Nomad Hordes*, Osprey, 2009.

Orwell, G, *Burmese Days*, Heritage Classics, 2005.

Ouspensky, P. D. *In Search of the Miraculous*, Routledge & Kegan Paul, 1983.

Parker, E. H. *A Thousand Years of the Tartars*, Dorset, 1987.

Rashid, *The Resurgence of Central Asia: Islam or Nationalism*, Zed Books, 1994.

Roy, O. *The New Central Asia: The Creation of Nations*, I.B.Taurus, 2000.

Sinor, D. (ed) *The Cambridge History of Early Inner Asia: From Earliest Times to the Rise of the Mongols*, Vol. 1, Cambridge, 2008.

Sitwell, N.H.H. *Outside The Empire: The World The Romans Knew,* Paladin, 1986.

Soucek, S. *A History of Inner Asia,* Cambridge, 2000.

Starrett, G. *Putting Islam to Work: Education, Politics, and Religious Transformation in Egypt,* University of California Press, 1998.

Starrett, G. 'The Varieties of Secular Experience', *Comparative Studies in Society and History,* 2010; 52(3):626-651.

Stewart, R. *Kyrgyz Republic,* Odyssey, 2004.

Tchoroev, T. 'Historiography of Post-Soviet Kyrgyzstan', *International Journal of Middle East Studies.* 34. (2002), 351-374. Teague, K. *Metalcrafts of Central Asia,* Shire, 1990.

Thesiger, W. *The Life Of My Choice,* Flamingo, 1987.

Van Der Leeuw, C. *Kazakhstan: A Quest for Statehood,* Caspian Publishing House, 2006.

Vassiliev, A, *Central Asia: Political & Economic Challenges in the Post-Soviet Era,* Saqi Books, 2001.

Weller, R. C. *Rethinking Kazakh and Central Asian Nationhood: A Challenge to Prevailing Western Views,* ARA, 2006.

Wheeler, G. *The Peoples of Soviet Central Asia,* Bodley Head, 1966.

Wheeler, G. *Racial Problems in Soviet Muslim Asia,* Oxford University Press, 1962.

Whittell, G. *Extreme Continental: Blowing Hot and Cold Through Central Asia,* London, 1995.

Yun, L. *Chinese Tea,* Better Link Press, 2010.

Zizek, S. *Living in The End Times,* Verso, 2011.

Printed in Great Britain
by Amazon